Peckham's Heritage – Past, Present & Future has been produced by the Peckham Heritage Regeneration Partnership through the Peckham Townscape Heritage Initiative, which ran from 2016–2023.

The Townscape Heritage Initiative (THI) programme is part of The National Lottery Heritage Fund's grant giving programme for the repair and regeneration of the historic environment in towns and cities throughout the UK. The nine buildings repaired and restored through the THI have been funded by Southwark Council and The National Lottery Heritage Fund, with contributions from building owners.

As part of the THI, the Peckham Heritage Regeneration Partnership (PHRP) developed a range of projects to support community involvement in Peckham's built and social heritage. With the completion of the THI, the PHRP has evolved into a new local community group, Peckham Heritage.

peckhamheritage.org.uk

Peckham THI funded by The National Lottery Heritage Fund and Southwark Council

Peckham's Heritage – Past, Present & Future
published by Peckham Heritage 2023

Typeset in Hypatia Sans & Europa

Designed by Laura Mingozzi-Marsh, mingomingo.co.uk

ISBN 978-1-3999-4029-0

PECKHAM'S HERITAGE
PAST, PRESENT & FUTURE

Derek Kinrade, with Benedict O'Looney
and the Peckham Heritage Regeneration Partnership

CONTENTS

"It's in perpetual change, with different people and cultures coming here"
Karin Greene, 'Grow Our Histories' oral history extract, 2022 (see page 212)

Welcome to 'Peckham's Heritage – Past, Present & Future' - a collaborative project by Derek Kinrade, Benedict O'Looney and the Peckham Heritage Regeneration Partnership (PHRP). This book is the Peckham Townscape Heritage Initiative's (THI) final project. It was produced through a partnership between Peckham communities and Southwark Council and so a variety of memories and perspectives have been shared.

This book gathers histories of Peckham people and buildings, shaping an account of how contemporary Peckham has developed. The exploration focuses on Peckham's historic centre, and roams as far north as the former Livesey Library on the Old Kent Road, and south to Peckham Rye Park. Embedded in the narrative is a sense that an exploration of 'heritage' can be wide ranging and inclusive, tapping into local interest, experience, and knowledge.

We start with a brief history of Peckham. Then, Part One explores the lost heritage of Peckham, those buildings from the 13th to the 20th century, which are now gone. Their stories chart the growth of Peckham from rural village to its absorption into the metropolis. Part Two examines buildings in need of restoration, consideration, and a more secure future – from modest everyday beauties to magnificent landmarks. Part Three celebrates buildings which are in better health, often with new or evolving uses. Part Four is a collection of extracts from interviews with eight residents of Peckham, produced through 'Grow Our Histories', an oral history project run in partnership with the South London Gallery.

A constellation of people from the 1970s to the present day, often with support from Southwark Council, have worked to protect and cherish Peckham as a living and evolving place. This is one reason that today's town centre, with its buildings from the 18th to the 21st centuries, reflects such a diverse and interesting built environment. The Peckham THI in particular is the result of years of hard work by Peckham Vision, The Peckham Society and Southwark Council to promote awareness of Peckham town centre's historic buildings.

A Peckham friend described their delight at the transformed view of the beautifully renovated group of 18th century cottages at 98 – 104 Peckham High Street. Our ambition is that the THI works to these and the other buildings forming the cluster of nine historic properties around the old village core at the junction of Peckham Hill Street and Peckham High Street, will capture peoples' imagination, set a high standard for future work to protect and enhance the Rye Lane Peckham Conservation Area, and unlock the potential of the town centre. The parallel community initiatives, providing advice, guidance, information, and inspiration can be found on peckhamheritage.org.uk.

Many thanks to everyone who has contributed to this book.

Claire Hegarty
Chair, Peckham Heritage Regeneration Partnership, 2016 - 2023

Tram track removal and signal installation by the Mowlem Paving Company outside Jones and Higgins, 1956

View of Rye Lane looking south with Holdron's
(now Khan's Bargains) in foreground, 1936

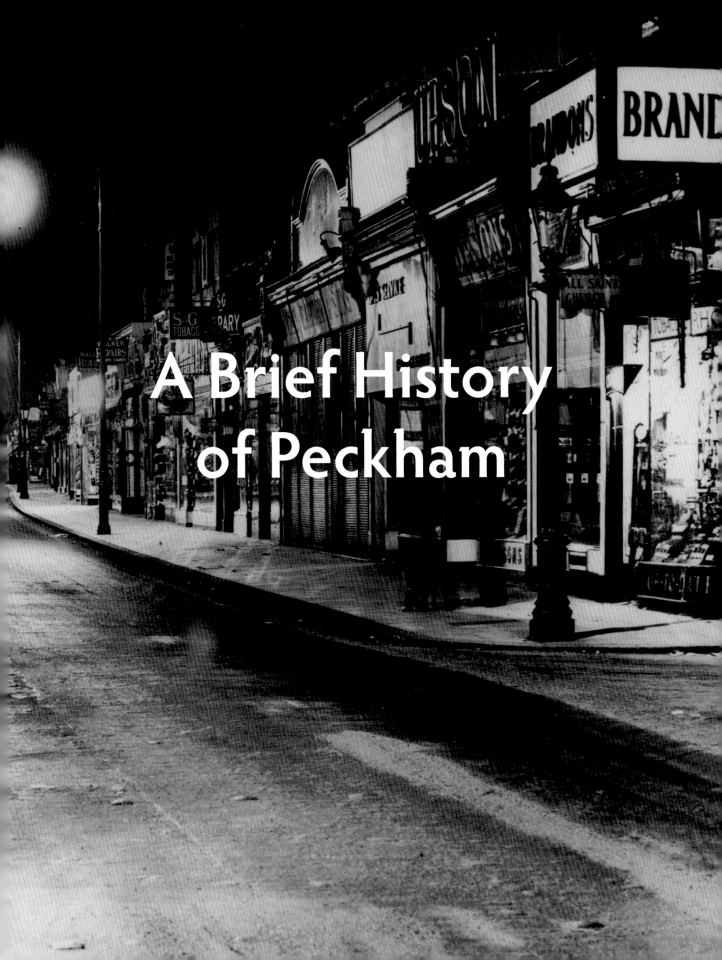

A Brief History of Peckham

PARTE OF

MIDDLESEX

LONDON *Shordich*

Stepney

Radriffe

Newington

Camberwell

PARTE

Diepeford

Lewsham

Raupus bourne

OF

Croydon

Addington

SVRREY

Layton

W. Ham

Ilforde parva

Ilforde magna

Barkynge

Dagenham

Romforde SA

E. Ham

Thamefis

Plumsted *Great Breach*

Wolwych *Lefnes* *Purfleet*

W. Comb *Charlton*

Greene wych 59 *E. Wykham* *Eryth*

Shooters hyll 58

Black heath *Cray ford*

Leigh *Eltham*

The Cray DAKFF *Wylm*

wellplace *Bexley*

Motingham *Footscray* *N. Cray*

Rookefley

Lathe 61

Bekenham *Scadbery* *Byrchen wood*

Bromley *Chyfelherft*

60 *Paulefcray*

Langley St MARYE

CRAYE

Keungtowne

Heys *Barhebert*

Farnborow *Orpyngton*

Chelffield *Loftyngfton*

W. Wykham *Kefton*

Addington

Downe 61

Halfted

Cowdham *Norbolt*

Chelfham Sutton *Maraux cort*

A BRIEF HISTORY OF PECKHAM

BEFORE 1700

This is a well-trodden path, but one not known to everyone. It begins with shards of Roman pottery found around the junction of today's Rye Lane and Peckham High Street, reminders of the route to Londinium, across the land that was to be become Southwark. Six centuries after the Romans' almost total withdrawal from Britain in the 5th century, an entry in the Domesday Book of 1086 indicates that 'Pecheham' was by then only a small settlement of 16 to 20 people.

In the 13th century it became part of an area known as Camberwell, which included the Peckham Manors of Basing and Bridenhurst. By the early 16th century many market gardens and orchards had been established, responding to the appetites of the nearby metropolis, while public houses in the town centre provided a convenient stop for cattle drovers en route to the slaughterhouse.

THE 18TH CENTURY

Daniel Defoe, writing in the early years of the 18th century, noted that from the hills of Clapham you could see "the pleasant villages of Peckham and Camberwell, with some of the finest buildings about London". He described these as "the palaces of the British nobility and gentry…houses of retreat, like the Bastides of Marseilles, gentlemen's meer summer-houses, or citizens' country houses; whither they retire from the hurries of business, and from getting money, to draw their breath in a clean air, and to divert themselves in the hot weather."

In this rural idyll, the illustrious Quaker botanist Peter Collinson tended his famous garden; until 1797 the manor house built for Sir Thomas Bond stood proudly; Peckham House, a grand mansion before it became

A View at Peckham Rye, in SURRY.   Vue de Peckham Rye, en SURRY.

an asylum, graced the High Street; and the eminent cleric John Wesley came to preach and recuperate no fewer than ten times.

But Peckham in the 1700s was also a dangerous place. Douglas Allport, writing in 1841, recalls a time when there were, indeed, many good houses in the parish, but scattered and isolated and owing to "the defective and ill-organised police of that period, far from secure". He tells of frequent robberies. One place with a particularly fearful reputation was the so-called 'Peckham Gap', located at the junction of Peckham Park Road and the Old Kent Road and intersecting the route between Peckham Village and the City. For some years until apprehended, two foot-pads (highwayman operating on foot), both residents of the nearby Turk's Head Inn, made rich pickings, ensuring travel to and from the City was a "rather formidable affair". In response, for a section of the route coaches were accompanied by a foot patrol. The journey, one way, took two hours and there were four such services a day.

Policing was locally organised, reliant upon a few constables and night watchmen chosen by a Justice of the Peace, and plainly insufficient to combat organised crime. Law enforcement relied more on the deterrent harshness of penalties than on the police. A search of the database of trials at the Old Bailey in the 18th century yields only three examples of offences in the environs of Peckham, each the theft of an animal, and each met with the death sentence.

There is an even bleaker side to Peckham in this era. It is now accepted that Britain's prosperity was sustained on the exploitation of the resources of its Empire, and this

not simply from its trade in commodities, but to a massive extent on enslavement, notably in the plantations of the Caribbean. In the BBC Two programme 'Black and British: A Forgotten History', historian David Olusoga revealed that the Duke of York (later King James II) who had a residence on Peckham High Street, was governor of the slave-trading Royal African Company, which between 1662 and 1731 is said to have arranged the transportation of around 212,000 men, women and children into slavery in the West Indies and the Americas, a fifth of whom did not survive the voyage. There they were brutally set to work in plantations. The extent of British involvement in the slave trade was meticulously recorded when slave owners were compensated for the freeing of their slaves. This register is now available online. It includes two Peckham residents: Benjamin Joseph Trueman Nightingale of 23 Cottage Grove: 52 slaves in Jamaica, £734 10s compensation paid; and James Clayton White of Shard's Place: 172 slaves in Jamaica, £3013 1s 6d compensation paid.

THE 19TH CENTURY

But in Peckham there was an honourable counter-attack. Quakers were prominent in the campaign for the abolition of slavery, and had a substantial presence in the area. In 1826, they opened a fine meeting house in Hanover Street (now Highshore Road), which survives to this day as a Royal Mail sorting office. Active among its members were the so-called 'Peckham Ladies'. Their Anti-Slavery Association was one of the first to be formed in the vicinity of London, and one of its members, Elizabeth Dudley, was co-secretary of the London Female Anti-Slavery Society. Another Hanover Street resident, William Naish, was a passionate supporter of their cause. His 32 tracts survive as a remarkable testimony of Quaker sentiment.

At the end of the 18th century Peckham was counted as a minor hamlet of 340 households. Pigot's Directory for 1823/4 indicates a significant expansion, as well as confirming the Duke of York's occasional residence in the High Street: it describes "a very populous village… celebrated for a great number of boarding schools, chiefly for young ladies, owing to the salubrity of the air, and the water, for drinking, considered to be more pure than any in the neighbourhood of the Metropolis."

London's population also continued to grow. Blackfriars Bridge, which had opened in 1769, provided an important additional link to the south and Peckham was progressively absorbed into this expansion, transforming from village to middle-class suburb. Better roads and transport facilities, the extension of the Grand Surrey Canal in 1826 (now filled in) and railway connections through Peckham Rye Station, built in 1865, conspired to reshape Peckham's economic and environmental character.

There was an important exception to this tide of urban development. In 1868, Camberwell Vestry, the local governing body responsible for the administration of Camberwell, Peckham, Nunhead and Dulwich, purchased Peckham Rye Common, passing the land into public ownership and ensuring its protection. This precious plot had been regarded as common land from medieval times, and it was here in 1760 that writer and artist William Blake famously claimed to have seen a tree filled with angels. The site was further enhanced in 1894 by the purchase of most of the adjacent Homestall Farm for use as a public park, an acquisition completed in 1907, and providing a sanctuary of nature that continues to delight.

RIGHT
Peckham High Street looking east, 1889

BELOW
Surrey Canal with Jones and Higgins'
clocktower in distance, 1925

Another sanctuary of the 19th century was the Licensed Victuallers Asylum, with its almshouses and central porticoed chapel, built between 1827 and 1833. Now known as Caroline Gardens, the complex was conceived to provide homes for aged and infirm public house landlords. The housing remains in use to this day, while its private chapel with its memorial tablets now serves primarily as a venue for weddings. Though gutted by enemy action in the Second World War, its stained glass windows survived and restoration has made a virtue of its damaged interior.

The irresistible advance of urbanisation was reflected in a proliferation of churches. Whereas prior to 1800, Peckham had only one place of worship - the Congregational Hanover Chapel - in the 19th century

OPPOSITE
25 inch Ordnance Survey map CIII, 1897 edition

Anglican, Baptist, Quaker, Methodist and Roman Catholic churches were established, as well as a synagogue.

Also striking was Peckham's growing reputation as a shopping destination centred around Rye Lane. In time, it would grow to become one of the leading shopping streets of South London with its 'golden mile' of celebrated stores. Of particular note was the founding in 1867 of a business manufacturing and supplying guns and associated equipment, later switching to the production of sporting equipment. This was the famous Bussey

Building, located behind 133 Rye Lane in a building that is still functional today. In the same year, Jones & Higgins began as a small drapery, a business which would expand to occupy a huge area at the northern end of Rye Lane. Holdron's, which opened in 1882 at 53, similarly grew to occupy a large slice of the east side of Rye Lane, south of the railway. In the 1890s, branches of famous London shops were attracted to Peckham, including Lipton's (98) and Dunn's (106). A large building behind 164 served as a public hall and included access to the wonder of the age: silent films.

ABOVE
Rye Lane looking north, 1905

OPPOSITE
Rye Lane, 1913

THE 20TH CENTURY

Expansion continued as the new century began. Shops included: the shoe shop Freeman, Hardy and Willis (1904); Austin's, which began in Brayards Road as a dairy before extending to the much-loved second-hand and antiques business in Rye Lane (1905); Boots at 20 Rye Lane (1907); the Electric Theatre at 133 (1908); a Lyons teashop at 26 (1910); Stead and Simpson at 89 (1911); Woolworths at 91 & 93 (1913); The Tower Cinema (1914); Marks & Spencer at 54/58 (1916) - where Argos is today; and Morgan & Collins drapery store at 61/67 - "all glass and chrome" and paying "the best wages in Peckham".

Despite the Great Depression of the 1930s, commercial development in Rye Lane continued. C & A Modes arrived in 1930 at 72/74 (now McDonald's). British Home Stores (now Primark) opened in the same year, and in 1931 Sainsbury's launched a new branch at 61/63 (now Clark's). In 1932, the impressive Co-operative House opened at 259/267, complementing its small 1913 store and its 1928 pharmacy at 202/204. In 1934, William Margree described Rye Lane as "the Oxford Street of South London", and argued that as a shopping street it had no rival outside Central London. This was Peckham's heyday, its prestige enhanced by the construction of

a cluster of fine art deco buildings around Peckham Rye Station from 1935.

That year is also remembered for a ground-breaking initiative at the aptly-named Pioneer Health Centre in St. Mary's Road. Known as the 'Peckham Experiment', it was based on a scheme that had run from 1926 to 1929 at a doctor's surgery at 142 Queens Road. It promoted holistic well-being through a range of facilities, including a gym and a swimming pool.

A less obvious event at the beginning of the 20th century heralded a far more profound change in the character of Peckham. In 1904, a young Jamaican student sailed to Britain to pursue a career in medicine at London's King's College. His name was Harold Moody. He was to discover deep-rooted racial discrimination in both his own experience and in the defining prejudice handed down to black

volunteers during and after the First World War. In that senseless conflict over 15,000 black volunteers travelled from the Caribbean and African colonies to serve their 'mother country'. Yet, even in this patriotic endeavour, apartheid prevailed. In October 1915, a segregated British West Indies Regiment was formed in which black soldiers, paid less than their white counterparts in other regiments, and led by white officers, were mostly employed as labourers.

After the cessation of hostilities, notwithstanding their legal claim to British citizenship, men from the British Empire were clearly not welcome in Britain. Unemployment was widespread and in the fierce competition for jobs, they stood little chance. In the 1918 General Election, David Lloyd George stood on a mantra 'Britain for the British, socially and industrially', and this clearly was intended to disadvantage men from the colonies. It was a message implicit in The Aliens Order, a Statutory Instrument of 1920, explicitly designed to safeguard jobs for indigenous residents. It required all 'aliens' seeking employment or residence to register with the police, and empowered the Home Secretary to reject or deport those who failed to register, were considered undesirable, or unable to establish their identity or nationality.

Moody, despite repeated rejection, had qualified as a fully-fledged doctor and in 1913 set up his own practice in Peckham. As a general practitioner in predominantly working-class Peckham, this was the hostile mindset which Moody encountered. He was to challenge this construct by example, building an abiding reputation in the community that he served. He moved his home and surgery to

Pioneer Health Centre, 1938

Sculpture of Harold Moody in bronze by his brother Ronald Moody, 1997, based on a work of 1946

the 'League of Coloured Peoples', set up to promote and protect the social, educational, economic and political interests of its members and the welfare of coloured people worldwide. Dr Moody remained its President until his death. Founding members included writer and activist C.L.R. James; Jomo Kenyatta, later President of Kenya; and cricketer and bass singer Paul Robeson. They held their first meeting at a YMCA building in Tottenham Court Road, primarily intent on the elimination of the colour bar routinely experienced by black people in British society. In 1933 the League founded a journal, 'The Keys', edited by founder member, writer and activist Una Marson, spelling out the quest for racial equality and opposition to colonialism, to which Moody contributed. He also had conspicuous successes in the League's cause. In 1940, his objection to the use of the N word by a BBC presenter drew an apology, and established a precedent: an object lesson that black people deserved respect. The war, however, exposed overt discrimination as many British families refused to accept black evacuee children. On 27 July 1944, the League published a 'Charter for Coloured Peoples' calling for an end to discrimination in the United Kingdom, and self-government for citizens of the British colonies. The quest for civil rights was far from over, and while Dr Moody's part in it was nearing its end, he had from his Peckham home helped arouse in thinking people a recognition of the need for action. A plaque to Dr Harold Moody was installed at 164 Queens Road by English Heritage in 1995.

164 Queens Road in 1921, where he cemented a bond with his patients, becoming universally respected for his kindness, expertise and, not least, the flexibility of his charges. During the Second World War, especially during the air raids, Moody saved many lives and was praised for his outstanding contribution to the war effort when in charge of a first aid post at Deptford's South-Eastern Hospital. When at midday on 25 November 1944, a V2 rocket obliterated the Woolworths store in New Cross, claiming 168 lives and injuring hundreds more, he was one of the first on the scene.

Moody's work extended beyond tending the sick of Peckham. In 1931, with Dr Charles Wesley of Howard University, Washington DC, and supported by Quakers, he founded

The chronicle of events in Britain after the Second World War was one of profound change: for the nation as a whole, and for Peckham too. The reforms of the post-war

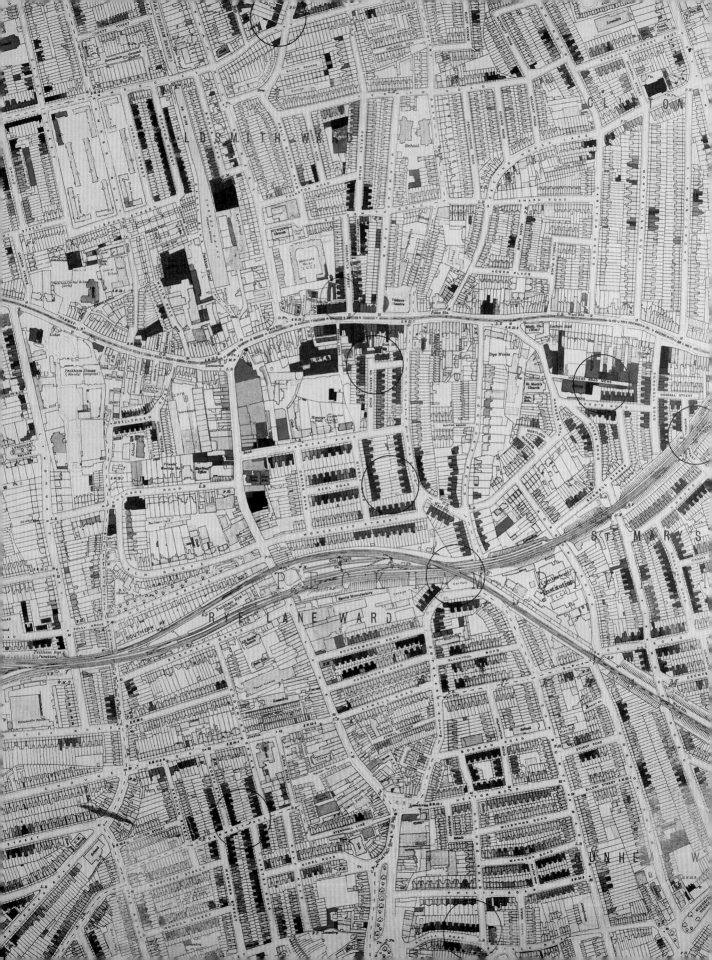

government not only introduced the Welfare State and the National Health Service, but also recognised pragmatically that the British economy had a need of workers. The British Nationality Act of 1948 created a new status of 'citizens of the UK and colonies' with a right to settle in the UK. This was followed by the Royal Commission on Population in 1949. Both measures made it clear that immigrants from the colonies 'of good stock' were welcome. Such encouragement attracted large numbers seeking a better life, not least on the famous HMT Empire Windrush, which docked in June 1948. By 1950, around 20,000 non-white immigrants had settled in Britain, mostly in London, especially in Brixton and Peckham.

The migration of workers continued, albeit somewhat restricted by government legislation after 1968. The 1991 census showed the number of non-white Londoners to be around half a million, and by 2011 this had increased to 1,088,640. Many settled in London, and by 2018, nearly half of Southwark's residents were non-white, with a much higher proportion in Peckham.

It cannot be said that the arrival of the first wave of immigrants was universally welcomed. Numerous accounts by early immigrants tell a largely negative story of prejudice, hostility, suspicion, and rejection. There were a few success stories and Peckham could boast one of these: Sam Beaver King, one of the Windrush contingent whose story is told in an autobiography 'Climbing up the Rough Side of the Mountain'. He was elected as a councillor in Peckham's Bellenden ward in 1982, and as Southwark's first black mayor the following year. In 2009, the people of Southwark voted for his achievements to be recognised by the award of a blue plaque at 2 Warmington Road, SE24, and in 2016, shortly before his death, he was honoured with the freedom of the borough.

RECOVERING FROM THE SECOND WORLD WAR

During the war almost everything had been put on hold. Dealing with destruction took precedence over creativity. Most of Rye Lane's famous traders survived but were diminished by inevitable post-war austerity. Holdron's closed in 1949, to be followed by the loss of Jones & Higgins in 1980. All but the clock tower at 1 and the HSBC Bank building at 47/49 were demolished, making way, five years later, for the multi-vendor Aylesham Centre.

North Peckham
Estate, 1971

The well-intentioned five estates of North Peckham, built between 1966 and 1975 to replace a network of run-down streets, rehoused a significant proportion of Commonwealth families. At first praised, they quickly came to be seen as examples of brutalist design creating ghettoes divorced from the wider community. SKY Magazine, in March 1988, described them as "a nightmare" and referenced a report by the European Economic Community, which named it "the most depressed housing area in western Europe".

One Peckham resident during the years 1969-75 has a special place in the town's social history. Rev. David Sheppard, already nationally famous for his achievements as a cricketer, came to live at 12 Asylum Road as the Bishop of Woolwich. Much has been written about his contribution to tackling the problems of social exclusion and injustice. Before coming to Peckham he had upset the cricket establishment by refusing to play against South Africa's all-white team. As Chair of the Martin Luther King Fund and Foundation from 1969, he brought a particular

focus on improving race relations. On 14 October 2016, eleven years after his death, a Peckham Society blue plaque was unveiled at his former home.

In 1989, Peckham faced an existential threat. British Rail came up with a plan to drive a rail link from Waterloo to the Channel Tunnel through the Holly Grove conservation area and Warwick Gardens. This scheme galvanised the local community and prompted a vigorous campaign, supported by Southwark Council, which focused on pride in the historic importance of the intended route. British Rail went so far as to purchase many of the area's 19th century houses, earmarked for demolition to make way for the envisioned rail line. But at the eleventh hour, Michael Heseltine, then Secretary of State for the Environment, proved an unlikely saviour, successfully championing a route from St Pancras through the Thames Gateway and Stratford. Announced on 9 October 1991, the change of plan frustrated British Rail but campaigners, who had all but given up hope, rejoiced in a victory that reawakened civic pride. It was a

Famous residents of Peckham and Nunhead including former Olympic swimmer Duncan Goodhew (left) and actor Terry Jones (centre), carrying a coffin into Waterloo Station where they joined the protest against British Rail's plans for a high-speed Channel Tunnel rail link, 1989

turning point for modern Peckham and one which encouraged talented activists to seek local renewal.

In 1994, Southwark Council devised a well-documented initiative to redevelop the North Peckham estate. By this time, the estate had become so unsafe that the Royal Mail had stopped delivering post, midwives needed protection, there were accounts of people being mugged three times in one day, and the police visited in pairs. A successful bid for funding from the government's Single Regeneration Budget introduced the 'Peckham Partnership', bringing together the Council, builders, housing associations, tenants, police, traders, and health services. The scheme led, over time, to the demolition of the five estates, replaced with a less-dense mix of lower-rise council, housing association, and privately owned - occupied accommodation.

But while redevelopment was still in progress, something happened that blighted Peckham far beyond anything that British Rail's scheme might have wrought. On 27 November 2000, a ten-year old schoolboy walking home from Peckham's new library, was stabbed in the leg with a broken bottle. He managed to stagger to the stairwell of one of the old, dilapidated

tower blocks of the North Peckham estate, before losing consciousness. He died on the way to hospital. His name was Damilola Taylor, and his death impacted across the national consciousness. Amelia Hill, writing in The Guardian ten years later, commented that the stabbing had "turned the neighbourhood into a byword for shattered communities". She quoted a Peckham resident saying that the improvements [to the estate] were cosmetic. This was evidenced by high youth unemployment and the worst take-up of education and training opportunities of all London boroughs. Another resident said that Peckham was seen as "the sort of place where violence happens".

The damage to Peckham's reputation was severe. These were troubled years. In 2003, listeners to the BBC's Today programme voted Rye Lane "the fourth worst street in London". And while Lewisham and Bromley prospered as shopping centres, one-by-one the famous high street names deserted Peckham. The financial crash of 2008 was followed in the summer of 2011 by rioting triggered when police officers shot and killed Mark Duggan, a young black man, in Tottenham. The resulting riots and fires across London, including Peckham, unleashed an outpouring of pent-up animosity to perceived racial prejudice in the Metropolitan Police.

There was an interesting reaction in Peckham. In August 2012, an artwork 'Peace Wall' funded by Southwark Council was installed in the town's central square. It had begun informally the previous year and consisted of some 4,000 post-it notes expressing people's love and respect for Peckham after the riots. Unveiling the tableau, Peter John, then Leader of Southwark Council, expressed

Peckham Peace Wall, 2011

a hope that it would serve as a reminder that Peckham's community had a strength of spirit that had and would always outshine the actions of a mindless minority. It remains a symbolic representation of the majority ethos and pride which, despite adversity, characterises this cosmopolitan area.

Nor was it the only positive development of 2011. Following the publication of a detailed Historic Area Assessment, commissioned by Southwark Council and undertaken by Historic England and supported by the Peckham Society, two new conservation areas in Peckham Town Centre were adopted.

Campaigning for change was given enormous impetus by Peckham Vision, a community action group formed by Eileen Conn with Jonathan Wilson, the co-owner of Copeland Park and with the support of the Peckham Society. Peckham Vision works 'to support Peckham town centre as a thriving and sustainable social and commercial centre, and to contribute to Peckham being a good place for all in which to live, work and visit'. Notably, it campaigned vigorously from 2005 to 2009 to prevent the demolition of the Bussey Building and other premises in Copeland Industrial Park, and in the Blackpool Road area between Copeland Road and Consort Road, to make way for a tram depot. And from 2012 to 2017, against what they believed was the inappropriate sale and redevelopment of the multi-storey car park built by Sainsbury's in 1983 (and vacated ten years later).

NOW

Today, Peckham is a diverse community ethnically and socio-economically. This includes traditional London working-class communities and professionals living in expensive Victorian properties, who coexist with communities that have their origins in among others: Afghanistan, Bangladesh, the Caribbean, China, India, Ghana, Nigeria, Pakistan, Turkey, Eastern Europe and Vietnam. Such a palette of cultures has had to learn to live together. In this, The Peckham Peculiar, and Southwark Council, (through its 'Southwark Life' magazine), have carved out a special place, consistently inclusive, focusing on the success stories of all citizens of interest. With the passage of time, it has become clear that the 'Peckham Partnership' has succeeded in reducing crime, providing better quality housing (that has aged well), reducing unemployment, and providing better and safer routes to the town centre. Health, social and postal workers have been able to do their jobs in the area.

Peckham has become a 'cool' place to live, with its own special character, invigorated by large numbers of aspiring young people of many backgrounds, choosing to make their

Local school children attending Our Hut workshop on the roof of Multi Storey Car Park, 2017

home in easy reach of central London. It has also become the place to visit for relaxation and entertainment, its night economy reflected in Network Rail's statistics, which logged 7.3 million journeys through Peckham Rye Station in 2017/18, an increase of 5.9 million since 2004/5.

As this book goes to press, ambitious proposals are being developed to upgrade the Peckham (Library) Square as a revitalized civic space with improved leisure and cultural amenities, further strengthening Peckham's identity as a focus of culture and creativity in London.

Southwark Council have played a pivotal role – through negotiations and financial support - in attracting Mountview Academy of Theatre Arts to relocate to Peckham, providing a world class performing arts school adjacent to Will Alsop's Stirling prize winning library.

At Peckham Rye Station, Southwark Council, in partnership with Network Rail, are working on a strategic upgrade, which includes restoration and extension of the current grade 2 listed Victorian station and creation of a new civic square in front. Already, local architect Benedict O'Looney has superbly restored the exterior of Peckham Rye Station.

The Bussey Building and revamped multi-storey car park have given rise to new bars, cafes, and restaurants, with more to come. Sophisticated artistic and musical pursuits have also flourished, hugely encouraged by the South London Gallery, and the presence of Mountview. The Townscape Heritage Initiative, proposed by Peckham Vision and delivered by The National Lottery Heritage Fund and Southwark Council, has led the way towards the appropriate refurbishment of historic buildings, bolstered by some

independent restoration of jaded premises such as the Old Fire Station and the flamboyant 133 Rye Lane.

The rooftop social spaces of the Bussey Building, the multi-storey car park, and Mountview give access to the magnificent panoramic views across from Peckham to central London. Daniel Defoe's description, in his travels through Peckham and the surrounding countryside in the 1720s, still resonates today: "Looking north, behold, to crown all, a fair prospect of the whole city of London itself; the most glorious sight without exception, that the whole world at present can show". From these high points, the experience of the expansive sky and wide sweeping cityscape give a sense of Peckham's location in the vast scale of the metropolis, and of the underlying topography of the Thames flood plain.

Peckham is, above all, a distinctive place, and stands in contrast to some of the sleepier suburbs that surround London. Since 1950, in all but two parliaments it has been represented by a woman. The area is well known for people with liberal, internationalist and open-minded sensibilities. It's distinctiveness and diversity is a large part of its charm, with many of its multi-cultural residents,liking it specifically because it caters to many contrasting appetites and lifestyles.

Former HSBC on corner of Rye Lane and Hanover Park, 2022

TO CLOSE

Most of the major buildings that graced Peckham in earlier centuries have long-since been demolished: these include Peckham House, turned mental asylum in 1826; Peckham Lodge, home to famous radicals; Marlborough House, which became a notorious workhouse in the reign of George III; the Crown Theatre, a late Victorian gem; Pelican House and Winchester House on the High Street; and Basing Manor, converted into a school in 1850. Only a few remnants survive: the iconic Jones and Higgins clock tower and, like a bookend, the remarkable former HSBC Bank building at 47/49 Rye Lane; Peckham Public Hall, dating from 1884, albeit hidden behind shops on Rye Lane; Central Hall in Peckham High Street; old houses in Peckham High Street, Peckham Hill Street, Queens Road, Woods Road and Rye Lane.

It is widely recognised that it is vital to conserve and nurture the historic buildings and places that are of value to Peckham. There is scope for further listing of historic buildings. The gem that is Peckham Rye Park and Peckham Rye Common will continue to be treasured, and the heritage and non-conformity of Peckham as a special historical place must be respected. Its character is precious, and excessive modernisation and gentrification could destroy what makes it unique.

Peckham's revival must honour its past, recognising that what we create today will be the heritage of the future.

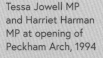

Tessa Jowell MP and Harriet Harman MP at opening of Peckham Arch, 1994

Corner of Rye Lane looking south before the demolition of the buildings on east side for the extension of Jones and Higgins premises, 1894

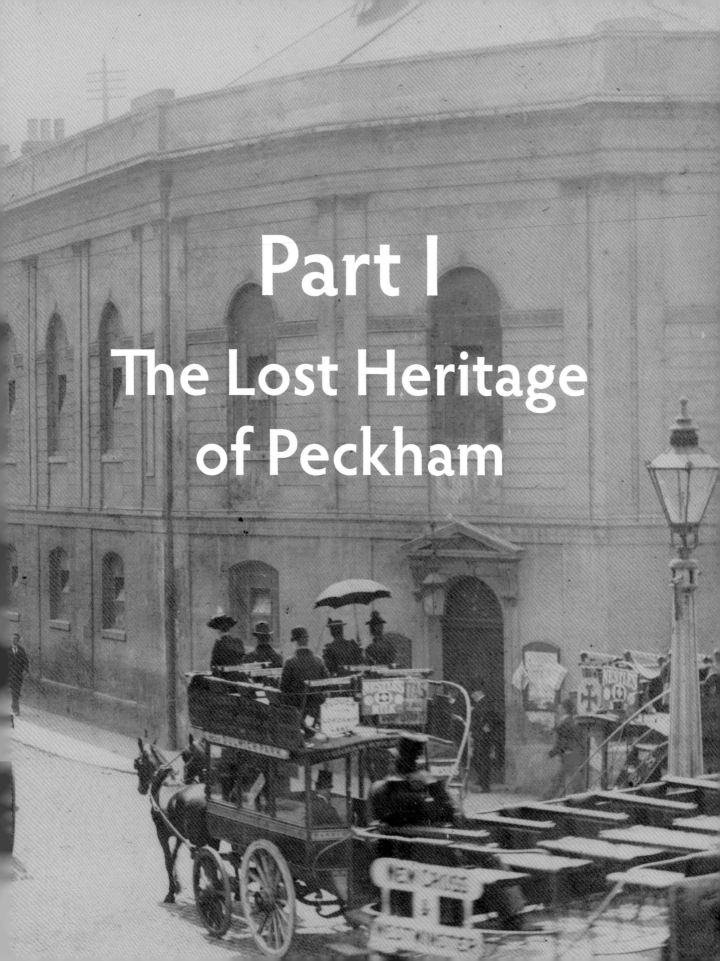

Part I
The Lost Heritage of Peckham

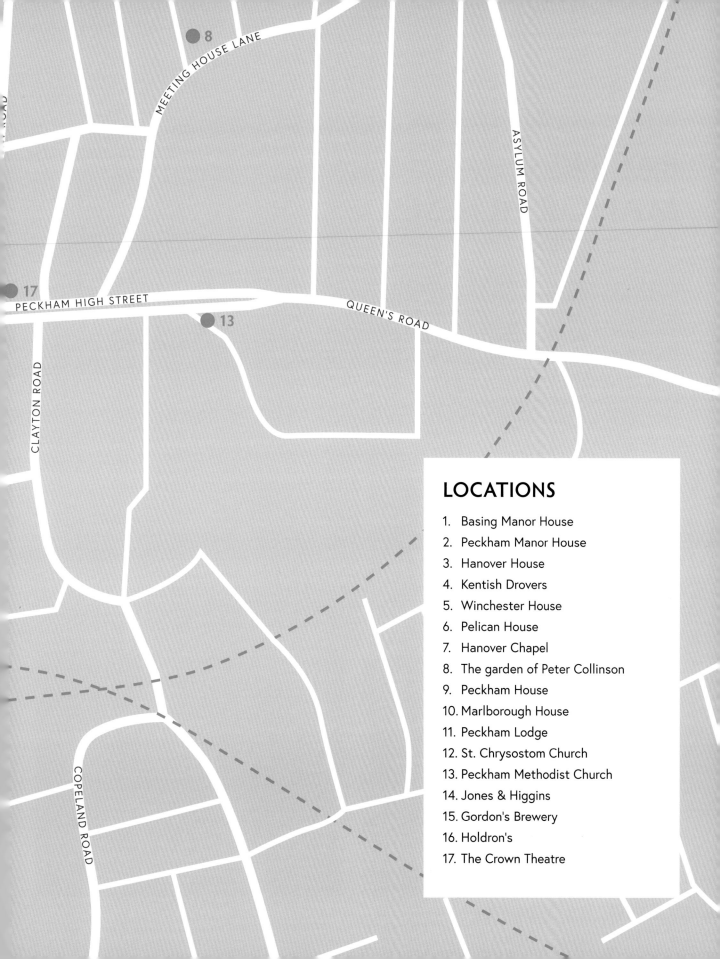

LOCATIONS

1. Basing Manor House
2. Peckham Manor House
3. Hanover House
4. Kentish Drovers
5. Winchester House
6. Pelican House
7. Hanover Chapel
8. The garden of Peter Collinson
9. Peckham House
10. Marlborough House
11. Peckham Lodge
12. St. Chrysostom Church
13. Peckham Methodist Church
14. Jones & Higgins
15. Gordon's Brewery
16. Holdron's
17. The Crown Theatre

BASING
MANOR HOUSE
13TH CENTURY

The site occupied by Lidl near the junction of Bellenden Road and Peckham High Street was once home to a fine mansion that dated back to at least the 13th century. It appears to have taken its name from the Basing family, who according to the late Peckham historian William Marshall, came to England with William the Conqueror from Port-en-Bessin near Bayeux in Normandy. They gained land in Wales and southern England, notably in London where Solomon de Basing was appointed a sheriff in 1215.

In the second half of the 17th century, Basing Manor House was bought by William Gardyner of Bermondsey and later passed to his grandson, Sir Thomas Gardyner, who has several mentions in Blanch's book Ye Parish of Camerwell. He is particularly remembered for a summons to appear before the Star Chamber, which he resisted on the grounds of infirmity, and for a bellicose letter warning Lord Dorchester of the territorial ambitions of Spain, which, he predicted, would cause its European neighbours "to sink and be as Sodom and Gomorrah". He added that he would have written a book on the subject, but was so busy with his melons and other fruits that he was unable to spare the time. Sir Thomas died in 1632 and his son George sold the manor in 1651. Its history thereafter evades detection until 1812 when Sir William East is recorded as the owner.

British History Online tells us: "the house was turned first into a farm and then into cottages". By the mid-Victorian era only part of the estate remained, having been used from 1850 as a girls' school overseen by a Mrs Tattersall. It was a wooden structure,

OPPOSITE LEFT
Weatherboarded
houses in Basing
Yard by John
Staines Babb, 1896

OPPOSITE RIGHT
Basing Manor House
photographed
in the fog a few
days before its
demolition, 5 Nov
1883

ABOVE
Watercolour of
Basing Manor House
by John Crowther,
1884

with moss-grown tiles, described by Blanch as "quaint", and by the South London Press as "picturesque", with a "general appearance of romantic antiquity".

Between 1883 and 1884, this historical gem was demolished and the land subsequently used as an extension of the depot of the London Tramways Company.

PECKHAM MANOR HOUSE (BRIDENHURST)

1672

Sometimes known as Bridenhurst, this manor house and superb garden formerly occupied a rectangular plot immediately north of Peckham High Street and west of Peckham Hill Street. Built for Sir Thomas Bond (1620-1685) on the site of an ancient manorial predecessor, here is history writ large.

Bond was a man of substance, but nothing is known of his early life or education. Records begin only when he became Treasurer, and in 1655, Comptroller of the Household of Henrietta Maria (1609-69), youngest daughter of Henri IV of France, widow of Charles I and mother of Charles II. He held the latter post until her death in 1669. The Earl of St. Albans is said to have introduced him at Court and to have received a bribe of 1,000 pistoles for procuring the appointment. Bond thus began his service during the Interregnum.

Henrietta Maria returned from France, as Queen Mother, when Charles II was restored to the throne in 1660, before leaving England for good in 1665. Inevitably, Bond must have spent much of his time in Paris and it was there in August 1655 that he married Marie Peillot de la Garde, daughter of Charles Peillot de la Garde, whose sister was a maid of honour to Henrietta, then Queen Catherine of Braganza. Two sons and a daughter were born, the eldest son Henry succeeding to the baronetcy. Johnson notices that, according to tradition, Bond was in great favour with Charles II, by whom he was created a

baronet, notwithstanding the fact that he was not of the Protestant faith. This may have been influenced by Charles's latent Catholic sympathies (he converted on his deathbed); but even more likely is that Sir Thomas was able to help the King financially. Entries in the State Papers mention large financial transactions including loans to the Crown amounting to £40,000 in the years 1667-8. Clearly Sir Thomas had become an important cog in the state machine.

According to Johnson, Sir Thomas had a house in Pall Mall and country estates at Peckham and Camberwell. Sir Thomas had purchased the large Peckham estate, situated roughly where Bonar Road is today. When they were determined in 1690, the Bond estates at Peckham and Camberwell comprised the manor of Bridenhurst, its mansion house in Peckham, ten other houses and 1,000 acres of land.

Settled back in London, in 1672, he had the existing manor house pulled down and replaced with an even finer house with splendid gardens. There he is said to have entertained Charles II, and his brother the future James II of England, who came to hunt with him. Another friend, the diarist John Evelyn, visited twice in June 1676 and September 1681. He wrote of Bond's home as "a new and fine house" with "a fine garden and prospect through the meadows to London". The famous garden was filled with

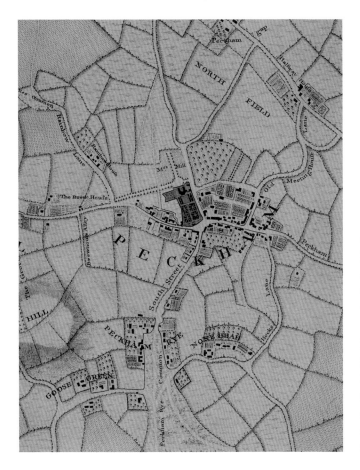

Peckham Manor House's location as shown on Rocque's plan of London and Environs, 1741 – 1745

trees, including many fruit varieties imported from France.

In 1685, shortly after the death of Charles II, Sir Thomas also passed away, whereupon his eldest son Henry, also a Catholic, succeeded to the baronetcy and inherited the properties in Peckham and Camberwell, albeit encumbered with mortgages. Charles II was succeeded by his brother James II, who in 1688 was famously allowed to depart to France in the face of fierce anti-Catholic sentiment.

Loyal to the defeated monarch, Sir Henry joined him in France, serving as Receiver-General and Pay-Master of his army. Meanwhile in England, under the Protestant William and Mary, the absent Sir Henry and several others were attainted of high treason, and stripped of all their land, property and chattels. The Peckham mansion had already been plundered by an angry mob in 1688, a

fate suffered by other properties owned by leading Catholics, while several of Sir Henry's creditors petitioned Parliament, arguing that the attainment of his estates should provide for the settlement of their debts.

In the face of this calamity, Sir Henry remained true to the Stuart cause. Indeed, in May 1692, he was among those who joined an attempt to invade England, led by the French and intended to restore James to the throne; an action that was decisively defeated in a naval battle off La Hogue.

Despite the strength of his allegiance to James, Sir Henry in 1695 made a petition to the British Crown, pleading various excuses for his residence abroad. He had not been able safely to return to England without the king's leave and pardon, but now desired to do so "with all duty and loyalty to the King and Government; therefore praying the King's pass to come to England and pardon of the said outlawry and reversal thereof, so that his estate may be the better sold to pay off his said debts".

The response to Sir Henry's petition was minuted in February 1696: "The King will grant these estates in trust to pay the debts, the residue to be in trust for His Majesty". This allowed him to sell the manor house and other property. There is evidence of a sale to Sir Thomas Trevor on 16 July 1700 of the house "built by the said Thomas Bond" for £11,947. And later, in 1708, during the reign of the passionately Protestant Queen Anne,

and with her consent, the Earl of Sunderland introduced a Bill to reverse Sir Henry's attainder. Henry's association with James was forgiven and his outlawry reversed. He was pardoned of all treasons and allowed to return to England.

Sir Thomas (later Lord Trevor) is said to have resided in the manor house occasionally, but after his death in 1731 the estate was purchased by Mrs Martha Hill, daughter of Sir Isaac Shard, a Sheriff of Surrey, and widow of a London merchant. She bequeathed it in trust to her youngest brother Isaac Pacatus Shard, but continued to live in the house until her death. It remained in the Shard family until its demolition in 1797 to make way for Hill Street (now Peckham Hill Street) and nearby developments. Thus a gem of Peckham's heritage was lost. Not even a painting remains.

But the land on which it stood has been put to good use. A Surrey Canal extension was dug, bringing supplies to Peckham's town centre, not least timber, through the business of the Whitten family, itself now historic. Eventually, the canal was filled in to become a popular walking trail and the Peckham Square complex was developed with its award-winning library and leisure centre, and most recently the vigorous Mountview Academy of Theatre Arts. At the time of writing, further construction is planned by London's University of the Arts (UaL) with the founding of a digital hub and college of technology, replacing the last home of Whitten Timber. Both Mountview and UaL promise to make a valuable addition to Peckham's considerable artistic heritage.

ABOVE
Canal Head, Surrey Canal, Peckham, 1925

OPPOSITE
Document describing the disposal of property relating to Peckham Manor, date unknown

Peckham's Heritage – Past, Present & Future

42.16422 PECKHAM, MANOR OF 2/5/72

Manor of Peckham between 1700 - 1850

Disposal of properties known as Muschamp's Quellotts, Dunston's Herne and Firs Field

In 1700 Sir Henry Bond released the properties to Sir Walter St.John of Battersea.

In 1722 Henry, Viscount St.John scattered each of above lands to various small holders, a selection of which is

Dunston's Herne to	(1)	Trustees of Battersea Free School
	(2)	Ann Field
	(3)	Francis East
Firs Field to	(1)	William Cartwright
	(2)	Thomas Moore

Muschamps Quellotts to Adam Laner for market gardens

HANOVER HOUSE
17TH CENTURY

Information concerning this grand house is sparse. Although clearly identified on the Greenwood map of 1830 adjacent to Hanover Chapel at the northern end of Rye Lane, the only detailed picture of its splendour seems to be a watercolour in the Lambeth Archives and a descriptive text in the memoirs of Mary Woolley, who lived there as a child between 1824 and 1831. This despite the fact that both sources attribute Hanover House to the venerated architect Sir John Vanbrugh.

Woolley was born Mary Pearce on 24 September 1822, at a small semi-detached house in Peckham Park. Her father was a lawyer, who was well-connected and successful enough to have a final resting place in Bunhill Fields. Woolley appears to have been taught at home. But this, and an appetite for reading, clearly implanted a facility that give her memoirs, written in 1895, a fascinating quality. They evoke a time when her uncles journeyed by stage-coach between Peckham Rye and the City, via the Old Kent Road, with guards who invariably carried pistols for fear of highwaymen attacking them on this lonely route. Her remembrance of visits to the old London Bridge and the original St Giles' Church, through streets without cabs and buses, gives us a rare sense of time and place. A special recollection, from the age of five, was of being taken to hear Elizabeth Fry address prisoners at Newgate. Woolley, alarmed at the rough appearance of the female prisoners, was taken on Fry's knee, and remained there throughout the service.

Woolley also gives us a glimpse of a different kind of heritage, one no longer in favour: a belief that strict parental discipline was beneficial. She recalls how, on one occasion, she had refused to learn a French grammar. In a tantrum she had thrown the book across the room, where it landed in her mother's cold bath. For this offence she was kept for three days in her room, on bread and water.

Woolley's mother was frequently ill and there were interludes at Ramsgate, Dover and Margate in pursuit of better health. By 1825, she had decided Peckham did not suit her and in March 1831 the family moved out. Woolley concluded that it must have been due to the damp, for she had a distinct recollection of water standing in the cellarage.

Woolley's recollections of those years, and of the house itself, remained acute. It was for her "the old fashioned house in Peckham, at the end of Rye Lane, on the way to my grandfather's at Peckham Rye…built by Sir John Vanbrugh in the latter part of the 17th century." She went on to describe it exactly: "It was of red brick with clamps of brick or stone work upon the four corners [which the adventurous girl used to climb], the walls were so solid that though large on the outside, in the rooms was not great space. "It stood in a garden [now roughly behind the present 56-66 Peckham High Street] and had a high gate of wood and iron work over the road, a stone flagged path to the door, at the top of several low, broad stone steps, with balustrades of stone." She adds: "The hall door was arched

round in brick and stone, and led into a wide hall, on each side, pillars to the roof and at the end a few steps down to the garden door, and a broad staircase in three sets of stairs, of dark mahogany, with long narrow windows to the garden.

"On each side of the hall were two rooms, one large and a smaller one to the back. I recollect that the two rooms on the right were made into a large dining room. There were two windows to the front in each large room, on the first floor, five windows, on the upper floor six, but not so large as below, the centre of this top floor window was a deep niche in the solid thickness of the walls, in which hung an alarm bell, on each side of this a small window to closet rooms, and two windows in each nursery at the sides.

"My parents' bedroom had two dressing rooms, my mother's to the front over the hall, my father's a nice room over the spare bedroom and dressing room. The first flight of stairs was very wide and handsome – on the landing, between the bedrooms was a large linen and store room. The upper flight of stairs were also in three sets like the first ones – but very narrow.

"Upstairs was a good landing, nurseries and servants' rooms, and those little closets were for coals, shoes or nursery supplies. The stone steps from hall to garden were also low and broad – on either side was stone work, ending with a solid slab, and our delight was to see who could be the best 'statue' on these bases, standing longest without movement.

"There was in the garden… a large summer house, such as was called, 'Queen Anne's', containing as much stone and brick as would now build two or three modern cottages. In the coach yard were all the buildings then needed for a family – brew house, bake house, laundry etc… there were on one side of the house made the third, and a wall to the lane completed it."

Mary's memories were "as vividly present" to her as they were 70 years before. By then, however, in about 1835, the historic house had been pulled down to make way for shops.

KENTISH DROVERS
17TH CENTURY

Information about this public house is scant. What can be said with confidence is that an ancient hostelry stood on the south side of Peckham High Street at its junction with South Street (now Rye Lane). This dated from at least the 17th century, perhaps earlier, for cattle were driven through Peckham for slaughter from the middle ages, and this location was a natural stop for the drovers, while their cattle grazed in nearby Cow Fields extending towards Nunhead. It was particularly popular during the Peckham Fair, until that festivity was banned after 1826.

Between 1856 and 1880 the pub had another somewhat macabre function. As one of a number of pubs near the Grand Surrey Canal, it became a receiving house for the Royal Humane Society, taking in corpses from the canal's waters, en route to Honor Oak Cemetery.

The building on the site is no longer a place either for refreshment or the recovery of mortal remains; the old house with its convivial frontage was demolished and rebuilt as a shop in 1954. But photographs record the former inn, and provide eloquent evidence of its past.

A public house of this name is now located on the opposite side of Peckham High Street, while the mediocre building on the former site next to the Jones and Higgins tower is quite out of character with the historic town centre.

Peckham High Street, 1920

WINCHESTER HOUSE
17TH CENTURY

This fine private residence, not to be confused with Winchester Palace, was located at 29 and 31 Peckham High Street, on the corner with Sumner Road. Little is known of its early history, when the main road was but a narrow country lane, though it has been claimed that Nell Gwynn once lived there. Solidly built, with walls of unusual thickness, it has been rumoured that a subterranean passage connected it with Basing Manor [add page ref once laid out]. One source says that without doubt there existed a passage of some kind, because in 1915 when a book-room was being created in the cellars, evidence of an opening was found revealing a circular hole about five feet in diameter filled up with bricks more recent than those of the original brickwork.

The building survived into the 19th century, having served as a grammar school before being purchased on 24 December 1873 by Thomas Tilling, the well-known transport pioneer. He had started his business in a yard of the Old Adam and Eve pub in 1850 and launched his first horse-drawn bus from Peckham to Oxford Circus in 1851. Winchester House became the headquarters of his thriving business, supplementing premises at 71. Eventually, as job master, he had stables for hundreds of horses for a variety of conveyances with depots across London.

The High Street was widened in 1890/92, leaving only a small front garden on each side of the main entrance of the old house. But workshops and a showroom were added on to the rear garden. It is said Tilling drove a landau daily between his home at Perry Hill and his Peckham base: an elegant office, boasting a lovely curving staircase, with niches for statues, and an enormous flagged kitchen.

After Tilling's death in 1893, his sons, Richard and Edward, made the business a limited company, and in 1920 moved to a new head office in Victoria Street. Though the company retained a presence at 71 High Street, they vacated the old house.

Sadly, during the Second World War, the Luftwaffe scored a direct hit on Winchester House. At one time, restoration was contemplated, but the building lay in ruins for

Present day view of site of Winchester House on the corner of Peckham High Street and Sumner Road, 2022

A dilapidated
Winchester House,
1953

some years before demolition. Eventually, the ground was cleared and used as a shabby, second-hand car lot.

A new and quite elegant building, Hollywood Nail and Beauty Supplies, has recently been erected on the site. Southwark's planning register record of its approval provides compelling evidence of a thoroughgoing respect for heritage following the designation of the town centre as a conservation area. The Planning Officer's report recognised that the location made the design of the building particularly important, where it "must preserve or enhance the character or appearance of the area" and, "must achieve a degree of detailing and materiality that matches the original buildings adjacent". It instructed that the design of the shop fronts should be timber with traditional features/proportions and detailing. It was also noted that the "consistency of the street frontage is key to the significance of the conservation area streetscape", and that the new development, including alterations and extensions, should respect the context of the conservation area and use complementary high quality materials. The issue of heritage was regarded as "key to any assessment of the proposal", as the open visibility of the site made "the impacts of its re-development all the more significant". This has resulted in the careful and appropriate reinvention of this site.

PELICAN HOUSE
LATE 17TH CENTURY

This imposing residence in Peckham High Street was best known as the home of Miles Stringer (1733-99), taking its name from ornamental pelicans at its entrance gates. Stringer was an eminent spice merchant in the City, and something of a celebrity in Peckham. He married Eliza Leach in 1761, fathered numerous children, and was evidently greatly loved. He is listed as one of the 'Obituaries of Remarkable Persons' in The Gentleman's Magazine of 1799. This tells us that he died at "his seat in Peckham" on the 1 April 1799 and was interred in the family vault at Greenwich. It said he had been simple and unaffected in his manners, just and upright in his dealings, merited the general regard of all who knew him, and the unbounded confidence of his friends. He was a liberal contributor to works of charity. The obituary

included the following glowing tribute:
"If these, with all the virtues in their train,
Be lov'd when living, and lamented dead
Then, Stringer, shall thy memory blest remain,
For these with thee resides, and are fled."

From 1825 to 1891, Pelican House was a grammar school for girls, after which it was occupied by the London Association for the Blind. By 1936, the original Georgian building was demolished, and the Association built workshops on the site, which it occupied until 1976. The former workshop building was then used as council offices until 1993 when it became vacant, disused, and derelict. Renamed Winnie Mandela House in 1989, that honour was reversed in 1995.

Planning applications for its replacement were made in 2000 and 2001, but withdrawn in the face of objections. Finally, in 2003, after negotiation, a revised application, conceding retention of the 1936 front ground-floor facade, the demolition of the rest of the building and the construction of a seven storey building behind the facade, was considered. Despite numerous objectors, the plan had support from, among others, The Peckham Society, and was successful. The compromise permitted the creation of 82 modern apartments, 19 of them said to be 'affordable', and was seen as bringing a vacant building back into beneficial use and providing additional housing. No mention was made of heritage.

ABOVE
The original Pelican House, though without the pelicans at the entrance gates

BELOW
Workshops built in the 1930s by the London Association for the Blind

Peckham's Heritage – Past, Present & Future

HANOVER CHAPEL

1717

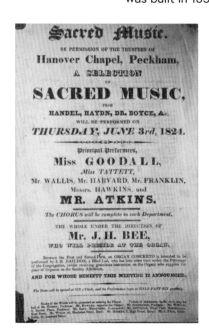

This story begins on the eponymous Meeting House Lane, where a meeting house or chapel was built in 1657 at the behest of the Rev John Maynard. Maynard had been appointed "to the sequestered vicarage of Camberwell" in 1646 and was there for some years but according to the author Edward E Cleal, his Puritanism made him so unpopular he was obliged to resign. So, he took up residence in Peckham, preaching at first in his own house "till the old meeting house which gave its name to the thoroughfare was erected".

In 1717, the congregation moved to a new, larger building at the junction of South Street (now Rye Lane) and Peckham High Street, where a succession of non-conformist ministers included Dr John Milner, "a solid but not attractive preacher", best known perhaps as master of the school where Oliver Goldsmith served unhappily as an usher.

The chapel was enlarged during Milner's 16-year tenure, but is said to have declined both materially and spiritually under the subsequent ministry of the Rev Richard Jones, who arrived in 1770 and stayed 30 long years. Blanch wrote of him as "not by any means successful as a preacher" and one whose "doctrine was not considered sound". By the turn of the 19th century the congregation had dwindled to "one old woman in the gallery, and 30 or 40 people downstairs", while the building was "in a most dilapidated condition".

Redemption came in the form of William Bengo Collyer (1782-1854), the son of a Deptford builder, who arrived at the chapel in 1800 as a teenager and showed himself to be an outstanding preacher. He was ordained the following year, when he accepted a pastorate that was to span more than half a century. At first, the number of church members was ten, but the congregation grew so rapidly that the building had to be extended. In 1816 the old chapel was deemed inadequate and was replaced the following year by a more impressive structure with seating for 1,000. It was opened by the Duke of Sussex, whose brother the Duke of Kent (father of Queen Victoria) donated the church organ. Such was the connection with the

Hanover Chapel in use as Peckham Picture Playhouse, c.1910 - 1914

ARCHITECTURAL NOTES

The site of Hanover Chapel is at the very nucleus of old Peckham on the prominent corner where Rye Lane meets Peckham High Street. The chapel was built in 1717 and then enlarged and rebuilt in the Georgian period when the more urbanised Peckham we know today was beginning to take shape.

This chapel is well documented in early photographs of Peckham and it also appears in a remarkable satirical print by George Cruickshank showing the Congregationalist preacher William Bengo Collyer and the opening of the rebuilt chapel in 1819.

The Georgian Hanover Chapel was a handsome Classical building with tall arched windows and well detailed masonry facades with slender pilasters, first floor rustications facing the High Street and Rye Lane. It must have had a bright and airy interior. With side galleries flanking a central space it would have accommodated 850 worshippers who came from across the capital to hear the sermons and hymns.

We think that the brick-faced west elevation with its arched windows partially survives to its west side and this can be seen from the Lidl car park. The distinctive chamfered plan form of the Hanover Chapel also survives in the present building on the site.

Edwardian Beaux Arts glamour arrived at the Hanover Chapel in 1910 when the chapel was converted in to one of Peckham's numerous early cinemas – 'the Peckham Picture Palace'. The chapel's front was transformed into a Triumphal Arch with the addition of a tall central niche. Bronze torcheres and ornamental sculpture on the facades beckoned Peckhamites to the flickering fantasy world of the early moving picture.

Hanoverian royal family that the building was given the name, Hanover Chapel.

Dr Collyer reigned supreme over all matters concerning the church and its congregation and his impact on Peckham was significant and enduring. The chapel remained at the centre of the town for the rest of the 19th century and beyond, through the years of Peckham's expansion and commercial success, as a symbol of Victorian and Edwardian values.

In time, its influence began to decline; in 1910 worship was transferred to Collyer Hall in Collyer Place, and later to a church in Bellenden Road. The chapel was converted into the Peckham Picture Playhouse, otherwise known as the Three Ps, opening in 1911, an incongruous change that was short-lived. In 1915, during the First World War, the cinema closed, and the former chapel was demolished to widen Peckham High Street.

Today there are only two reminders of this once-famous building: part of the rear wall of 1817, which is visible from the Lidl car park, and a plaque above a pawnbroker shop in the Central Buildings, 2 Rye Lane, which now occupy the Hanoverian corner. How's that for non-conformity?

This reinvention of the Hanover Chapel as a cinema did not last long. The present, practical and attractive 'Central Buildings' was constructed during the First World War. The style of the current 1916 building remembers the Georgian Chapel with its confident Classical detailing. The commercial building type of shops on the ground floor with residential accommodation above is emblematic of the sharp rise of real estate value as Peckham town centre became one of South London's foremost shopping destinations in the early 20th century.

Central Buildings is an extremely attractive, compact example of London's Edwardian Baroque Revival. Note the three pretty projecting bays, two on Rye Lane, one on the High Street. The first floor windows have pediments supported by Tuscan columns. Elegant Palladian windows are featured on the second floor. (The lovely gauged brick arches to the latter hints at the influence of the Arts & Crafts Architect Sir Edwin Lutyens on England's early 20th century commercial architecture). The middle part of the elevation to Rye Lane was damaged in the post-war years when the shoe shop Peter Lord installed a glass curtain wall in this location. Happily this is now removed. The lost architectural details could be easily restored!

Plaque still visible on Rye Lane today denoting the site of Hanover Chapel, 1981

SITE OF THE OLD
HANOVER CHAPEL.
1717 — 1910
MADE FAMOUS UNDER
THE MINISTRY OF
DR W. B. COLLYER.
1801 — 1852.

THE GARDEN OF PETER COLLINSON

1724

Peter Collinson (1694-1768) can arguably be claimed to be Peckham's most distinguished past citizen. Merchandising cloth was his trade, but botany and natural history his calling. A Fellow of the Royal Society, a member of the Society of Antiquaries, a founding member of the Foundling Hospital, and much involved in the foundation of the British Museum, Collinson was a key player in the evolution of British gardening, engaging with the public men of his time across the world: none more so than Hans Sloane and Benjamin Franklin.

As an importer, he sought first to enhance his own garden by asking his American suppliers, many of them fellow Quakers, to include plants and seeds with their rolls of cloth. Famously, in 1734, this informal practice led to a long and mutually beneficial relationship with John Bartram, a Philadelphian farmer, which developed into a botanical trade across the Atlantic Ocean. This introduced many new species to Britain, to be supplied-on to grace the gardens of stately homes and offer inspiration to countless gardeners.

Collinson, at the age of two, was brought to the care of his maternal grandmother Martha Tomson, in what is said to have been "the attractive and salubrious" village of Peckham. One of the features of her home was a formal garden famed for its topiary and exotic plants. In his diary he wrote: "I often

Portrait of Peter Collinson, F.R.S, 1780

went with them [his relatives] to visit the few nursery gardens round London, to buy fruit and flowers, and clipt yews in the shape of birds, men and ships." Thus was awakened his liking for gardens and plants, and his lifetime interest in collecting all things natural.

In 1724, he married Mary Russell, setting up home in Peckham in what Peter called "the most Delightful place to Mee". He continued to live here until 1749. Here the mystery begins, for although local records confirm his presence in Peckham, they do not identify the precise location of his home. We know he had a very special garden, stocked with exotic plants, and land sufficient from which to supply trees, but quite where it was sited has defeated many researchers. And this despite his garden being internationally renowned at the time, visited by fellow botanists, including Linnaeus, Sloane and Kalm, and described in print by the latter.

Collinson left a considerable correspondence, but none from his Peckham address. Two local historians place his home and garden as having been on Meeting House Lane, and this vague setting features in the Camberwell Golden Jubilee Guide for 1950. But evidence is lacking. Here is heritage lost, not only by redevelopment, but by the passage of time.

Ultimately famous in England, Europe and America, Collinson thought of trees as providing "a pleasing scene for a man of fortune to behold the rising groves, barrenness made fertile, our country improved, ourselves made useful and happy, and posterity enriched." Dr John Fothergill described him as having "a pleasing and social aspect - open and communicative… ready to relieve and sympathise." He would have delighted in Peckham Rye Park. Odd that we have done nothing to honour him.

RIGHT
Great Martigon …from Pensilvania painted by Georg Dionysius Ehret. Originates from the library of Peter Collinson, who noted on the back that the Martigon was sent to him by John Bartram and flowered in his 'Garden at Peckham' in September 1736.

PECKHAM HOUSE

1740s

This splendid mansion once stood between Peckham Road and Highshore Road on the site now occupied by Harris Academy Peckham. It is unusual in that there is a clear historical record from its inception through to its demolition.

The story begins in March 1742 with the lease of a six-acre portion of French Field – as the land was then known – from Peter Bronsdon, a shipwright from Deptford, and James Collinson, a dealer in textile fabrics and brother of the botanist Peter Collinson. The indenture in the Minet Library in Lambeth has various covenants, including one requiring Collinson to build, within two years, a "substantial brick dwelling house on part of the said land".

In 1751, the site and buildings, "lately erected thereon", passed to Charleton Palmer and subsequently, in 1787, to five individuals including Charles Lewis Spitta, to whom the land and buildings were released. The historian Blanch tells how Spitta and his family lived in great style, holding fêtes – or what would now be termed garden parties – for their neighbours. They also gave generously to the local poor. However, the family's luxurious contentment was not to last. A lease of 1816 lists Spitta as "a bankrupt", and in 1824 Peckham House was advertised for sale as "a most respectable and commodious residence".

Failing to attract a buyer, in 1826 it was acquired for development as a private mental asylum. Three years later Peckham House was licensed to receive 172 pauper

Interior view of hallway in Peckham House, 1953

Exterior view of Peckham House, 1953

patients and 40 private patients and so began an inglorious chapter in the building's history. Charles Mott, its half owner and controlling mind, was a man of extreme parsimony and the asylum is still infamous for the meagre diet of its unfortunate residents. Mott left to become an assistant Poor Law commissioner in 1834, but his spirit appears to have lingered. In 1844, the commissioners noted that the diet of the pauper patients had always been "a source of trouble". An inquest on one inmate found death attributable to severe neglect. Cholera broke out in October 1848, by which time the asylum accommodated 317 paupers and 50 private patients. In 1866 the commissioners again commented "very unfavourably" on its condition.

Standards began to change with the appointment of a new superintendent in 1872. Dr Alonzo Henry Stocker was a man of high medical qualifications with experience gained at another asylum. He made improvements both to the building and to the care of patients. A journalist, given a guided tour in 1874, found that patients were treated with the utmost kindness and attention, and that "nothing that can tend to ameliorate the medical condition of the patient is left undone".

Over the years, Peckham House became a "private hospital for the treatment of patients suffering from nervous and mental illnesses". Provision steadily improved, and photographs from the 1920s in a brochure held by Southwark Local History Library and Archive testify to a well-run and quite opulent establishment. It continued under the direction of members of the Stocker family until 1952, when financial difficulties are said to have forced the family to put the house on the market.

The London County Council (LCC) saw the site as an irresistible opportunity and the ideal location for a new school. The cost of purchase, clearance and partial redevelopment was in the region of £100,000. LCC planners gave consent for a change of use, and in 1954 a precious part of Peckham's heritage was lost.

Peckham Secondary
School for Girls,
Camberwell,
London: view of the
gymnasium from the
east, 1958

ARCHITECTURAL NOTES

The Peckham House was an attractive Early Georgian mansion, one of a number of similar houses which could be found in the Surrey villages surrounding south London. Most of these houses are now lost.

To get a sense of what it looked like, see the slightly earlier Ranger's House on the west side of Blackheath or Vanbrugh Castle on the east side of Blackheath. Other elite houses from this period in Peckham's history can still be seen in the listed buildings at 4-10 Queens Road, further east along the High Street.

The present architectural interest of the Peckham House site stems from the replacement modernist Harris Academy school which was built in 1957 by the noteworthy 'Brutalist' architects Lyons Israel & Ellis, well-known for their school projects from the 1950s to the 1970s.

It was built as a Girls' Comprehensive School by the London County Council to accommodate 1,590 pupils.

The elements of the school were carefully deployed to preserve the existing mature trees and lawns of the former Peckham House. In this way something of the 'place' of Peckham House survives.

The school is noteworthy for its advanced use of precast and in-situ concrete elements, typical of this progressive, Le Corbusier-inspired practice. The celebrated architect Sir James Stirling was the assistant in charge of building this school for Lyons Israel and Ellis, so this could be considered his first built work. When seen with the adjacent Pelican Estate one is reminded of the radical transformation of Peckham's townscape toward modernism in the post-war period.

In the early 2000s the school was reworked by Curl la Tourelle Head architects when it became the Academy @ Peckham. About half the 1957 school was lost; however the original 1950s concrete framed structures are easily distinguishable from the newer buff brick buildings, of less aesthetic significance.

Edward Hassell's 1831 image of the front of Marlborough House

MARLBOROUGH HOUSE
18TH CENTURY

This "fine old mansion" was situated north of Peckham High Street, where Marmont Road is today. The location is shown on the Dewhirst map of 1842. Curiously, while information about the building itself is scant, there is a proliferation of material relating to its eventual use as a workhouse. What is clear is that any glory attached to its long residence as a family home is in striking contrast to its final inglorious chapter.

We are indebted to the assiduous Blanch for some description of the house. Writing in 1875, not many years after its demolition, he related that it "contained a noble entrance-hall and a fine oak staircase, and frescoes adorned the walls and ceilings". He saw the tradition that the mansion was once the residence of the Duke of Marlborough as "more than doubtful" but thought that it may be assumed to have been home to some

members of the Marlborough family. While there is no proof, there are pointers, which suggest that the Marlboroughs did indeed have a connection with Peckham:

David Johnston, who lived in Peckham between 1830 and 1848, wrote in his autobiographical reminiscences (1885): "In Peckham stands Marlborough House, the ancient seat of the hero of Blenheim, with all his deeds emblazoned on the walls, in good preservation."

Elizabeth, wife of Charles, the 3rd Duke of Marlborough was the granddaughter of Sir Thomas Trevor, the one-time owner of Peckham Manor.

According to John Beasley's Peckham in the 19th Century (1973), Lady Edward Spencer Churchill, daughter-in-law of George, the

6th Duke of Marlborough sang in the second concert given at Peckham's public hall, an engagement which seems improbable without a prior connection with Peckham.

There is a painting of Blenheim House, across the road from Marlborough House, which shows it to have been a grand mansion, evidently home to prominent occupants. Smith and Roethe say that it predated the 18th century, and was set within its own grounds.

Deborah Elliott notices that Leopold Wagner in his book Names and Their Meaning: A Book for the Curious (1892) notes: "Marlborough Road, Peckham, covers the ground plot of a Marlborough House, residence of John Churchill, Duke of Marlborough." She also observes that Arabella, John's sister, was the mistress of the Duke of York and had four children from him. She was a lady-in-waiting to Anne Hyde, the Duke of York's first wife. Might Peckham have been a convenient hideaway for royal mistresses? Was this, perhaps, the purpose of the Duke of York's occasional residence in a house on Peckham High Street?

Marlborough House became vacant around the beginning of the 19th century, when it was made one of a number of remote, privately managed locations to which the City of London's "indoor paupers" could be farmed out. In 1837, following the 1834 Poor Law Amendment Act, these disposals were brought under the control of the newly formed City of London Union, and restricted to two poor houses: Marlborough House and Stepney Green. The former provided a refuge for some of the City's indigent, homeless people and also catered for casual,

sometimes violent vagrants, in conditions that were to become the focus of intense scrutiny.

Big trouble began with a letter to The Times, published on 15 July 1846. This referred to a report from the London Fever Hospital which stated that considerably more than one fifth of all its admissions came from Marlborough House, said to be "the most easily accessible asylum for the house-less poor in or near the metropolis". It was filled to excess every night, and on particular occasions, as at the end of harvest and hopping, significantly overcrowded in a poorly ventilated room with a sloping roof, closed at night, with no separation of those with fever or other diseases and those without. The letter went on to castigate the Poor Law commissioners for lack of attention and supervision, adding that "it is left to the medical officers of a valuable charity to detect and describe an evil of so alarming a character as to seem to call for immediate and even parliamentary interposition". The named commissioners, included Mr Mott, one-time infamous superintendent of Peckham House Asylum.

This indictment prompted a flurry of reports, mostly defensive, but nevertheless revealing. One that Marlborough House was home to "the lowest class of vagrants and prostitutes, mingled with the most destitute of the more deserving poor", with as many as 30,000 temporary admissions in the previous year. Other reports admitted that at certain times the numbers had been for a short while very large. At such times additional accommodation was provided by deploying two sheds used for oakum picking and stone breaking as sleeping wards. The number in excess consisted chiefly of Irish paupers under orders of removal.

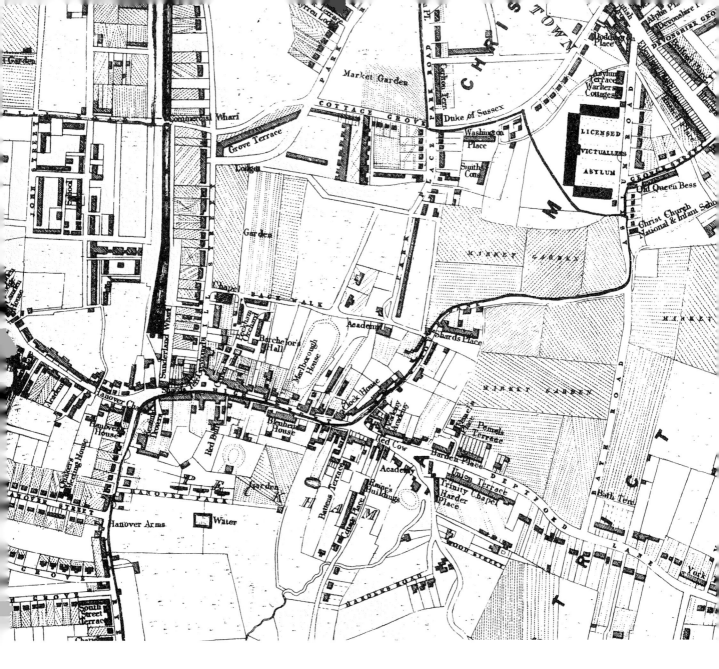

Detail of Dewhirst map, 1842

The "casuals" slept on a straw mattress, with a blanket and rug. Their food generally consisted of bread and cheese for supper and bread and porridge for breakfast. During the day the men would break stones or pick oakum "according to their ability", and the women picked oakum for four hours after breakfast.

Medical officer Henry Fidler concluded that "the circumstances which the paupers were accommodated in the wards would not originate fever if they were clean and healthy, but were favourable to the development of fever where the seeds are already sown". He believed the fever originated out of the establishment, not in it, "for the most part".

Such was the fate of the homeless of Peckham and its environs, and such the prelude to the eventual demolition of Marlborough House.

PECKHAM LODGE
18TH CENTURY

One of the most historically interesting of Peckham's buildings, this opulent residence in South Street (now Rye Lane) is thought to have been built by Isaac Heaton (c.1705-1774), a wealthy malt distiller. It is mentioned in an Act of 1776, which defined the arrangements for lighting and watching the villages of Peckham and Camberwell as not applying "beyond the House of Isaac Heaton Esquire in South Street", referring to the second Isaac Heaton (1733-1810), who had inherited his father's land and properties. This was the local philanthropist best known for giving employment to some 500 destitute men, c.1800, to dig an enormous hole in his estate, creating a lake, and building the famous Heaton's Folly (at some distance from the lodge). He never married, and when he died, Claude Champion de Crespigny, husband to Isaac's step-sister Mary, inherited the lodge.

The buildings in Rye Lane have been renumbered more than once. It will be clearer to say that three houses were situated on the east side immediately north of Hanover Park. These were Champion Lodge, White House and Peckham Lodge. They are clearly indicated on the OS map of 1871, and also on a plan in the 'De Crespigny Terrier' (1840). These indicate the shape of Peckham Lodge and its garden, and distinctive crescent-shaped entrance gates. The 1840 plan even gives the names of the neighbours to the north.

No picture exists; instead The Lodge is remembered for what went on there. One of its occupants, from 1808, was Timothy Brown, a Lombard Street banker and a partner with Samuel Whitbread in the famous brewing firm. He was no ordinary businessman, being ready to explore new ideas, challenge orthodox thinking and champion human rights: so much so that he was known by the soubriquet 'Equality Brown'. These were turbulent times. Britain had avoided the violence of the French Revolution, but a dissident thirst for social and political reform was gaining ground. Charles Darwin had yet to enter the scene, but there were some radical thinkers already questioning the rationality of fundamental religious beliefs. Brown's interest in the Enlightenment was evident from his choice of friends, notably John Horne Tooke and Sir Francis Burdett. He helped to finance a number of radical, freethinking publications, including Thomas Paine's 'The Rights of Man' and Baron d'Holbach's 'Ecce Homo', befriending their publishers when they were charged, imprisoned and pilloried. He was also a regular member of a Sunday dinner group of intellectuals who met to explore radical and reformist ideas at Tooke's home in Wimbledon. When Tooke died in 1812 Brown hosted these meetings at Peckham Lodge. He also famously befriended William Cobbett during the latter's confinement in Newgate, and stood surety for him on his release in 1812. They remained close friends; when

ABOVE
Aquatint of Heaton's Folly by John Hassell, 1804

BELOW
Detail of Peckham town centre shown on OS Map, 1871

Peckham's Heritage – Past, Present & Future

Cobbett moved to London in 1815 he lived for a time with Brown, continuing to write his 'Political Register' from Peckham Lodge.

Brown died on 4 September 1820, and was buried at Camberwell's St. Giles. The lodge became home to Richard Heale, and from 1830 was leased to Richard and William Pulford. They left no remembrance. The 1871 OS map shows Peckham Lodge clearly, but the version by 1894 has a building in front of it, and there is a record that the lodge was demolished in 1900 for an extension of the Jones and Higgins department store.

ST CHRYSOSTOM CHURCH

1814

There is more than one way of preserving heritage, but the following example is particularly appropriate for a Christian church - resurrection! Located on the east side of Peckham Hill Street, everything about this place of worship was unusual: not least its striking design by an unknown architect and the fact that it came to be named after the soubriquet of a 4th century bishop of Constantinople.

It opened in 1814 as a proprietorial church known simply as Peckham Chapel, owned by some 41 shareholders who each committed £100 to its creation. Impressive, with a crypt, galleries and an upstairs chapel, it is said to have been built as a 'chapel of ease' for St. Giles. As the number of proprietors dwindled it became possible in 1864 for the church to be purchased and brought into use as the parish church of St Chrysostom, much the same time as the railways reached Peckham. At some point in the 20th century the church fell into disuse, its vicar sick, reviving only when a Franciscan priest, George Potter, arrived in 1923. He has described his remarkable tenure at St Chrysostom's in two autobiographies, spelling out his dismay in finding the church closed and the churchyard a rubbish dump. The inside proved to be "spotlessly clean" but there was no heating, parts of the ceiling were missing and pots and buckets were strategically placed around the sanctuary. All previous vicars had lived outside the parish, but Potter aspired to live among the people, sharing their difficulties. He decided to reside in the dilapidated parish hall, until 1925 when an invasion of rats from the next-door factory proved too much. Gradually, with help, he overcame extraordinary difficulties by extraordinary means, and remained as vicar until 1938.

His foundation of the Brotherhood of the Holy Cross, which strove to improve the lives of difficult, deprived and delinquent boys, is another - and well-known - story.

Moving from the parish hall to the derelict Eagle Pub, and onward to a series of hard-won premises in Peckham and Nunhead, Potter and the brothers, celibate and without salary or stipend, followed the aims of

Interior view of St Chrysostom, date unknown

Exterior view of St Chrysostom, date unknown

St. Francis through practical action. After leaving St. Chrysostom's Father Potter went freelance, often attracting very large congregations. His dedicated, frequently improvised, achievements led to him being made an Honorary Canon of Southwark Cathedral. St Chrysostom's was not so fortunate. Damaged by bombing during the Second World War, it survived, but again deteriorated. Attempts at restoration were made in 1960/61, but it became evident that the roof timbers were severely decayed by dry rot. In 1962 the building was declared unsafe, and in the following year was demolished. Later, the site later was sold, to make way for shops and flats.

This was not the end. In 1960, the parishes of St. Chrysostom and St. Jude had been amalgamated, the latter parish church having been destroyed in the war. It was decided that the new church and parish centre of St John (Chrysostom) and St Andrew being constructed in Meeting House Lane should replace the demolished and bombed-out churches, incorporating the Hill Street bell and the crucifix which had been fixed above its front door. New life was generated in a modern setting replete with art works, suitable for both religious and secular use: worship, music and drama.

PECKHAM METHODIST CHURCH

1865

Peckham is notorious for its religious non-conformity. That inclination is evidenced in the divergence of Congregational, Baptist, Quaker, Capuchin Franciscans and Methodist adherents. The latter version of Christian thinking can be traced to John Wesley, who visited Peckham on at least ten occasions between 1783 and 1791. According to John Beasley who has written two accounts of the emergence of a Wesleyan Society in Peckham, believers of that persuasion first came to this prosperous village in 1805, thinking it a "quiet and pleasant spot in which to retire". Previously they had been part of a boat-building community along the south side of the River Thames, some of whom had become connected with a meeting house attached to the old Silver Street Chapel in Rotherhithe.

This informal affiliation, first joined in a private house, expanded to a Wesleyan meeting place: Providence Hall, in Harder's Road (now Wood's Road). Soon this building, with seating for only 60 worshippers, proved inadequate. A new chapel was proposed, provided the cost of the land should not exceed £100 and the cost of erection and fitting less than £420. A site, then surrounded by fields, was found in Stafford Street which, albeit at greater cost, was brought into use in 1834.

But this was merely a prelude to the building of the Peckham Methodist Church. John attributes its principal genesis to Rev. John S. Workman, appointed to work in Southwark in 1862. He contended that Wesleyan Methodism was not represented as well as Peckham deserved, given its population of around 30,000, and proposed that a more suitable church was needed. Notwithstanding concerns that this was financially impossible, he succeeded in forming a committee to

Peckham's Heritage – Past, Present & Future

LEFT
The Burning of Peckham Methodist Church, Queen's Road, 1972

RIGHT
Present day Peckham Methodist Church rebuilt behind Cherry Tree Court, 1985

Peckham Methodist Church before the fire, 1972

time, while the building remained steadfast, the society around it changed. By 1939 the attendance at services diminished to the extent that the church now seemed too large for the congregation. The Second World War brought new challenges, as a number of Peckham's churches were devastated by Nazi bombs. The Methodist chapel was one of those most severely damaged, compelling its closure. Only after extensive repair did it reopen on 6 November 1954. Thereafter, its trustees did all they could to keep it going, but became painfully aware that the cost of maintenance was increasingly beyond available resources. A souvenir programme produced for the centenary in 1965 acknowledged this and made it clear that the trustees were giving serious thought to ways and means to aid the work of the church. A "bold and imaginative plan" was needed if the work of the church was to continue.

The conclusion reached by the trustees on 30 November 1969 was that the only realistic course of action was to replace the burdensome church with a "new building designed to meet new needs", constructed in conjunction with the sale of half the available land to a housing association. On 23 September 1972, a last service was held to give thanks for the church's past, but also to look forward to a continuity of God's work in a new home.

This was not quite the end. On 26 October 1972, soon after the land had been sold, a fire engulfed the building, as though a token of its fate, attributed to two boys who were never apprehended. The site, including two cottages in Harder's Road dating from 1902, which had once accommodated Providence Hall, was cleared, making way for the present community church.

seek a suitable site, and two years later the necessary land was purchased for £1,600. Despite formidable difficulties, John Workman raised the funds and the foundation stone was laid on 5 May 1864. Remarkably, the top stone was placed on the spire less than seven months later. The new chapel was opened on 9 February 1865, when Workman led "the congregation out of the little foursquare chapel in Stafford Street into the spacious and beautiful sanctuary in Queen's Road".

The new chapel, which cost a little under £7,000, attracted a much larger congregation; so much so that a lecture hall and classroom were added in 1874/5. It stood as a conspicuous local landmark, and reached out to a generally affluent section of Peckham's population into the 20th century, through and beyond the First World War. But, over

JONES & HIGGINS

1867

Though neither of the founders of this famous department store were born or brought up in Peckham, their influence on the town centre was long and profound.

George Randell Higgins, born in Oxford in 1844, lost his father at the age of eight. Four years later he had to leave school to make his own living. After a six-year apprenticeship with Nathaniel Sweetman, an Oxford draper, George moved to London. Aged 18, he found a job with Spencer, Turner & Boldero, a retail and wholesale drapers on Lisson Grove in

Marylebone at a salary of £20 a year. But he did so well that his annual pay was soon increased to £80.

In those days employees often lived in the shop, and it so happened that the young Higgins slept in the same room as 25-year-old Edwin Jones. Though markedly different in temperament, they were to become lifelong friends.

In 1867, having saved £210, they decided to strike out on their own, renting a small (12 feet square) draper's shop at 1 Coburn Terrace, Peckham, previously kept by one Madame Shute. The terrace, which ran south along the east side of Rye Lane, comprised a row of small shops culminating in an old-fashioned country house with a large garden.

Living frugally, sleeping under the counter and without domestic help, Jones and Higgins started with just one customer: their previous employer. The first week's turnover was a mere £13.19.4d. But a blend of cautiousness (Jones), enthusiasm (Higgins) and hard work soon proved successful. A year later they were able to acquire 5 Coburn Terrace, and over the next ten years they added seven further shops.

By then their original shop had become 3 Rye Lane, and eventually they were to own 1 to 49 Rye Lane as well as 68, 70 and 72 Hanover Park and 76 and 106 Peckham High Street.

LEFT
Founders George Randell Higgins (left) and Edwin Jones (right) on Rye Lane, date unknown

OPPOSITE
Jones and Higgins Rye Lane, date unknown

High Street, Peckham.

Some of the estate was rented out, not least the late-Victorian building on the corner of Rye Lane and Hanover Park, which was built and leased in 1895 to Midland Bank at an annual rent of £250. The manager was paid £200 a year, with a bank house attached.

In 1890, Jones left the partnership to devote more time to his duties with the London County Council. The store's acquisitions then extended to 23 Rye Lane, and would continue to grow in his absence. As a guest, he joined the 25th anniversary celebrations in 1892, contributing a speech which encapsulated the singularity of this remarkable business. Other houses, he pointed out, could claim as long a life. Nor was there anything peculiar to the business of Jones & Higgins in the mere matter of success but there were some features it would not have been easy to parallel elsewhere. The firm had started in what was then one of the most unpromising neighbourhoods in London. It had been a success gained by a strict adherence to practices and principles that alone can win and hold the confidence of the public. The object in business, he concluded, is not solely to make money – there is something more to do in the world than that, and Mr Higgins had shown qualities of the heart other than a mere desire for gain.

As though to salute their success, Jones & Higgins acquired 1 Rye Lane and the adjacent property on Peckham High Street and built the iconic structure that everyone knows now. It opened in 1894 and remains today as Peckham's landmark building, albeit with its Victorian central clocktower replaced with a plainer version.

In 1896 it was decided to form a limited company. This began with a capital of £250,000 and attracted some 11,000 applications for shares. Jones returned to chair the board, and with Higgins as managing director the store became legendary, maintaining its reputation for honourable trading, courtesy to customers, value for money and staff relations that secured loyalty and esteem from employees. The deaths of directors and employees were faithfully recognised and the deaths of monarchs prompted special announcements and store closure. Annual sales were a strong feature, with a big emphasis on the opportunity to secure "very cheap goods" and "substantial remarking of regular stock throughout all departments". Sometimes sales would extend to the entire stock required from failed competitors. By 1906, the scope of the business had expanded to be advertised as "complete house furnishers".

ABOVE LEFT
Jones and Higgins on corner of Peckham High Street and Rye Lane with its Victorian clocktower, 1910

ABOVE RIGHT
Entrance to Jones and Higgins workshops and stables on Hanover Park, date unknown

BELOW
Text reads *'Messrs. Jones and Higgins'* original shop 3 Rye Lane, formally 1 Coburn Terrace, March 16 1867'

MESSRS. JONES & HIGGINS' ORIGINAL SHOP
No. 3 Rye Lane, formerly No. 1 Coburn Terrace
MARCH 16, 1867

During the war years, the management did all they could to support the war effort. So did the staff. Every male employee of eligible age joined up. Of the 210 who served, 39 made 'the supreme sacrifice' and were subsequently honoured by a war memorial plaque. In the absence of most of the male staff, their accommodation in Hanover Park was made available to the War Office and first housed Belgian refugees, and then in December 1915 became the Hanover Park VAD Hospital. Consisting of two houses with a large garden, the company made the rooms ready for conversion, and added a generous donation. The hospital served until the end of the war, finally closing in April 1919 and later becoming a car park for Morrisons supermarket.

In the meantime, in June 1916, Edwin Jones also passed into history. He left no children, so the business continued in the Higgins family alone. But Edwin's name lived on, and with his former partner as chairman, Jones & Higgins went from strength to strength. By 1920, it was the largest department store in Greater London, with more than 40 separate departments. This was the year of George Higgins' death, but by then his son Charles had joined the directors, and the business continued on its firm foundations of integrity and high moral principles.

By 1923, Jones & Higgins employed 1,000 staff, and in 1925 the store spanned more than three acres, with a frontage of over 400 feet, featuring an arcade almost equal in length to the whole shop front. Recreational opportunities for staff included a lending library, an athletic association and the use of a nearby public hall for concerts and dances. Its popularity with customers showed no signs of slowing down. Mabel August, writing in 'Life in Old South London', observed: "As time went on they had to have a policeman to control the crowds wanting to enter. Regular customers were given a card to enter by the back door half an hour before the front doors opened."

Alas, war was looming once again and in 1943 Peckham was heavily bombed. Two hits caused great damage at both ends of the Jones & Higgins estate, closing the store for 11 weeks. Austerity prevailed both during the war and in its aftermath. The damaged buildings were renovated in 1953, but the reconstructed symbolic clocktower now looked out on Peckham's austerity.

In 1955, the business was taken over by Great Universal Stores, albeit retaining the Jones & Higgins brand name until 1980, reopening the following year as The Houndsditch Centre. But the glory days were over and worse was to follow when in 1985 the greater part of the famous Rye Lane estate was demolished to make way for the Aylesham Centre. Only the former HSBC Bank building and the renovated clocktower with its ornate appendage remain. The latter remnant is now iconic and precious. At the time of writing, this historic facade and the rooms behind it are dirty and neglected.

In Southwark Council's appraisal, following Peckham town centre's designation as a conservation area in 2011, the remnants of the Jones & Higgins store were recognised as being a "significant legacy" of historic importance. The building until recently used by HSBC Bank was judged "of particular note", and the clocktower, with most of its original Renaissance detailing, described as "one of Peckham's most important landmarks". It is to be hoped that, as part of the plans for a newly restored Peckham, this pairing will continue to be given the respect and esteem they deserve.

ABOVE
Jones and Higgins cafe, date unknown

OPPOSITE
Jones and Higgins entrance below clocktower on corner of Peckham High Street and Rye Lane, date unknown

ARCHITECTURAL NOTES

The Jones & Higgins site, where Rye Lane meets Peckham High Street, is the most conspicuous in Peckham. This is the nucleus of the village of Peckham, and as the high street bends slightly north here, the tall landmark clocktower can be seen from the approach to Peckham from the west, marking the town centre's finest architectural landmark. It has an interesting history. Built in 1893, it was designed by the leading lights of Southwark's Victorian architects, Henry Jarvis & Son, based in Trinity Square. Perhaps wishing to give a continental panache to the new building, the architects chose to base the Portland stone-clad facade on the Torre dell'Orologio (St Mark's Clocktower) in Piazza San Marco in Venice. Like Jones & Higgins, its arched doorway leads to an important city market.

Unlike the Torre dell'Orologio, which is surmounted with a large bell, Jarvis & Son chose to add a further three stages to the Jones & Higgins tower, culminating in a dome and cupola, adding a measure of baroque chutzpah to Peckham's town centre.

The people of Peckham and beyond flocked to the renewed department store and the architectural extravagance of the new building handsomely paid off for the firm's company directors. Sadly the top of the tower and the elaborate stone and metal mansard roof were taken down in the 1950s after wartime damage. They were then replaced by the present, rather simpler stone dome and weathervane. The 1950s marked a nadir of regard for Victorian architecture and as London rebuilt in a new style after World War Two, exuberant Victorian domes, decorative urns, spires and balustrades

were removed from buildings across the capital. Some of the architectural drama and eclectic detailing of the original Jones & Higgins ensemble can be seen by visiting the St Saviour's Union Infirmary (Dulwich Community Hospital) on East Dulwich Grove. This was built by Jarvis & Son a few years earlier in 1885.

There are a number of other noteworthy projects by this prolific practice that survive: they rebuilt Borough Market in the 1860s after the Southeastern railway constructed three railway lines across the site. They designed the Globe Tavern in the market itself. They also built the former Walworth Town Hall on Walworth Road and St John's Church on Larcom Street just behind it. Also look out for the Grade-II* listed St Augustine's Church (now converted into flats) on Lynton Road in Bermondsey, and north of the river a handsome Gothic Revival commercial building at 109 Farringdon Road, also listed.

The Clocktower on St Mark's Square, Venice, as drawn by Francisco de Holanda in his Álbum dos Desenhos das Antigualhas, 1538-1540

GORDON'S BREWERY

1876

This imposing brewery once occupied a huge site on the north side of Chadwick Road, behind the houses of Lyndhurst Way. It opened in 1876 and was the second venture of Alexander Gordon, who had struck success with a similar business in Islington. Designed by Frederick Meeson, it was depicted in The Building News in 1877 with a drawing that captures the brewery's architectural splendour.

The brewery came to Peckham in the heyday of the temperance movement. In Victorian Britain drunkenness was seen as a scourge, frequently leading to violence, crime, gambling and prostitution, and a threat to civilised progress. The temperance movement urged moderation and more often, total abstinence backed up by a pledge.

This was a period of rapid urban expansion. Between the censuses of 1871 and 1911 London's population grew by more than 86%, from just over 3.8 million to nearly 7.2 million. Peckham, with the opening of a railway station in 1865 and Tilling's horse-drawn tram, lay within relatively easy reach of central London and became more densely populated. The number of public houses also increased exponentially. Such was the backdrop of social conflict for Gordon's Brewery, a confident and massive riposte against puritan protest, dividing opinion.

Information about the conduct of the business is sparse. The Brewery History

Society has a record of an annual outing in June 1888, when nearly 300 employees had a bean feast in Clacton. And there are some details of the beers brewed in the 1890s. Alexander Gordon died in 1895, and the business passed to his nephews, George William Gordon and Alexander Duncan Gordon. The latter gentleman died in 1915, and shortly afterwards the site was requisitioned by the army.

But Gordon's Brewery has one considerable claim to fame which has nothing to do with beer. In 2015, a project led by Melissa Jo Smith recreated a famous photograph taken 100 years earlier by Frederick Finch. It showed horses and soldiers of the Royal Field Artillery assembled in Lyndhurst

ABOVE
Brewery worker with a glass of beer, 1860

OPPOSITE ABOVE
Gordon's Brewery, in The Building News, January 12th 1877

OPPOSITE BELOW
Soldiers and horses from the Camberwell Division of the Royal Field Artillery on Lyndhurst Way (formally road), 1915

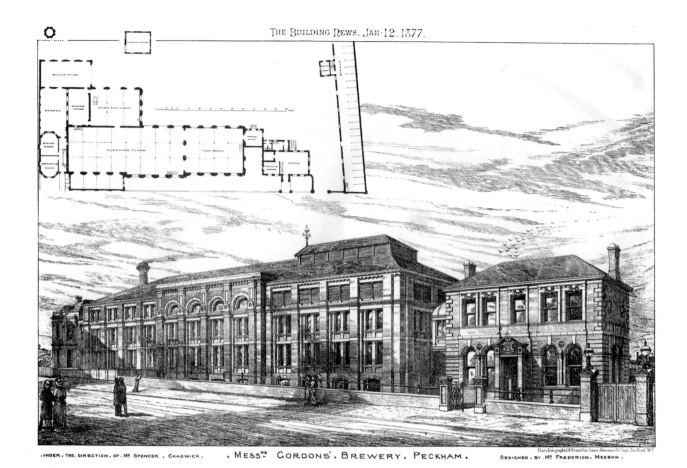

THE BUILDING NEWS, JAN. 12. 1877.

·UNDER·THE·DIRECTION·OF·M^R·SPENCER·CHADWICK· · MESS^RS· GORDONS'· BREWERY· PECKHAM· DESIGNED·BY·M^R·FREDERICK·MEESON·

Road, now Lyndhurst Way. These horses, destined for the front, had been removed from temporary stables at the requisitioned brewery to escape an infection. Dubbed the War Horse Project, research yielded further evocative photographs from 1915, discovered and released by the late historian Stephen Humphrey. They show the horses in the brewery grounds, and add to a particularly obscure part of Peckham's history.

After 1915, suburban directories make no mention of a business on the site until 1929 when the headquarters of George Mence Smith Ltd, a "grocer and household storekeeper", is first listed. A map from the 1930s shows a large building, clearly new, though some of the outbuildings close to the railway are unchanged from the OS map of 1914.

Today the site is home to Print Village, a miscellany of modern, light industrial units that are somewhat protected by Article 4 of the Town and Country Planning Order 1995, directing anyone seeking a change of use to apply for planning permission. Would that such enlightened legislation had existed in 1915.

LYNDHURST ROAD IN WAR TIME.

HOLDRON'S
1890s

Very little of this famous department store survives, and thus it must be regarded as belonging in the "lost" category of this book. Its founder, Harry Thomas Holdron, was born at Fressingfield, Suffolk in around 1854. His father was a draper and tailor. The 1871 census has him working and boarding as a draper's assistant at Hoadley's, 73-75 Buckingham Palace Road, along with 20 others.

In 1879, he married Kate Standwell Mayne and the 1880 street directory lists them at 1 Campbell Buildings on the east side of Rye Lane, a little north of the railway crossings. This is confirmed by the 1881 census, which describes him as a draper, with three assistants and three apprentices. It is generally accepted that circa 1882, he opened a shop at 53 Rye Lane and between 1885 and 1888 expanded this to join with the neighbouring premises, creating a group of single-storey shops at 51-57. By 1891, Harry Holdron had moved up in the world and was living at 204 Denmark Hill, with three servants and a groom. The ensemble shop premises, located between the railway crossings, had by then been renumbered: 117-125.

The business evidently did very well, for in the early 1890s Holdron acquired 137-139 Rye Lane and then 135. These single-storey structures were redeveloped as two red brick, three-storey buildings with Dutch gables, separated by a splendid arcade accessed beneath an ornamental metal structure with the name "Holdron" picked out in gold. It is said that the store catered for a class of customers somewhat higher in the social scale than those of Jones & Higgins. An edition of Yesterday's Britain published by the Reader's Digest in 1998 has a photograph of a female customer sitting on a chair by a counter, with staff bringing goods for her perusal.

By 1910, the main store extended from 135 to 147, with 117-125 as a branch. The land behind was developed into single-storey warehouses for the store and still remaining today – now used by the new cultural and leisure businesses in what is known as Copeland Yard. It has been said that by trading on a cash-only basis, and therefore avoiding bad debts, the business prospered. Retrospectively, the South London Press contended that Holdron achieved this success by "strict attention to business, and by leading a godly life", catering for "the top-hatted plutocracy that lived in the large houses of Camberwell".

OPPOSITE
Interior of Holdron's Arcade at 147 Rye Lane, circa 1927

ABOVE
Holdron's Arcade, 117-125 Rye Lane, circa 1930

RIGHT
Exterior of Holdron's main building, 135-147 Rye Lane, circa 1927

Khan's Bargain Ltd,
135 Rye Lane, 2013

In the 1920s, Holdron's was considered one of Peckham's principal attractions, a much-loved part of the town's social and architectural eminence. In 1926, at the height of this achievement, Harry Gordon Selfridge seized the opportunity to acquire a controlling interest in the thriving business. Its prestige was further enhanced by the addition of a massive ensemble of showrooms in the adjacent 1-15 Bournemouth Road, in around 1927.

Harry Holdron left the scene (he died in 1929 in Elham, Kent), and Selfridge embarked on a phased remodelling of the main store. Four possible designs were produced, the choice being decided by a public vote. In practice, this internal and external redesign was not taken beyond 135, but when the store reopened in September 1935,

notwithstanding the impact of the Great Depression, it boasted a striking modernist facade of tiling and metal-framed windows. The interior, likewise, had been upgraded, with a staircase designed by Selfridge himself, a "club lounge" and, on the top floor, Sir Henry Segrave's model electric railway, said to be the largest in Europe.

The business continued to prosper through the 1930s until, with the outbreak of war, things changed. In 1940, the John Lewis Partnership acquired Selfridge's provincial shops, including the Peckham store, which continued to trade as Holdron's. Nine years later John Lewis, claiming that government restrictions had made trading unviable, ceased business there, and sold on what remained of Holdron's to an investment company. Littlewoods Mail Orders and, over

Peckham's Heritage – Past, Present & Future

Holdron's department store and arcade glass concrete roof, 1936

time, other retailers took up parts of the site, putting an end to its coherence and elegance.

In 2001, the decline was compounded by a fire that swept through the premises at 137-141, which was demolished in 2003 and replaced by modern housing with shops below. Khan's Bargain took over what was left of 135, retaining the stylish frontage on the upper floors.

The final chapter played out in 2011 when a planning application was submitted to replace the Bournemouth Road showrooms with flats. The Peckham Society raised a spirited objection, arguing that restored and reinhabited 1-15 "could show that Peckham's future is not just coarse new developments, but could include the attractive and inventive re-use of the best of its stock of historic buildings". To no avail; this fine building was consigned to history.

Some fragments remain. The grand facade above 135 is capable of restoration, and the original gabled frontage of 143-147 is intact, albeit with Betfred and Barclays bank on the ground floor. And Holdron's Arcade (135a) survives, opening on to an array of small businesses.

To his great credit, Akbar Khan, of Khan's Bargain has worked to uncover a hidden curved art deco vaulted ceiling in his store dating from the 1935 remodelling. Preserved in concrete, with glass lenses, the precious section offers a glimpse of the grandeur that was Holdron's.

ARCHITECTURAL NOTES

Holdron's department store has left a rich and complex legacy of buildings in central Peckham, with more of its original architectural archaeology yet to be uncovered.

The oldest surviving part of Holdron's is at 143-147 Rye Lane. This building dates from the late 19th century and is an exuberant example of the Edwardian "free Renaissance" style, typical of the advanced, "artistic" commercial architecture of that period. Sadly, it is the only fragment of Holdron's former city block-long frontage that exists today. What is left at 143-147, with its picturesque Flemish gables and elegant decorative detailing in Bath stone hints at the former architectural splendour of this store.

It is likely that the Holdron's parade was designed by Henry Jarvis & Sons, who built the equally large department store Jones & Higgins at the north end of Rye Lane. What remains of the Jones & Higgins building uses similar materials and detailing to Holdron's and both stores were constructed in the 1890s, so were contemporaries of each other.

Retail spaces occupied the ground and first floors of Holdron's, with residential accommodation for the shop staff on the upper floor. In the 1890s expansion of his shops, Harry Holdron made the most of the deep site he had pieced together, by constructing a shopping arcade at a right angle to Rye Lane, opening up the interior of the site for commercial use. Historic maps make clear that the east side of Rye Lane was generally developed later than the west side, with plant nurseries surviving on this site until Holdron acquired the land.

Shopping arcades were a new feature in 19th and 20th century British cities. They have their roots in Roman architecture, but found their characteristic form in late 18th and 19th century Paris and London, where advances in glazing technology allowed developers and retailers to create bright, day-lit, all-weather shopping spaces, unlocking the commercial use of the centre of city blocks.

Old photographs of the arcade at 135a Rye Lane show it to be a bright, inviting passage of a comparable width and height to the fine Burlington Arcade on Piccadilly, which opened in 1819. At Holdron's Arcade, tall plate-glass windows were set in beautifully detailed bronze framing, which showed off Holdron's goods to great effect. The arcade was covered by a barrel-vaulted glass roof, while electric lighting further enhanced the shopping experience. The glazed roof of this Parisian "passage" still survives, awaiting its rediscovery, stretching out into Copeland Yard, behind the current arcade.

The Arcade was rebuilt in the 1930s, building on the identical footprint as that in the Edwardian shop; indeed part of the Edwardian floor can still be seen at the back of the Arcade. A refurbishment in 2021 revealed its 1930s art deco ceiling. After the Second World War it was subdivided into small shop units, and these remain in use today by start-ups and small businesses. The Arcade, along with the building at 135 Rye Lane, forms part of the Copeland Park property and like other former Holdron's buildings along Rye Lane would have been demolished if the tram depot plan had gone ahead (see The Bussey Building, page 104). In 2014, the Wilson family, owners of the Arcade, gave Peckham Vision use of a unit as a community shop, in recognition of its work to save the Copeland Park site, including the Arcade, from demolition.

In the late 1920s, Harry Gordon Selfridge bought Holdron's thriving retail business and set about modernising the site. Such was the stature of Holdron's that the architects TP Bennett and Son presented a series of different designs for the people of Peckham to choose from, in classical, neo-Georgian and modernist styles. Not surprisingly, the striking modernist design was the one selected.

Details of the project were published in The Builder in 1935 and show a design for re-fronting the whole block of Rye Lane, from the railway bridge to Bournemouth Road. What we see on Rye Lane today is the first phase of this new vision, built at 135.

The publication of the completed project in the Architects' Journal (2 April 1936) makes clear that some of the most fashionable and progressive building materials were used in its construction: the steel and concrete frame was supplied by Kahn's Trussed Concrete Steel Company's patented system from America (this is also seen at 117-125 Rye Lane and an earlier version of this fireproof construction can be found at the Bussey Building too). The new facade was clad in Leeds Fireclay glazed terracotta and the modernist ribbon windows were made in the Crittall factory in Essex.

Perhaps the most remarkable feature of this new wing, which was carefully restored by the art deco-enthusiast shop owner Akbar Khan in 2014-15, is a glass and concrete vaulted ceiling. This was made by Lenscrete and contains more than 1,000 circular glass lenses set into precast concrete panels on curved steel beams. This luminous vault brings architectural drama and masses of daylight into the middle of the shop floor's deep plan. Another contemporary example of this unique Lenscrete system can be seen in the iconic domed entrance hall at Eltham Palace.

An escalator lifted shoppers to the first-floor retail areas, with the open gallery giving views over the ground level shop floor below. A jazz-modern stair with escalator-like detailing survives at 135, and now gives access to a mosque and martial arts studio on the first and second floors.

The 1930s photographs of Holdron's new wing show it to be a beautifully detailed, glistening glass and terracotta building. Its ground level was permeable, with well-lit showcases that you could circulate around, day and night, admiring the artistically displayed merchandise. Projecting canopies with glazed lay-lights sailed over the pavement, culminating in lettering announcing Holdron's as "the store of the people". The Holdron's Arcade, built at the turn of the century, was given a makeover too in this period.

The decades following the completion of the 1935 extension have not been kind to the Holdron's site.

In 1950 the shop closed and 135 Rye Lane became the Times Furnishing Company. The recently revealed black glazed tiling on the shopfront fascia dates from the facade's rebranding at this period.

In the 1980s the subtle, cream-toned Leeds Fireclay facade was unfortunately painted over. It was first blue, likely from its spell as a Blockbuster Video, and was later painted the present light yellow.

The late Victorian building at 137-141 Rye Lane burned down in 2001 and was replaced by the Sky Shopping City market and another retail unit with flats above. In 2011, Holdron's beautifully detailed, five-storey, late 1920s showrooms on Bournemouth Road were demolished and replaced by a large and unremarkable block of flats. Both these setbacks for the architecture of Rye Lane strengthened the local campaign for the Rye Lane Peckham Conservation Area.

At the time of writing, the restoration of the faience facade of 135 Rye Lane has started and Akbar Khan was commended by Historic England for his careful work in restoring the building's art deco interior. The rear of Holdron's is now part of Copeland Park where, at its centre, a truncated chimney survives, the remaining letters on it spelling 'RONS'. This chimney is the last vestige of a power plant that probably supplied electricity and heating to the once extensive Holdron's department store site.

Sketch by Benedict O'Looney, 2022

THE CROWN THEATRE

1898

This Victorian theatre opened in 1898, on the north side of Peckham High Street between Marmont Road and Staffordshire Street. One of a number of new theatres in this period, the Crown challenged more famous houses for decor and comfort, with a striking exterior and highly decorative auditorium. The design of its ceiling is said to have been influenced by the elderly Queen Victoria's imperial crown, and this was matched by painted panels displaying the arms of Britain's colonies. The stage, at 140 feet, was unusually wide, and seating was provided for 2,600 patrons.

Initially, theatregoers came by train from London, attracted by artists of some repute. The first offering was actor/manager Wilson Barrett's hugely popular 'The Sign of the Cross'. Even more prestigious was the first Christmas pantomime, starring music hall singer, comedian and actor Marie Lloyd as Dick Whittington. She was enticed to appear for two more seasons. Other notables included the tenor Courtice Pounds, famous for his appearances in the Savoy operas; John East, who produced many of the pantomimes, also appeared in Jack and the Beanstalk; and in 1906-7 musical theatre actor Violet Loraine (who can be seen in 23 photographs

LEFT
Crown Theatre (left) on Peckham High Street, 1905

OPPOSITE ABOVE
Crown Theatre, date unknown

OPPOSITE BELOW
Gaumont Picture House on site of the Crown Theatre, 1979

plus a lithograph in London's National Portrait Gallery) made an early appearance as principal boy in Mother Goose. Musical attractions were provided by the Carl Rosa and D'Oyly Carte opera companies.

This was the staple fare of its day, but neither its supply nor demand was sufficient to continue enticing theatregoers from central London, where such entertainment was abundant. Peckham was just too remote to rival the glitz of the West End, and the number of local enthusiasts insufficient to sustain such a large theatre. Following Queen Victoria's death, the Crown was downgraded to become the Peckham Hippodrome. By 1912 audiences had so declined that live performances gave way to the emerging silent screen. The great theatre survived as a cinema until 1932 when it was demolished to make way for the purpose-built Gaumont picture house. With the rise of television even this venture was abandoned in 1961. The building was transformed into a bingo hall, which survived until November 1998. Two years later the Gaumont building was taken down to be replaced by the present block of flats.

The Crown Theatre, Peckham. 1898

Scenes from the past. Series 3. No. 11

Published by the Libraries Department, London Borough of Southwark, 1977

ARCHITECTURAL NOTES

Along with the nearby Wesleyan Methodist Church, the demolition of the Crown Theatre is one of the greatest losses to Peckham's architecture. The Crown was built by one of Edwardian London's leading theatre architects, Ernest Runtz. It was constructed during a boom in theatre-building in London between 1885 and 1915, when more than 200 theatres opened their doors across Britain. Had this theatre survived into the 21st century it would rank among Peckham's most significant, and listed, buildings.

Runtz was well-known for his flamboyant designs. He collaborated with the architect Norman Shaw on the Gaiety Theatre, Aldwych and designed the Holborn Empire and the Pavilion Theatre and Wonderland in Whitechapel, both now demolished. Unfortunately the enthusiasm for building theatres in the fin-de-siècle period was matched with a similar passion for knocking them down post-1945.

The Crown Theatre was a powerful example of the "free" Renaissance style often found in this era of ambitious theatre and pub building. Much of the detailing was executed in cast terracotta, also known as faience – a hardy material that was well suited to London's gritty environment. The faience for the Crown was made in Doulton's terracotta factory on the Albert Embankment in Lambeth. Examples of similar architecture include Frank Matcham's fabulous Coliseum Theatre on St Martin's Lane and the Palace Theatre on Shaftesbury Avenue by Thomas Collcutt. In Peckham, similarly flamboyant terracotta detailing can be found on the Old Kent Road at the Royal London Buildings. Nice Edwardian terracotta detailing can also be seen to the west in the shopping parade on the south side of Camberwell Green.

Peckham's Heritage – Past, Present & Future

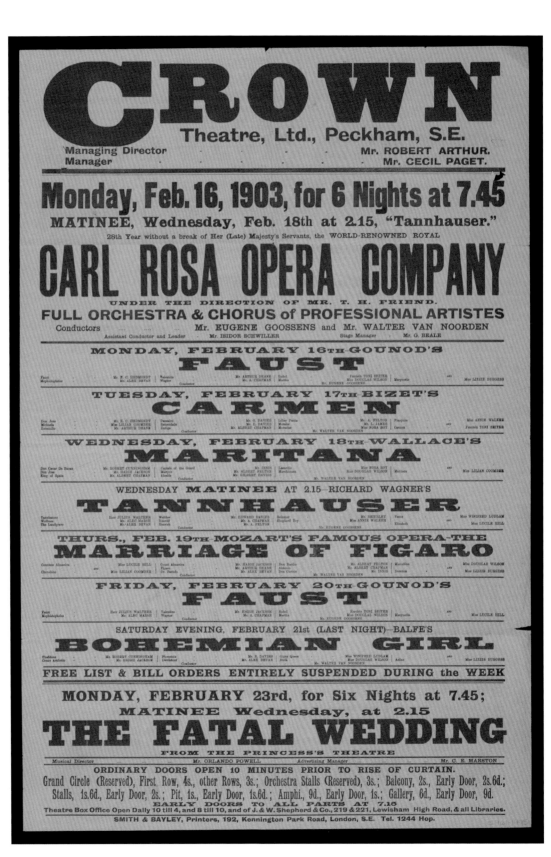

Peckham Rye Station forecourt, 1969

Part 2

In Need of Restoration

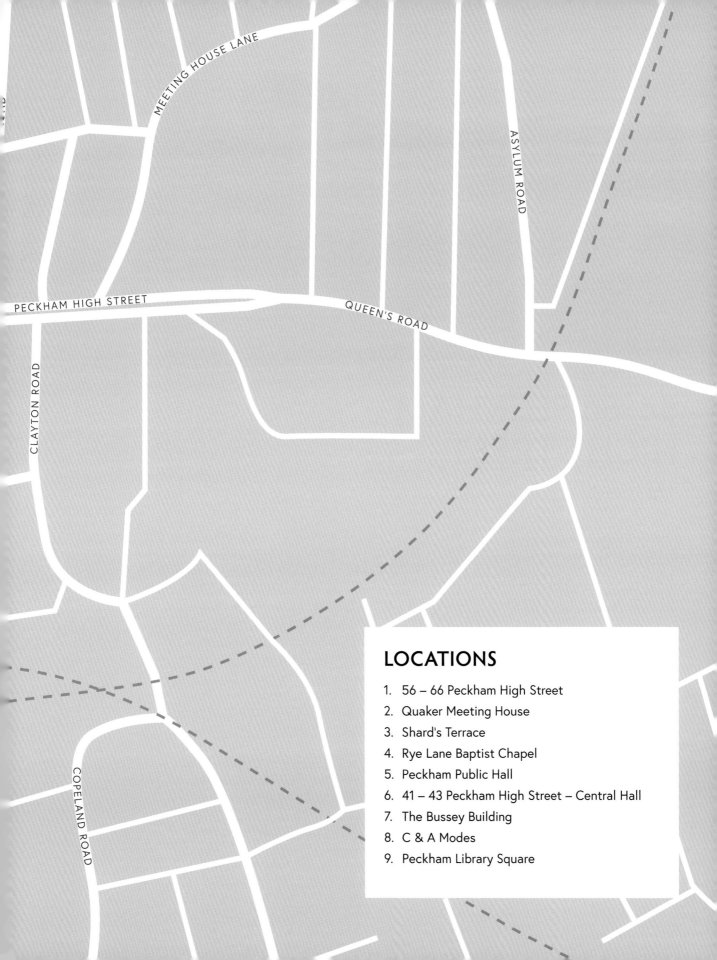

MEETING HOUSE LANE

ASYLUM ROAD

PECKHAM HIGH STREET

QUEEN'S ROAD

CLAYTON ROAD

COPELAND ROAD

LOCATIONS

1. 56 – 66 Peckham High Street
2. Quaker Meeting House
3. Shard's Terrace
4. Rye Lane Baptist Chapel
5. Peckham Public Hall
6. 41 – 43 Peckham High Street – Central Hall
7. The Bussey Building
8. C & A Modes
9. Peckham Library Square

56-66 PECKHAM HIGH STREET
18TH CENTURY

"The very early 18th century wood-framed buildings in Peckham High Street are vulnerable to demolition and this, our old village centre, is the focus of the Central Peckham Conservation Area for which the Peckham Society has been campaigning for some years." This summary offered by Dr Peter Frost, Chair of The Peckham Society in Autumn 2007, endures today. These old vernacular houses are among the most important of all Peckham's remaining historic buildings.

Along with 98-104 Peckham High Street (see pages 122-123), the buildings at 56-66 were included in the 1998 survey by the Royal Commission on the Historic Monuments of England. Of the group to the west of Rye Lane, only 58-64 still exist; the last of them gutted by fire. The Commission found that 60-62, probably built as a single house, appeared to have the earliest origins,

incorporating the rural village architecture of the 17th century – a type of broad-fronted two-cell two-storey house that had once been standard and widespread. The tallest and most westerly of the group, 58, was described in the survey report as "a particularly remarkable survival, perhaps of c.1725-30". When built, it had the garden of Peckham Manor to the north, Basing Manor House to the south, and Hanover Chapel to the east, and was a house "for which no close comparisons are known".

Records of occupancy of all four houses suggest that they had been "successful in finding better-off inhabitants". The Commission's report observed that while it was obvious that bigger houses were generally of higher status, "a small house might carry respectability to varying measures depending on its context".

In 2009, the Grade II listing of 58 marked the happy conclusion of a long campaign by The Peckham Society. It was followed shortly afterwards by a remarkable discovery. A copy of an 1830 painting by Charles Kirshaw was sent from Perth, Western Australia, by a Mr John Doddemeade, seeking to identify the location of the houses it depicted. It came, via the Local History Library, to John Beasley then editor of the Peckham Society News, who was astonished to realise that he was looking at an historic portrayal of 56-66 Peckham High Street. Doddemeade later explained that Kirshaw, a distant family member, had lived in Coldharbour Lane and that the terrace he had painted had been owned by his great great great grandfather Edward Early. Originally a peruke (wig) maker, Early spent his married life in Peckham where he had prospered, owning a successful bakery business and several other premises. The painting, carefully wrapped in waxed paper, had come to John through several generations of the family. It confirmed the Royal Commission's view that these modest houses could have been home to wealthy people.

These rare and precious 18th century survivors have degraded over time, not least as a consequence of their conversion and forward extension as shops. A kiosk on the pavement near the corner with Rye Lane further blocks the prospect. The Peckham Society, after a long campaign, persuaded Southwark Council to protect these and other historic buildings by the creation of a town centre conservation area, but it has yet to make the most of these treasures located at the heart of the former village of Peckham.

ARCHITECTURAL NOTES

The old timber-framed houses of Peckham High Street are picturesque survivors from the beginning of Peckham's transition from a quiet Surrey village to its absorption into what was by 1700, Europe's greatest city.

The architecture of these late 17th and early 18th century houses and shops gently speaks to us of Kent and Surrey's rural, 'vernacular' building traditions and also show themes in architectural fashion and detailing in early modern London.

London's domestic architecture was transformed in the late 17th century by sweeping building regulations in the City and Westminster following the Great Fire of 1666. Prior to this most people lived in timber-framed houses clad in weatherboarding, plaster, with clay-tiled or thatched roofs. Only elites lived in brick or stone buildings. With new building regulations, London was rebuilt with fireproof brick-clad facades, sturdy brick structural walls and timber roofs faced in clay tiles or slate, usually concealed behind brick parapets. These new building laws shaped the townscape of London we know today.

In the outlying villages around the capital people were still using older building techniques. Vernacular building uses materials locally available. At 56-62 and 102-104 Peckham High Street note the tall, pitched, clay-tiled roofs - Georgian maps show a brickfield just south of the Peckham High Street; clay for bricks and tiles was abundant here. Note also the traditional timber sash windows and the timber weatherboarding, particularly to the rear elevations.

62 Peckham High Street was damaged in a fire in 2018. The heat caused the plaster to fall off the walls revealing a beautiful, hand-hewn, timber structure, parts of which were reused from an even earlier house. Structural timber was valuable, often re-useable, and would have come from nearby sources.

As the 1830s Kirshaw watercolour wonderfully shows, the fronts of these houses are quite formal, architectural, with symmetrical paired windows neatly arranged in the Classical manner. In Peckham, these five surviving houses are handmade, timber versions of the smart new brick-clad town houses being built in London's expanding West End. In contrast, the backs of these structures were usually more irregular with clay-tiled 'cat slide roofs' containing later lean-to rear extensions. A picturesque group of similar early 18th century timber-framed houses and shops survives nearby at Tanner's Hill in Deptford.

The setting of the two groups of timber-framed houses on Peckham High Street has changed considerably! When originally built, circa 1700, 56-62 Peckham High Street had tall, vertically proportioned, weatherboarded fronts. By the end of the 19th century the front gardens had been built over forming a shopping parade. Rye Lane and the Peckham High Street had become busy shopping streets for a wide catchment area. Peckham had become a hub for buses, trams and the railways. All across London in the 19th and 20th centuries the front gardens along London's 'high streets' were built over for shops. Steel beams and iron columns created deep retail spaces to the ground level with residential or storage spaces in the old houses above. This can also be seen nearby on the Walworth Road, the Camberwell Road and the Old Kent Road where handsome Georgian terraces are set back behind later shops.

Early topographic views of Peckham show many timber-framed houses, shops and pubs from the 16th, 17th and 18th centuries. These buildings on Peckham High Street, 84 Rye Lane, and the old house on Wood's Road are the only survivors from this early period of Peckham's history and should be carefully protected.

A late nineteenth century painting (exact location unknown) showing the timber framed houses that characterised the village of Peckham, 1890

QUAKER MEETING HOUSE

1826

Quaker beliefs, promulgated by George Fox (1624-1691), spread out from the north of England in an organised campaign from 1654. Two of the earliest travelling ministers, Francis Howgill and Edward Burrough held a meeting in Southwark that year and by 1656 meetings were taking place in several private homes. In 1674, a meeting house was built in Ewer Street. Beck & Ball in their 1869 history remind us that friends quickly became "large and influential" in Southwark, with adherents drawn from a wide cross-section of society: "many rich and many poor". This social mix was no less disparate in its religious commitment with "many faithful and zealous", but also "many lukewarm and disorderly".

Through the 18th century, the Society of Friends continued to have a large following in Southwark. In 1723, no fewer than twelve

Quaker ministers were recorded as living in the area and in 1763 the original meeting house was replaced with a building located between Red Cross Street and Worcester Street. By the early 19th century increasing numbers of Friends had moved out of the City to settle in this desirable location and in 1821, it was decided that a new meeting place was needed. A carpenter's shop in Baker's Row was leased for a price of £28 per annum, and fitted up at a cost of £144.

In just three years these makeshift premises had also become too small and inconvenient; a new and larger meeting house was required.

A site was found in Hanover Street (now Highshore Road) and the handsome building, of which the frontage still remains, opened in 1826. The final cost was at least £2,167 and in the following year the freehold was purchased for a further £350. There is evidence pointing to the construction and fitting out of the new meeting house having been undertaken by Frederick Farrand, perhaps with the co-operation of John Wooley. Both were Peckham residents.

Frederick Farrand, (1786 - 1858) - Quaker and builder, who lived at Elm Grove, Peckham

Several notable people were associated with the Peckham meeting house in its early years. Not least Elizabeth Dudley who as Clerk of the Women's Yearly Meeting was regarded, according to an article in The Friend, as: "second only to her friend, Elizabeth Fry, as a preacher in the Society. So popular was her ministry that the meeting house was enlarged in 1844 in order to accommodate the many people who attended to hear her." No less celebrated was her sister Mary, prominent in the Peckham Ladies Anti-Slavery Association; also William Naish who published numerous booklets in support of their campaign.

The "suburban offshoot" in Hanover Street soon outstripped the Southwark meeting house at Red Cross Street. In 1860, this property was sold and Peckham became the headquarters of the Southwark Monthly Meeting. Particularly striking is the fact that at this time five women sat as ministers at the head of the Meeting: Caroline Norton, Rachel Savory, Elizabeth Cash, Ellen Masters and Agnes Grimshaw. Even more memorable is the name of Elizabeth Mary Taylor, who was to marry chocolate manufacturer George Cadbury at the meeting house on 19 June 1888.

Attendance numbers peaked in the 1890s and began to fall off during the following century. There was a particularly serious setback on 16 December 1907 when part of the meeting house, including the library, was destroyed by fire. Fortunately, the minutes of the Monthly Meetings were saved, and none of the books lost were unique. Meetings continued at Peckham through the 20th century until 31 December 1961, when the meeting house was sold to the Ministry of Works, and became, as it is today, a Royal Mail sorting office. The last meeting was held on 31 December 1961. Back then, the site included a burial ground described by Basil Holmes as "beautiful, [illustrating] what can be done with a disused and closed graveyard, not even visible from the road, when it is treated with proper care and respect". The ground had been made into a garden in 1935 (after which only the interment of ashes was permitted) and upon the closure of the meeting house the remains were reinterred at Camberwell Old Cemetery in a section for Friends. A bench said to have been used by Peter the Great during his visit to Deptford was transferred to a new meeting house in Bromley and then in 1972 to Blackheath Meeting House, from where it was stolen a few years later.

Quakers still meet in or around Peckham and while it is undoubtedly a pity that their historic meeting house should have been sold for secular purposes, at least its old frontage has been retained.

SHARD'S TERRACE

19TH CENTURY

REPAIRED AND RESTORED THROUGH THE
PECKHAM TOWNSCAPE HERITAGE INITIATIVE

• 105 Peckham High Street - Manze's
• 130 Peckham Hill Street

This semi-circular block of twelve three-storey buildings at 91-107 Peckham High Street and 126-130 Peckham Hill Street, is a Georgian survivor from the early 19th century. Once part of Thomas Bond's manor, it is named after Charles Shard, who inherited the land.

To date, it has survived the road widening of the High Street in 1880/82, the threat of demolition to make way for a tramway, and the modern development of nearby Peckham Square. Steven Robb, an Historic Buildings and Areas Inspector, writing in the Peckham Society News in 2006 noticed that the terrace

must have remained in a single ownership for some time as around c.1900 it was given "an attractive Edwardian makeover with elaborate shop-fronts featuring timber carved pilasters and sturdy console brackets". Since then, he observed, the terrace had deteriorated, with many shops being badly converted with large fascia boards.

Despite such neglect, the terrace retains something of the character of the old village of Peckham. In 2006, it benefited from a £120,000 Southwark Council facelift, designed to help shopkeepers improve the appearance

Shard's Terrace located at the junction of Peckham High Street and Peckham Hill Street, 1979

Peckham's Heritage – Past, Present & Future

Manze's after repair
and restoration,
with newly painted
signage, 2021

of their properties. The eel and pie shop at 105 Peckham High Street, one of the Manze chain since 1927, is conspicuously well-preserved with some original features. In 2005 it came top in the annual vote for a Southwark blue plaque. Perhaps even more deserving is 99, where Alfred Harman had a photography shop before he set up Ilford Ltd, and 101, which was the first shop of Charles Harris, the linoleum and carpet business taken to dizzy heights by his son Lord Philip Harris of Peckham.

Two buildings in Shard's Terrace, Manze's at 105 Peckham High Street, and 130 Peckham Hill Street (now Filishack), have been repaired and restored through the Peckham Townscape Heritage Initiative (THI).

Manze's at 105 Peckham High Street was in a reasonably good condition. The pitched roof was in a poor state of repair and required a full replacement with traditional materials,

including Welsh slate, and lead. Readdressing the iconic Eel & Pie House signage on the brickwork was a priority piece of work, as the previous signage was in a poor state and was unsympathetic to the handsome host building. After testing several ideas, a simple, effective drop shadow design was agreed and carefully hand painted using stencils to bring it to life and complement the historic nature of the building. Several other items required careful repair and decoration works - the new sash windows were painted green on the outside whilst being kept white on the inside, the stone cornice parapet was lime washed and later painted to match the brickwork signage, and the shopfront piers, pilaster heads and shopfront itself were carefully sanded down, repaired, and repainted.

130 Peckham Hill Street was repaired and restored to improve the building's condition and appearance. Lost and damaged historical

features were restored, with the aim of bringing back some of the unifying features that give architectural clarity to Shard's Terrace. 20th century render on the front elevation was removed and new 'breathable' render and finish was applied. The parapet cornice was restored, and the roof covering was extensively repaired and upgraded with new slate tiles, and lead flashings. A new timber shopfront and sliding sash windows were made to fit carefully into the existing revealed openings. An internal shallow ramp has created level access between the shop unit and the public realm.

At the time of going to press, proposals are being developed to restore and adapt 91 – 93 Peckham High Street, on the western end of Shards Terrace, as a base for Peckham Platform. The proposal is to adapt the buildings so they have two frontages - maintaining the historic form and character of the on Peckham High Street, and creating a lively contemporary presence on Peckham (Library) Square.

Rye Lane Baptist
Chapel, 1972

RYE LANE BAPTIST CHAPEL

1863

In the years immediately prior to 1800 the residents of Peckham had access to three places of worship: the old church of St. Giles in Camberwell; Camden Church in Peckham Road; and the Congregational Meeting House (Hanover Chapel) at the junction of Rye Lane and the High Street. As the population of Peckham grew through the 19th century new places of prayer proliferated. These included: Peckham Chapel (Anglican), Hill Street, 1814; Rye Lane/Blenheim Grove Chapel (Baptist), 1819; Meeting Place (Quaker), Bakers Row, 1821; Wesleyan Chapel (Methodist), Stafford Street, 1834; Park Road Chapel (Roman Catholic), 1855; and the South East London Synagogue (Jewish), Lausanne Road, 1889.

The Rye Lane Baptist Chapel came gradually and by degrees. Many attempts had been made to establish a Baptist cause at Peckham but none succeeded until the arrival of William Spencer (1751-1816), a renowned maker of mathematical and navigational instruments, made wealthy as a partner in Spencer, Browning and Rust. Spencer committed his life to the Baptist cause. In 1786, after a time at Southwark's Maze Pond Chapel, he came to the company of Church Street Chapel in Blackfriars Road, worshipping there for almost 30 years, 25 of them as a deacon. Sadly, his enthusiastic commitment was not rewarded by perfect health. In his later years he suffered from

HARVEST FESTIVAL RYE LANE CHAPEL

Harvest Festival at Rye Lane Baptist Chapel, 1905

an unspecified but debilitating and painful affliction; and in about 1815 he moved to what Blanch called "the quiet little village of Peckham", hoping its salubrious air might encourage an improvement. It did not. But while his physical health declined so that he could barely speak, the serenity of his mind appears to have been unimpaired. Finding no Baptist sanctuary in Peckham, he and his wife Ann opened their new home in Hill Street to prayer, and soon were allowed to preach on Sundays and weekday evenings in a room at the nearby Lancasterian school.

Though intent on establishing a more permanent church, Spencer's health declined so fast that he became confined to his house and died on 5 April 1816. Others took up the cause, but not without opposition. In a note to his published funeral sermon, James Upton observes that one (unnamed) minister was very angry and, "wished to root the Baptists out". But Dr Collyer and his friends at the Congregational Chapel displayed "the most friendly disposition of mind": this was the same Dr Collyer, of a dissenting persuasion, whose preaching attracted many wealthy and

fashionable people, peers, and members of the Royal family, not least Princess Victoria.

On 15 December 1818, seven of the Baptist group, including Spencer's widow, formed themselves into a "Particular Baptist Church", followed on 27 January 1819 by the administration of believer's baptism to a further six followers. On 22 February, a lease was taken out on a building at the junction of Rye Lane and Blenheim Grove for use of "Strict Communion Baptists of orthodox sentiments", opening on 1 September 1819 for public worship. In June 1831, the sudden death of the ground landlord George Choumert, afforded the opportunity to buy the land on which the chapel stood and in 1839 it became financially possible to secure the freehold.

Friendly relations with Hanover Chapel persisted. Blanch recounts an exchange of letters dispelling any possible disquiet from the two chapels being so close to each other, a Protestant amity cemented by Dr Collyer giving the first sermon in the new Baptist chapel.

In fact, the enemy turned out to be the South London, and London, Chatham and Dover Railways, whose lines and station obliterated the hard-won chapel. It was said that the pastor and his flock were called away "by Providence" but the reality in 1863 was a compulsory purchase order. Alternative land was found on the other side of Rye Lane, purchased from Claude de Crespigny for £550. The present, impressive chapel was very swiftly built at a cost of £1,734, with a school hall and manse for a further £920. The new chapel opened on 18 November 1863 and its subsequent history has been the subject of an admirable book by Barry Evans. The whole building was listed Grade II on 27 September 1972.

The chapel remains well attended and vigorous as a place of worship but there are problems. In 1943, much of the chapel was devastated by the Luftwaffe. It remained unusable until July 1948, when repairs allowed a partial reopening. The school hall, which had been the most badly damaged did not reopen until April 1960. Today, several parts of the estate are in poor condition. There is no disabled access to the sanctuary and roofs in some parts are no longer fit for purpose. The floor plan of the restored building at the rear is poorly laid out and inefficient with structures reaching the end of their serviceable life. While the guardians of the chapel focus on the continuity of the chapel's holy mission, the community as a whole has a stake in its wider salvation.

Rye Lane Baptist Chapel, date unknown

Baptist Chapel, Rye Lane.

PECKHAM PUBLIC HALL

1884

Situated behind 166 Rye Lane, this multi-purpose hall opened in November 1884 to serve what had by then become a busy, densely-populated town. Reportedly, access was gained via a spacious, glass-covered corridor from the main road. Capable of accommodating 12,000 people in comfort, the South London Press believed it helped make Peckham "all the more attractive as a residential neighbourhood".

The event, which attracted a huge turnout with many people having to be turned away, was the occasion of a celebratory concert with the band of the Scots Guards and various soloists. These included the famous tenor Edward Lloyd, who sang 'Then You'll Remember Me' from Balfe's 'The Bohemian Girl' (which he recorded for the Gramophone & Typewriter Company in 1904); several ballads such as 'Come into the Garden Maud'; and other ditties representative of the fare popular at that time.

The hall survives, though hidden. While it cannot be seen from Rye Lane, you can catch a glimpse from the former Asda car park in Alpha Street. The passageway, presumably original but no longer spacious or glass-covered, lies inconspicuously between 164 and 168 and leads into the hall, which is now used by the Christ Apostolic Church as a place of worship.

Exterior of Peckham Public Hall, 2022

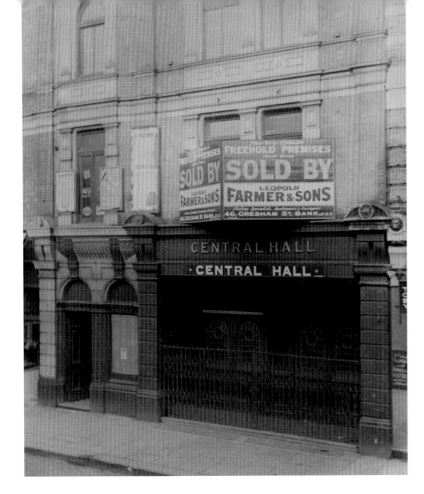

41-43 PECKHAM HIGH STREET – CENTRAL HALL

1894

Central Hall, Peckham High Street, 1935

This fine Victorian building at 41-43 Peckham High Street marks the centrepiece of a once magnificent terrace. Designed by the architect Robert Whellock, the huge structure included two halls, entered from number 43, the largest capable of accommodating 1,000 people.

The main hall, with its fine arched ceiling and gallery, opened on 11 November 1894 as the headquarters of socio-religious mission, the People's League. This organisation had been founded a year earlier by Robert James Lees, a Leicestershire-born spiritualist, medium, writer and healer who is said to have been the recognised leader of the Christian Spiritualists of Great Britain. He reportedly had psychic visions of Jack the Ripper and offered his assistance to Scotland Yard in tracking down the killer.

From the League's 'Central Hall' in Peckham, Lees and his followers provided improving lectures, popular concerts and what historian

John Beasley has described as, practical objectives supporting local people in need. Lees' life story and reputed psychic powers have been chronicled extensively online by Stephen Butt, who records Lee as having lived at 67 Ondine Road in 1892. The same timeline shows that in 1895 Lees moved to Cornwall (evidently due to ill health), which marked the closure of the People's League – so the span of his much-vaunted enterprise was quite brief.

From January 1896, the hall was used by the congregation of the local Baptist Tabernacle, and then in 1908 by the Rev G Ernest Thorn as the 'Church of the Strangers'. For some years from 1910 the New Bioscope Trading Company of Cecil Court, Charing Cross Road ran a permanent cinema at the hall, and several other groups performed or met there, apparently alongside Thorn's ministry, until in 1932 the building was converted into a refreshment depot by Express Dairies.

The Central Hall, a grand space to the rear of 41-43 Peckham High Street, 2018

Sold on again in 1935, the activities of the hall changed direction in the post-war years, becoming a venue for rock and roll bands. One of its incarnations was as the Wild West-themed Maverick Casino, probably based on a popular television series of the 1950s and remembered by one Peckham old-timer as having been opened by Diana Dors. Peckham resident Barry Jenkins, knew it as the Bouncing Ball Club, and remembers appearances by The Animals and Screaming Lord Sutch. Bob Marley and the Wailers are said to have played at the club in May 1973.

Into the 21st century, a number of nightclubs, some notorious, flourished at 43. In 2003, following a report by DTZ Pieda Consulting, it was proposed that the building and its entire surrounding terrace should be demolished. The Peckham Society disagreed, recognising the terrace's historic character and potential.

In 2011, 41-43 Peckham High Street was included in the newly created Rye Lane Peckham Conservation Area. In April 2018, Eileen Conn of Peckham Vision was alerted by a local resident of the hall's imminent sale at auction. She went along to the pre-auction visit and discovered the magnificent hall at the back of the building. The building ended up being sold just before the auction could took place but the Southwark News used photographs taken by Eileen to carry the story that local people wanted to contact the new owner to discuss ways the hall could be restored and brought back into use as an event space.

By then it was in a very poor state of repair, with a particularly dilapidated entrance on the Peckham High Street elevation. The sale was followed by a planning application in 2019 seeking permission for redevelopment to the frontage buildings on Peckham High Street, including refurbishment of the front façade, to reflect the building's special architectural and historic qualities. These works have been completed, revitalising the building's handsome presence on the street.

Central Hall, to the rear, was not included in the 2019 proposals – an omission strongly regretted in objections to the planning application. The magnificent hall remains in limbo, aching for renovation and inviting exciting future possibilities.

Blackjack table at
Maverick Club at
Central Hall, 1966

ARCHITECTURAL NOTES

Amongst Peckham's many fine Renaissance revival
buildings, Peckham's Central Hall really stands out.
It was built by the noteworthy architect Robert
Whellock in 1894, who also designed the beautiful
Queen Anne-style public library nearby on the Old
Kent Road.

Central Hall's four-story façade to the Peckham High
Street features a tall central pavilion flanked by
symmetrical wings with paired windows.

Elaborate Renaissance-inspired detailing in stone and
stucco make this one of the liveliest buildings in the
town centre. The stone detailing is complemented by
the vivid Kent red facing bricks.

Central Hall's design shows it to be a smaller cousin
of the (exactly contemporary) Jones & Higgins
across the street. The four immense console brackets

survive to the shop front marking the former
generous entrances to the public halls behind.

Internally the magnificent swept arch of the
celebrated hall shows the use of an early steel frame.
This wide, column-free space could accommodate
1,000 people. With their wide spans and deep
cantilevered galleries, the architecture of London's
theatres was revolutionised by the introduction of
American steel frame technology in the late 19th
century. (The Coliseum on St Martin's Lane is an
impressive example of this.)

Central Hall is the centrepiece of an excellent
collection of Victorian buildings on the north side of
the Peckham High Street. The old houses and shops
were cleared on the entire north side when the High
Street was widened in the 1870s.

The Bussey Building,
2011

THE BUSSEY BUILDING

20TH CENTURY

Though this huge building to the rear of 133 Rye Lane is not pretty, it has considerable heritage value. It is a story of protean development which deserves to be told in some detail.

George Gibson Bussey was born in about 1829 in Ripon, North Yorkshire. He began his working life as a saddler's apprentice before moving to London in 1851 where he established himself as a leather gun-case maker operating from a series of addresses. In 1864, he began a company making gun wadding and cartridges and a few years later moved his business to Peckham. He appears first to have constructed a rifle range on the east side of Rye Lane, alongside the most southerly railway embankment, then in 1867 to have added a factory.

Named the Museum of Firearms, it exhibited guns and associated accessories on the ground floor, while the range was used to test the accuracy of guns, rifles and revolvers, the strength of gunpowder and other explosive compounds. The rest of the building was

Interior in the Bussey Building, with tall cast iron columns and pairs of steel windows

given over to the manufacture of firearms. A directory of 1870 lists the business as "firearms, ammunition & shooting tackle manufacturers", and a building is clearly shown on the Ordnance Survey map of 1871, with the remainder of the rifle range to the rear.

By 1876, Bussey had patented two designs for roller skates and in addition to firearms, was making leather goods of every description. At some point in the 1880s, he and his son William added sporting equipment to their inventory. As an article in the South London Press in 1887 put it: Bussey "was not slow in finding out that the gun trade and accessories in connection with it was not the most profitable groove for the employment of capital, nor the most suitable for a man of restless energy and great inventive skill".

George Bussey died in 1889 but the business continued to thrive. By 1898, sporting equipment had taken over from guns, and the factory was known as the Sports Manufactory making cricket bats, stumps and balls; lawn tennis rackets and tennis balls; footballs and other paraphernalia. The business soon came to be recognised as London's leading manufacturer of sports goods.

Exactly when the present monolith was built on the site of the old rifle range is uncertain. Smith and Roethe, usually authoritative, say it appears to date from the early 20th century. The building in front of the Bussey Building, now known as Market Peckham at 133a Rye Lane, was constructed in 1908, and both it and the Bussey Building appear on the OS map of 1916.

What is certain is that the Bussey business continued until the 1930s, when it was leased, first to Holdron's and then to that store's successors, Selfridge Provincial Stores, and later to John Lewis. How it was used during this period is unclear, save that the basement is known to have served as an air raid shelter during the Second World War; for which purpose its concrete structure was admirably suited, though thankfully never tested. A completely separate purpose-built bomb shelter still exists in the car area of Copeland Park; its ventilation system can be seen on the wall of Block D of the Bussey Building.

In the years following the Second World War, the Bussey Building was vacated, neglected and fell into disrepair. By the 1980s it was being used for a variety of purposes including clothing manufacturing, printing and as artist studios.

In 1994, Jonathan Wilson began with his then business partner, to purchase run-down but structurally sound warehouses in what is now Copeland Park, including the Bussey Building. By 2001, Wilson had acquired much of the present estate and by 2013, the Wilson family were owners of CIP, Copeland Park, and set about working to further revive the site.

This required a leap of faith with a series of potential set-backs. In 2005, Transport for London (TfL) proposed a cross-river tramway, Camden to Peckham, with the terminating depot occupying Copeland Park and another large site around Blackpool Road. Southwark Council supported the cross-river tram project and included it in the unitary development plan then being prepared for submission to the Government for its public hearings in 2005. The scheme also received strong support from an

independent Ipsos MORI consultation of more than 5,000 people and organisations.

Eileen Conn appeared at the public hearings and discovered the extent of the demolition the tram depot would require, and the issues for businesses, jobs and culture it raised. She worked with the artists on site and Jonathan Wilson to arrange public meetings in January and March 2006. These attracted large numbers of locals who saw the plans as a threat to an historic part of their town. Peckham Vision as a community action group, led by Conn, grew out of this early work. Campaigning went on for years. Finally, in 2008, TfL recognised that the site was unviable for the tram depot, after reviewing technical issues, cost and the damage to Peckham town centre, and chose a more suitable site near Burgess Park.

In November 2008, the new Mayor of London, Boris Johnson, announced the cancellation of the entire tram project due to funding problems. Peckham Vision's campaign was not a factor in the decision but the plan for the Copeland Park site that Peckham Vision had developed in its long campaign provided the alternative plan that the Council then adopted.

Geo. G. Bussey manufacturers featured in Tatler Magazine, 1906

The 2012 Peckham and Nunhead Area Action Plan recognised the asset value of Copeland Park and the Bussey Building in particular, stating that "mixed-used development should be centred around the retention of the historic Bussey Building" and "should conserve and enhance its heritage setting". It added: "In the past few years a number of creative industries have appeared on the site and in the Bussey Building. There is opportunity to build on this and create a new cultural and creative quarter for Peckham to attract visitors from outside the area."

Since 2011 the Bussey Building has come within the Rye Lane Peckham Conservation Area and it has been nominated for inclusion in Southwark's draft "local list" of all buildings of townscape, architectural or historical interest. The Bussey Building's historic importance has been confirmed in the Southwark Plan, which was adopted in February 2022.

The Bussey Building and Copeland Park have gone from strength to strength and are now the hub of Peckham's cultural quarter. In the building you can find creative workshops, studios, yoga classes, a radio station, a gym and a rooftop film club with stunning views of central London. It has also been used as a venue by the London Handel Festival. All in all the Bussey Building is a prime example of regeneration: preserving and respecting, indeed improving, Peckham's rich heritage.

Table Croquet sets produced by Bussey's, date unknown

ARCHITECTURAL NOTES

The Bussey Building is central Peckham's outstanding example of industrial architecture. The present building was built in stages from the 1880s onward. With the new railway lines profoundly reshaping central Peckham in the 1860s, the enterprising George Bussey saw the potential for a long, linear rifle range on the newly re-ordered land east of Rye Lane, parallel to the railway lines, set behind the busy shops and department stores on the Lane.

The footprint of his rifle range gives the Bussey Building its most striking characteristic: its extreme proportions - very long, tall and very thin.

The Bussey Building's remarkable proportions places it in the development of the factory building type of which Britain was one of the world's pioneers. In the eighteenth and nineteenth centuries the emergent factory building was principally lit by daylight. Consequently, a distinctive plan form evolved, which was narrow in footprint with tall windows in the walls letting in as much daylight as possible to the internal work spaces. In cities, the taller you built, the better the light.

The architectural and engineering goal was thin, largely glazed side walls. From the late 18th century onward factory engineers and architects began to use 'frame construction'. This allowed the weight of the building to be supported internally removing the need for thick, load-bearing, walls. Initially timber frames were used, then as Britain's Industrial Revolution took off, cast-iron and wrought-iron frames prevailed. This allowed the factory designers to create much lighter and more open external elevations, throwing daylight into the interior from both sides of the building. Soon engineers were tying the external walls into the building's frame making the enclosing walls lighter still, becoming by the 1920s almost entirely glazed.

This frame construction, pioneered in Britain in the 18th century, eventually led to the steel-framed skyscraper making dense, tall townscapes like Manhattan possible.

The Bussey Building is an example of the innovative and evolving building type of the urban factory. Here modern structural engineering combined with the latest in industrial power - 400 horse-power boilers drove engines fuelling the factories' machinery and delivering electric lighting throughout the site.

The Bussey Building is a significant work by the otherwise obscure architect W.J. Easton. The main

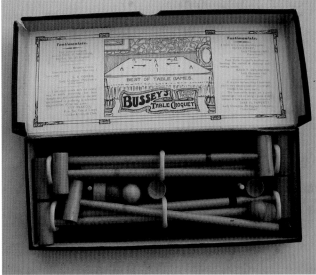

show façade can be viewed from the raised railway line on the north of the building - seen by thousands of commuters each day. This six-story elevation is a spirited classical arrangement of two wings of seven bays flanking a raised central feature five bays wide. This extended eastwards with a taller three-bay element, a big brick chimney and ten further bays, three stories tall, making a building almost 600 feet long and only 35 feet wide.

The upper part of the walls were rebuilt in the post-war period in the brick 'moderne' style; however, period pictures show the magnificent original design with a big central baroque gable with terracotta detailing. Tall white brick letters set into a field of red facing bricks proclaimed to travellers on the railway lines 'George G. Bussey & Co, Sports and Games' (some of this 'super graphics' survives to the east part of the range).

Luckily the attractive original elevation survives much better below the altered upper storey. Here, turn of the century steel windows are set in pairs, separated by a brick pilaster. A large 'red rubber' brick arch with a keystone catches the eye on the taller central element.

The architectural interest of the Bussey Building carries on internally. The floors feature a central line of tall, slender, cast-iron columns. For a factory filled with woodworking machines and sawdust, fire-proof construction was a necessity. The Bussey Building used the Kahn's fire-proof, hollow-pot floor system, patented in the United States. This is a lightweight and immensely strong assembly of hollow terracotta blocks tied together with steel reinforcement, vaulting between steel or concrete joists.

A later, all-concrete, version of the Kahn structural system known as 'Trusscon' can also be seen at the art deco former Holdron's Building at 135 Rye Lane, and its annexe the former C&A at 117-125 Rye Lane.

It is hard to overestimate the importance of the survival of the Bussey Building in modern Peckham. Once London's largest sporting goods factory, its robust, flexible interiors have been wonderfully repurposed. The Bussey Building has incubated much Peckham talent over the years and has been a rallying point for architectural preservation in the town centre.

The re-use of this factory is a powerful marker of the benefit of conserving our industrial heritage.

C&A MODES, 117 - 125 RYE LANE

1949

This well-known business was founded by the Brenninkmeijer brothers in northern Holland in 1841 - C for Clemens, A for August. They drew on a family heritage of linen merchandising to build an empire based on selling fashionable, ready-to-wear clothing at affordable prices. The firm's first venture beyond the Netherlands, in 1911, was a store in Berlin, expanding during the 20th century to much of Europe, Brazil, Mexico and China.

ARCHITECTURAL NOTES

117-125 Rye Lane marks the highlight of the Southern Railway's development of its Peckham estate on both sides of Rye Lane, begun in 1935.

By the 1930s, Rye Lane was in its heyday as one of South London's most popular shopping streets. The railway junction at Peckham Rye Station contributed to the Lane's success. The Southern Railway capitalised on this by creating the station arcade and two- and three-storey commercial buildings on the Holly Grove and Blenheim Grove corners of Rye Lane, to the north and south of the station.

Plans recently discovered in Network Rail's archives show that this integrated development was a late work by the noteworthy Anglo Scottish architect John

James Joass (1868-1952). This ensemble of Peckham buildings should be seen in the context of the contemporary, bold, modernist developments by the Southern Railway at Surbiton and Richmond stations.

The architect J. J. Joass first came to prominence in London in the 1890s as the chief assistant, then partner, to John Belcher RA (1841-1913), one of the leading lights of the Edwardian Baroque revival.

Joass was particularly skilful at combining unique, Michelangelo-inspired, Classical detailing with space saving modern steel frames, and the generous glass and bronze shopfronts beloved of early 20th century retailers.

C&A came to Britain in 1922 and to Peckham in 1930, opening a store at 72-74 Rye Lane in the building that is now occupied by McDonald's. In 1949, C&A opened a second, larger, store on the other side of Rye Lane (117-125) in a fine building, which was constructed as part of the art deco development around Peckham Rye Station. Both stores traded in tandem until 1971, when the original store closed and was taken over by a furniture shop.

Details of the second store are sketchy. Nevertheless, most older Peckham people remember the building as a typical C&A store, memories reinforced by photographic evidence, which shows a huge property with an impressive frontage.

C&A Modes at 117-125 Rye Lane, 1981

There is no doubt about its eventual destiny: deemed no longer viable, it closed on 17 January 1987, an early casualty that presaged the entire withdrawal of the company from the United Kingdom on 15 June 2000 (though still flourishing elsewhere in the world). In 1998, the South London Temple, a Pentecostal church, moved into the upper floors, while retail outlets trade from the ground floor. In 2023, works were carried out to repair and clean the artificial stone to the front of the building. The fine Crittall windows, with beautiful bronze ironmongery, remain in place, and require further care. This landmark building is a prime candidate for a full restoration project.

In Joass' later years, when 117-125 Rye Lane was designed, he had mastered the then fashionable Art Deco style for commercial building. However his classical background informs his design for Rye Lane. An imposing three storey symmetrical frontage was built with taller chamfered corner 'towers' and a higher central feature. These vertical elements were further heightened by immense flag poles now lost, though their steel brackets still survive; period photographs attest to their scale.

The latest construction techniques were used at 117-125 Rye Lane. As at the neighbouring Holdron's department store, the American, Kahn's ferro-concrete structural system created wide, fireproof, spans to the retail floors.

Externally wide, steel, Crittall windows delivered plenty of daylight to the shop interior and a stylish modern shopfront, now lost, created an alluring base to the building. The whole ensemble, on both sides of Rye Lane, are visually unified by the use of projecting horizontal bands of masonry at the corner elements

At 117-125 Rye Lane the Art Deco facade that faces the Lane is executed in a fine grained artificial Portland Stone.

Similarly elegant artificial stone cladding can be seen in Robert Lutyens' former Marks & Spencer building at 54 Rye Lane, another landmark of Peckham's 'Art Deco Quarter'.

PECKHAM LIBRARY SQUARE

1994

The genesis of what is now Peckham Library Square is complex. Its starting point lies in the fate of North Peckham's five estates, begun in 1937 as a London County Council initiative to provide social housing to replace run-down properties in the so-called Sumner area: the streets between the High Street and Commercial Way. These were to be 'homes for the future' and were followed by similar estates in the post-war years: high-rise tenement blocks which, though initially welcomed, would come be seen as synonymous with defective design and in some parts, desolation.

Refurbishments achieved some improvements, but in the early 1990s, with Sally Keeble as Leader, Southwark Council grasped the need for something more decisive. Having fought off the Channel Tunnel Rail Link, regeneration was in the air. In 1994, Southwark's Labour Council made a bid for funding from a government scheme dubbed the Single Regeneration Budget, and were awarded £65 million to launch an initiative largely directed to the redevelopment of the council-owned estates. To oversee this bold programme of renewal the Peckham Partnership was founded, bringing together a consortium of council officers, statutory agencies, housing associations, voluntary organisations and local tenants, headed by Malcolm Smith, a town planner. Its priority was to replace the estates with less dense, mixed tenure, low-rise housing, beginning with the Sumner area. They also wanted to tackle Peckham town centre, which was seen by many as declining commercially, unattractive, unsafe, and difficult to access. The Partnership planned to build a new health and fitness centre, and a library and media centre. Their site would be identified on Ordnance Survey maps as Canal Head Square.

The history of this area went back a long way. This was the location of Sir Thomas Bond's illustrious 17th century garden, of Nell Gwyn's reputed house, and would lead on to the so-called linear park, the green corridor of the former Surrey Canal. Nearby was the exact location of the former Peckham Manor House, dating from the reign of Edward III, rebuilt in 1672 and sacked in the Glorious Revolution of 1688. Here was 'Heritage' writ large for those who had the wit and imagination to take advantage of it, and develop it into the future.

The first construction was an imposing arch, spanning 35 metres between historic buildings on Peckham High Street. It was opened by local Members of Parliament Harriet Harman and Tessa Jowell in 1994, and served as the threshold to the new centrepiece of the ancient village.

View looking north from Rye Lane towards Peckham Library Square, canopy for Jones and Higgins department store in foreground with Whitten Timber Yard beyond, 1979

The Peckham Pulse followed on 6 June 1998, built on the site of the Victoria Baths. Its exterior did not attract awards but it fulfilled a healthy revolution with two swimming pools, a large gymnasium, exercise studios and a spa. The centre proved popular, and two years later the area fronting the building was enhanced by four globes designed by Duncan Hoosan, representing earth, air, fire and water.

The crowning glory of the square was its new library on the east side of Peckham Hill Street. Architect Will Alsop was known for futuristic design and had been joined by Jan Störmer in 1991. Work began in 1995 and was completed in 2000; it was opened by the Secretary of State for Culture, Media and Sport, Chris Smith on 15 May.

Its design was carefully considered but unconventional. Alsop said "The first thing I thought of when I saw the plans is the view from the library looking across the former Thames floodplain towards the centre of London. It's one of the reasons I designed it that way". Alsop already had a reputation for breaking with tradition, and Peckham provided an opportunity to respond to a diverse community, which was itself free-spirited. Its most obvious peculiarity was the relatively meagre footprint of the lower floors, with the library area projecting above it to make an inverted side elevation

Interior view of Peckham Library under construction, 1999

Peckham's Heritage – Past, Present & Future

Peckham Square shortly after construction of Peckham Arch, 1994

in the shape of a letter L. Experts loved it, showering the concept with awards, including the prestigious RIBA 2000 Stirling Prize, and the 2002 Civic Trust Award. The cladding in pre-patinated copper was also admired, and the multi-coloured panels on the rear elevation afforded a striking view of the City.

Particular praise was expressed by parents and childminders for the Children's Section with its glass lift and large glazed wall. Spacious separate areas could be used for sessions devoted to singing nursery rhymes during term time, with 'pods' on the top floor for music and stories.

A more recent addition to the Square is the purpose-built Mountview Academy of Theatre Arts. This world-renowned

theatre school offers a wide range of courses and performances in two theatres, and subsidised space for local groups, supporting Peckham's status as a cultural hub. Next to Mountview, and occupying part of Peckham Hill Street, University of the Arts London (UAL)'s 'Digital Hub' provides student workspace for individuals and small businesses in the creative arts, with accommodation for almost 400 students. The Hub is on the former site of Whitten Timber and the former manor house (see pages 36-39). At the time of writing, plans are being developed for further enhancement of the Square, as described in 'A Brief History of Peckham' (see page 27).

ARCHITECTURAL NOTES

The Peckham Library and the Peckham Arch are two exceptional works of contemporary architecture: much-loved by locals and the subject of pilgrimages of fans of modern architecture from around the world.

THE PECKHAM LIBRARY

The Peckham Library was designed and built by Will Alsop RA (1947-2018), the enfant terrible of the British architecture scene in the late 20th and early 21st century. Alsop was also a keen painter and saw his built work as a natural extension of his painting and sculpture.

I worked for Will Alsop for a number of years *(writes Benedict O'Looney)* and witnessed his design process intimately - architectural ideas leapt from his sketchbooks and canvases both of which were produced in great quantities in the studio. Our challenge was to transform his bold, colourful ideas into something you could build and inhabit. At the Peckham Library, Alsop's 'architectural expressionism' is given momentum by an excellent technical design and robust, well-considered detailing and painterly colouring.

The inspired Director of Regeneration for Southwark Council, Fred Manson, was key in commissioning Will Alsop for the Peckham Library. He really understood how working with a first-rate architect could powerfully improve the then run-down town centre. Manson went on to mastermind the re-use of the Bankside Power Station into Tate Modern and helped connect Bankside to the City of London with the Millennium Bridge.

The Peckham Library is a great example of the modernist 'object-building', bold eye-catching architecture set on tall legs, so city life can flow under and around it. With the development of steel or concrete-framed architecture in the modern period, buildings no longer needed thick structural walls to support them. The celebrated Swiss architect Le Corbusier (1887-1965) pioneered buildings lifted up on legs, called pilotis, that could let people use the spaces below buildings.

This worked perfectly for Peckham's Canal Head site where the bright green verdigris copper cladding and orange 'beret' can vividly be seen above the brick facades of the Georgian and Victorian Peckham High Street. Alsop believed his buildings should be at least 10 meters off the ground. The inventive structural engineers Adams Kara Taylor devised a way to lift the library's reading room off the ground creating a bridge-like truss supported on an exposed concrete frame to the north and slender steel 'dancing' legs to the south.

Peckham Library is also an example of environmentally conscious design. Each side of the library responds to its unique environmental setting. The south side has small windows to guard against overheating in the summer, and the building's big overhang helps shade the southern elevation. The north elevation, which gets less direct sun, is entirely glazed in different coloured glass panels. This ensures the excellent natural lighting, and natural ventilation, penetrates deep into the library, minimizing the requirement for artificial lighting. Before the Mountview building arrived, this glazed wall offered panoramic views of London's skyline to the north. The carefully detailed exposed concrete structure in the Peckham Library absorbs the cool night-time air, helping chill the building in the hot summer months and helping retain the building's warmth in the winter months.

The building type of the 'public library' is one of the noblest of civic building types with a long architectural history going back to antiquity. The Peckham Library makes a unique contribution to this genre with its incredible aerial reading room, so popular with the Peckham community. This tall, double-height hall has inventively placed windows offering readers views out across Peckham. Three organically shaped, and inhabitable, timber 'pods' delight the eye in the reading room: a music library, a children's play space, and a well-used local meeting space.

At the Library, Will Alsop's sense of fun, delight and architectural poetry shine brightly, and this is backed with considerable technical skill and innovation. It is no wonder that the building won the Stirling Prize in the year 2000. It is perhaps the greatest example of Southwark Council's determination to use progressive architects for their public buildings.

The Alsop story continues just down the Queen's Road in New Cross. Following the success of the Peckham Library, Goldsmiths University commissioned Will Alsop to design the Ben Pimlott Building housing the Art, Computer Science and Psychology departments. The Pimlott Building is a wonderful update of the Peckham library with its elegantly detailed glazed north elevation rising up behind the Baroque-revival Town Hall. Like the Peckham's Library's orange beret and rooftop letters saying 'library', an immense, 9 meter tall, steel 'scribble' sculpture, illuminated at night, sits on the building, offering a playful, cheeky landmark.

THE PECKHAM ARCH
The Peckham Arch is unique in Britain and has become an iconic symbol of Peckham Town Centre since its construction in 1994.

It forms a cheerful covered public space, used by all, at the meeting point of north/south and east/west movement, in the heart of Peckham.

The Peckham Arch was bravely built by Southwark Council under the leadership of Fred Manson as a marker of the renaissance of Peckham Town centre after years of decline. For a number of years, the arch stood alone, framing the view to the old village centre to the south and the timber yards and industrial archaeology of the canal head to the north. It created a sense of place and announced that something special was going to happen here – by the end of the decade the arch was complemented by Will Alsop's Library and one of the final works of the Southwark's own architecture department, the excellent Peckham Pulse.

The Peckham Arch is a splendid example of the British 'High Tech' movement and was designed by Troughton McAslan, who were protégés of the best-known High Tech architect Richard Rogers.

It has all the features of the High-Tech Movement - particularly bold structural expression: the compressive forces of the wide-span tubular steel structure are counter balanced by (elegantly detailed) slender steel rods handling the tensile forces. The mechanism of the arch's structural equilibrium is beautifully shown.

Like so much British High-Tech architecture - the Lloyds Building or Stansted Airport, for example – this confident and expressive use of structure is inspired by the Victorians. The Peckham Arch is a compact version of the great iron and glass roofs at St. Pancras or Victoria Stations. Another characteristic of High-Tech architecture is the separate articulation of structure and skin – note how the arch's cladding sits on top of, clear of, the structural system.

The arch is playfully lit by four lighting 'trees'. The lighting design is by Ron Hasleden and modulates from warm to cool tones based on barometric pressure.

The Peckham Arch is an important early work by John McAslan whose practice has flourished since, working on some of London's most significant buildings including the restoration of the Roundhouse in Camden, and King's Cross Station.

Another way to look at the Peckham Arch is in the tradition of open but covered public spaces in Europe. They are both popular gathering spaces and a part of local commercial life. Think of the Tudor market halls with open undercrofts at Faversham and Ledbury, which form a focal point for the town. Consider even the similarity with the Loggia dei Lanzi in Florence or the porch of the Pantheon in Rome. The Peckham Arch is our own unique and iconic public 'loggia' in the core of old Peckham.

View from the top of Witcombe Point
with Peckham Levels in foreground, 2022

Part 3

In Better Health

COMMERCIAL WAY

PECKHAM HILL STREET

MARMONT ROAD

● 6

PECKHAM HIGH

PECKHAM ROAD

● 10

● 20

14 ● ●

● 15

● 3

● 13

17 ●

● 16

● 4

CLAYTON ROAD

HANOVER PARK

LYNDHURST WAY

BELLENDEN ROAD

RYE LANE

● 23

● 8

● 21

COPELAND ROAD

LYNDHURST WAY

12 ●

● 19

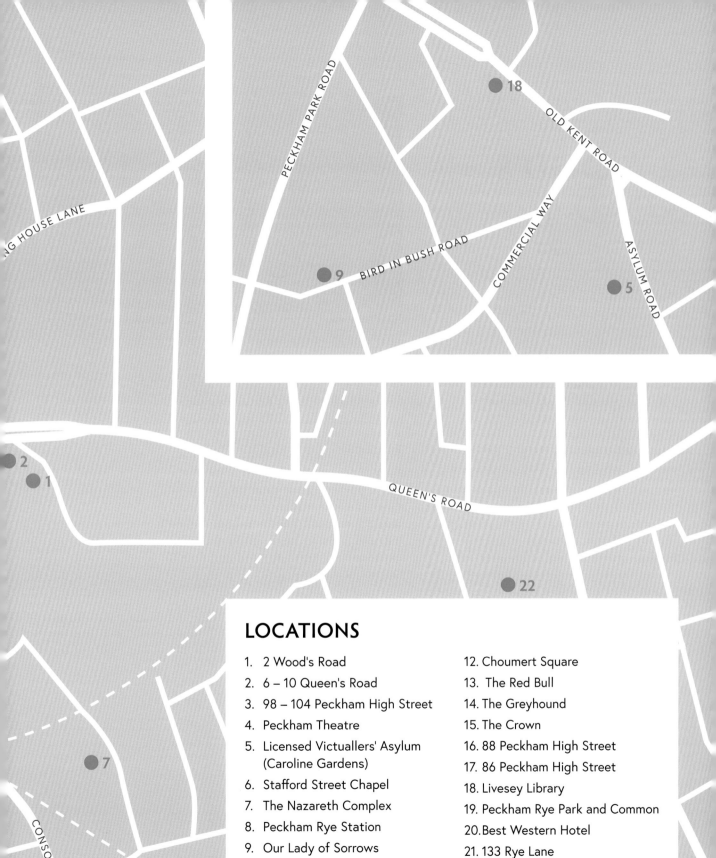

LOCATIONS

1. 2 Wood's Road
2. 6 – 10 Queen's Road
3. 98 – 104 Peckham High Street
4. Peckham Theatre
5. Licensed Victuallers' Asylum (Caroline Gardens)
6. Stafford Street Chapel
7. The Nazareth Complex
8. Peckham Rye Station
9. Our Lady of Sorrows
10. The Old Fire Station
11. The Old Mill Building
12. Choumert Square
13. The Red Bull
14. The Greyhound
15. The Crown
16. 88 Peckham High Street
17. 86 Peckham High Street
18. Livesey Library
19. Peckham Rye Park and Common
20. Best Western Hotel
21. 133 Rye Lane
22. Pioneer Health Centre
23. The Peckham Multi Storey

2 WOOD'S ROAD
17TH CENTURY

This detached weatherboard house, originally built as a rural residence in the late 17th century and listed Grade II in 1972, is probably the oldest of Peckham's very few remaining secular buildings. It belongs to the area described in Pigot's Directory as a village with "one principal street, which is well lighted with gas, and inhabited by very respectable persons."

With the urban spread of Peckham in the late 19th century, 2 Wood's Road lost its residential character. In 1894, it was used as a dye works and in 1919 was acquired by Thomas Colyer, trading as Carty & Son vat makers – their beautiful cedar wood vats still occasionally turn up for auction. From 1989 to 2014, MR Scaffolding Ltd established its offices there. By October 2016, when an application for planning permission was made, the building was in a sorry state of repair with the ground floor vandalised, the stairs rotten, the roof leaking and some features including an historic fireplace, removed.

Notwithstanding a refacing in stucco around 1820, significant alterations and a change to industrial use, this building is defined by the National Planning Policy Framework as a 'designated heritage asset'. Standing apart in what was previously Harders Road, it was evidently in need of sympathetic restoration.

To this end, a scrupulous planning application backed by Nick Collins, former Principal Inspector of Historic Buildings at English Heritage, was approved in January 2017. It granted a change of use from offices to four self-contained flats and the erection of a single-storey rear extension to replace a dilapidated one dating from 1937. The case officer noted that the building retained sufficient of its original condition to be immediately recognisable as dating from before the 18th century.

The planning application was supported by DLG Architects, with carefully considered commitments for the building's restoration: historic features were to be preserved and the front of the property converted to a lawned garden contained within railings, to reflect its Georgian character.

Wood's Road following renovations, 2022

6-10 QUEEN'S ROAD
1715

6-10 Queen's Road with neighbouring premises of Carter & Son vat makers (now 2 Wood's Road), 1980

This is a good news story. These impressive Grade II listed 18th century houses, somewhat neglected by local historians, were lovingly restored c.2005. They date from about 1715 and were constructed as a pair of residential villas.

The restoration, secured by architect Eleni Makri, achieved a commendation at the Georgian Group Architectural Awards in 2007. The adjacent smaller and less imposing house at 4 is said to have been built in 1700.

ARCHITECTURAL NOTE

The group of old houses 2-10 Queen's Road and 2 Wood's Road are some of the most historically interesting buildings in Peckham.

The oldest, the Grade II listed, 2 Wood's Road was built in the Stuart period and has an elegant brick facade covered in stucco with Renaissance inspired symmetry.

The architectural star of the group is 6-10 Queen's Road, once a terrace of three houses, later shops and offices, recently restored and returned to residential use. With its tall, baroque-proportioned facade and red rubber dressed bricks framing the windows, this group is an exemplar of elite town houses in the Queen Anne period, circa 1700.

6-10 Queen's Road is a good example of the new urban architecture of London shaped by the building regulations that were drafted after the catastrophic Great Fire of London in 1666. These regulations required all new houses to have brick facades and thick brick party walls to contain the spread of fire. 6-10 Queen's Road shows this new, stylish, London domestic architecture arriving in Peckham. The beautifully detailed, counterbalanced, timber sash windows were another architectural innovation of this period, possibly invented by the architect and polymath Robert Hooke.

Although these houses show a new architectural fashion, the materials are all local: quality facing bricks and a tall, pan-tiled, roof from nearby Surrey Brick & Tile Works. It is not until the Industrial Revolution and the construction of canals and railways that Peckham's building materials came from more distant sources.

As Peckham lay well outside Central London in 1700, older, timber-framed, vernacular, houses were still being built by less affluent people, away from the watchful eyes of the official surveyors in the City and Westminster. This is shown by the houses at 98-104 and 56-62 Peckham High Street. Further east, you can see a picturesque surviving group at 19-25 Tanner's Hill, Deptford.

The whole south side of Queen's Road from Consort Road to the boundary with Lewisham, to the east, is filled with architectural interest, with developments of fine brick houses from throughout the Georgian and early Victorian periods. Thankfully, many of these houses are listed.

98-104 PECKHAM HIGH STREET
18TH CENTURY

Among the most significant historic fragments that remain in Peckham town centre is the picturesque group formed by 98-104 Peckham High Street, a survival of Peckham's past as a rural village. This early group of buildings, (along with 56 – 66 Peckham High Street, see pages 86-89), was considered important enough to be mentioned in a report by the Royal Commission on the Historical Monuments of England, published in 1998, which noted that 98-104 Peckham High Street remain "very much at the centre of the old settlement".

Two buildings in this group, 100 and 102, were included in the Peckham Townscape Heritage Initiative (THI) programme of repairs and restoration works. The intention was to repair and restore this group of buildings as a whole, stitching together this fragment of historic townscape.

The house at 98, parts of which date from circa 1700, was evidently built alongside an open passage – a right of way which gave access to the ancient Peckham Theatre, located at the rear of 100 (see following pages), with the site later used as part of Peckham Boys School from 1822 to 1884. 102 and 104, recorded as from the late 17th century, were originally timber-framed, one-room-plan houses. These are rare surviving examples of a plan that was widespread in London in the 18th century, intended as "standard and respectable housing for artisans and labourers".

102 (The Peckham Cobbler) is a two-storey circa 1830s cottage. It is almost certain that the building was damaged by a WWII bomb blast, and a later shopfront was installed. In the THI works, the eaves level was lowered, and the dormer window was recreated. The timber pilaster heads were reinstated, and the shopfront roof was completely overhauled. The new decorative ironwork above the shopfront is a close interpretation of the original. New sash windows were designed

98-104 Peckham High Street, 2023 - at the centre of this historic group, numbers 100 and 102 were repaired through the Peckham Townscape Heritage Initiative

for the existing openings dating from the post-1945 version of the building, which is different from its original early 19th century form. This references the SPAB (Society for the Protection of Ancient Buildings) principle of acknowledging changes that take place in the building's lifetime. The asymmetrical arrangement of the two doors arose from the need to provide a separate access door for tenants living above the shop. The tiled stall riser and new timber-framed shopfront were configured to combine client needs with due deference to the original shopfront.

100 Peckham High Street was the final building completed in the THI scheme, and

though small in scale, its transformation has perhaps been the most dramatic of all the THI projects. The first-floor extension, built in the 1950s, was removed, and the first floor and roof were reinstated to align with neighbouring buildings. A new street elevation was created with a traditional shopfront and distinctive clay tiled gambrel roof. The building opens up to the rear to the former Peckham Theatre, later the British School (Boys) building, which was repaired and retained as an integral part of the project.

Great efforts by local people and Southwark Council have contributed to the valuing and protection of 98-104 Peckham High Street. In 2020, while the THI works to 102 Peckham High Street were underway, a planning application to demolish 104 and replace it with a four-storey residential building with commercial space on the ground floor, was rejected by the Council, a decision that was supported by the Peckham Heritage Regeneration Partnership, Peckham Vision, and others who sought to support the protection of this important historic group of buildings. As this book goes to print, Southwark Council is using its planning enforcement powers on the owners of 98 High Street to carry out repairs, as the building has been left derelict for many years.

ABOVE
100-108 Peckham High Street, 1928

BELOW
Peckham High Street, 1979

PECKHAM THEATRE
18TH CENTURY

To the rear of 100 Peckham High Street, and visible from the service yard of Morrisons supermarket, is the shell of Peckham Theatre. The official Camberwell guide listed this site as demolished, but it was rediscovered by local historian William Marshall in 1983.

Originally a rather primitive wooden building, the theatre was rebuilt in brick probably in the late 18th or early 19th century. Playbills show that it boasted boxes, a pit and a gallery. Between shows the building was also used as a stable and barn. There is a belief that Nell Gwyn appeared there after leaving the London stage but this is highly unlikely. Edward Jerningham's play 'The Peckham Frolic: or Nell Gwyn' reinforces the view of Peckham as a place of frolic and fun, but is plainly fictitious.

Solid evidence for the establishment of Peckham Theatre dates only from 1780, when the rates book for the area lists Ann Wakeland at £10 for a house and the same amount for a "play house". Almost certainly, this is Ann Wakelin, an acrobatic dancer at Sadler's Wells who had managed a theatrical company in London and on tour. She was the mother of Sarah Baker (1736-1816), a well-known actress and manager with many distinguished connections in the profession, who after the death of her husband in 1769 embarked on a managerial career and toured regularly in Kent, with her mother joining the troupe until 1777. She is known to have

organised the building of several theatres, and to have transitioned gradually to offer 'straight' drama and even operas. A notice in the Kentish Gazette of 19/22 July 1780 indicates that she would close in Deal on 12 August, "as she is obliged to open her theatre at Peckham at that time".

Among Marshall's papers is a handwritten, undated, but evidently contemporary account of the theatre [punctuation as written]: "Theatre Peckham = a Wooden building formerly belonging to Mrs Baker they go there every year play thee there fair days and every night for a month afterwards and have very good business the house is very neat inside though shabby without will hold about twenty five pounds no benefits there Boxes two and sixpence Pit one and sixpence Gall.y one shilling halfprice taken."

Playbills found by Marshall from 1807, 1808, 1816 and 1817 indicate a varied programme. On 8 September 1807 Shakespeare's Hamlet was followed by a "musical entertainment". Richard III was presented on 28 September in the following year, followed by a "comic song" and a "laughable entertainment". Boxes for these performances cost three shillings, the pit two shillings and the gallery one shilling. The final playbill for 2 June 1817 suggests a rise in the status of the artists with Mr Cobham, late of the Theatre Royal Covent

Plaque from school that occupied 100 Peckham High Street from 1822 until 1880s uncovered during restoration, 2019

Garden, the promise of Mr B. Nathan from the King's Theatre, the Misses C. J. and A. Bennett of the Theatre Royal, Drury Lane, and Mr Jones of the Theatre Royal, Liverpool.

Shortly after these performances, the Peckham Theatre welcomed an actor who was to become one of the giants of the English stage - John Baldwin Buckstone, made his first appearance on any stage first as a walk-on, then as Captain Aubri in a melodrama The Dog of Montargis (a number of other sources attribute Buckstone's debut to Wokingham, but the Peckham engagement came first). He went on to fame as the writer of 150 plays, as a leading comic actor and from 1853 to 1877 as manager of the Haymarket.

But just as the reputation of Peckham Theatre appeared to be in the ascendant, so came its demise. The fairs at Peckham and Camberwell attracted increasing public criticism and it seems this disapproval extended to the Theatre too. In 1822, the building was handed over to a local school founded by members of the Society of Friends. Allport commented: "the school of morality has succumbed to that of sound, scriptural, enlightened education, and the old playhouse is now appropriated to the instruction of the poor". The school still had 200 boys attending in 1871, but new legislation led to its closure by the 1880s.

Historically, the school is of interest. A so-called Lancasterian system of education was introduced to Britain when Joseph Lancaster (1778-1838), an English Quaker, opened a school for poor children at his father's house in Kent Street, Southwark. This was followed by a free school in Belvedere Place, Borough Road. Lancaster pioneered a monitorial system of teaching in which more advanced pupils – "monitors" passed on knowledge to those below them, with some supervision. It was thought this began because Lancaster was unable to afford an assistant but that he subsequently made a virtue of necessity, proclaiming the system's advantages with considerable success.

Britannica has it, however, that "he proved to be vain, rash, and soon fell heavily into debt". Fellow Quakers bailed him out, organising the 'Royal Lancasterian Institution for the Education of the Poor of Every Religious Persuasion' in 1810. It was under this direction that the school was established in Hill Street, Peckham in 1812. However, concerns about Lancaster's conduct persisted, and in 1814 the threat of an investigation prompted his resignation. The Royal Institution had by then been renamed the British and Foreign School Society, omitting any reference to Lancaster, and the monitors were gradually replaced by trained teachers. Over a thousand British schools were established, hundreds of them in London. The Society is now a grant-making body but two 'Lancasterian' schools remain, in Manchester and Tottenham. In Peckham, the school's premises were used commercially before falling into their present-day decay, a forgotten remnant of Southwark's history.

LICENSED VICTUALLERS' ASYLUM (CAROLINE GARDENS)

1831

Built on a six-acre site in Asylum Road purchased from the Hill family in 1827, the Asylum is near to, but in striking contrast to the Old Kent Road on a charming, sequestered byway of North Peckham. The buildings were listed Grade II in February 1962, and designated a Conservation Area in 1978. Here the term 'asylum' means sanctuary.

Credit for its conception is given to Joseph Proud Hodgson, who envisaged it as a place where retired, poor, aged publicans and their wives or widows – 'decayed brethren' – could pass their final years in tranquillity. This was at a time when people in need of relief found it extremely difficult to get help under the Poor Law, meaning occupational charities played a significant role in assisting distressed former workers. The Society of Licensed Victuallers was founded in 1793 as a friendly society and embarked upon a number of philanthropic endeavours; launching the Morning Advertiser newspaper to raise its profile, and establishing a school in Kennington for the children of licensees. But building the almshouses in Peckham is its defining legacy.

Much written about the early years of the Asylum has been taken from William Harnett Blanch's 'Ye Parish of Camerwell'.

Blanch was a fastidious historian, close to the events of his day, with unparalleled access to contemporary documents. He commended the work of the charity, which he noted would surely: "place the Asylum in a position altogether unequalled amongst Trade Societies".

On 29 May 1828, the foundation stone of the Asylum was laid by its patron, Augustus, Duke of Sussex, the sixth son of George III. The original building comprised 43 dwellings, and between 1831 and 1833 two more wings were added, each of 29

Archival photograph of Licensed Victuallers' Benevolent Institution, date unknown

Licensed Victuallers' Asylum, 1830

houses. In 1835 the Society was able to provide its residents with small grants, which later extended to coal, medicine, medical advice and a small pension - 8 shillings for single people, and 13 shillings for married couples. Two entrance lodges were added in 1839 and on 15 December 1842, the Society was incorporated by Royal Charter. In the following year, on the death of its first patron, the Duke of Sussex, the Asylum welcomed Albert, the Prince Consort, in his place.

Driven by demand, expansion continued. In 1849, 16 homes were added as a Ladies' Wing, with seven more additional homes built the following year, along with a chapel, board room and a spacious court room. Another wing of 15 homes, named after and launched by Prince Albert, was built in 1858, with six more added in 1859.

Prince Albert died in 1861, but the Asylum pressed on with the provision of almshouses, building 13 more on the Albert Wing. In 1864, a 16 foot statue of the Prince

Consort was erected in front of the chapel; unveiled on 9 August by his son the Prince of Wales, the future Edward VII. In 1866, another wing was commenced in the name of William Smalley, General Secretary of the Society of Licensed Victuallers (1844-1880), who contributed £1,000 towards the cost of its erection. Again there was royal involvement, the foundation stone was laid by Alfred, the newly created Duke of Edinburgh, second son of Queen Victoria. Finally, six houses were built on the grounds of the chaplain's house.

By 1875, the Asylum consisted of 170 two-storey homes, which would later rise to 175. It had become London's largest nexus of almshouses, with a chapel enriched by exquisite stained windows, and walls adorned by marble tablets in memory of its donors. Its services were said to have been "bright", with singing strengthened by members of the Licensed Victuallers' Choral Association, and an organ supplied by Bovington & Sons of London.

So endowed, the Asylum fulfilled its worthy purposes without incident, save that in 1921 it was given a change of name. Recognising that 'asylum' was now commonly associated with mental illness, it was renamed the Licensed Victuallers' Benevolent Institution.

From 1940, the grounds were used as a barrage balloon site, and most of the tenants were evacuated to accommodation on a new site in Denham, Buckinghamshire, remote from the danger posed by German bombers. It proved to be a sensible precaution for in 1943 a stray incendiary bomb hit the chapel, leaving its interior and roof severely damaged. Remarkably its stained glass windows and most of its memorial tablets remained intact.

After the war, the reconstituted National Victuallers' Homes developed new accommodation in Denham Garden Village, to which the remaining residents of the Asylum Road site were removed in 1959, along with the statue of Prince Albert. The entire Peckham site, with its buildings intact, was sold to the Metropolitan Borough of Camberwell in 1960 and passed to Southwark Council on its formation in 1965. No longer connected with licensed

PRINCE ALBERT LAYING THE FOUNDATION-STONE OF THE NEW WING OF THE LICENSED VICTUALLERS' ASYLUM.—(SEE PRECEDING PAGE.)

ABOVE
The wedding of
Nancy Coleman-
Frank and author
Derek Kinrade at
the Asylum Chapel,
2018

ABOVE
The wedding of
Nancy Coleman-
Frank and author
Derek Kinrade at
the Asylum Chapel,
2018

OPPOSITE
Illustration of Prince
Albert laying the
foundation stone for
the new wing of the
Licensed Victuallers'
Asylum, published
in The London
Illustrated News,
10 July 1858

victuallers, the site was renamed Caroline Gardens, after Caroline Secker, a former resident, whose late husband was one of the marines reputed to have caught Horatio Nelson when he fell in the Battle of Trafalgar.

The almshouses continue to be used as social housing, but the story of the chapel is less straightforward. Dilapidated, but retaining a certain charm, it was suggested in 1960 that it might be used as a theatre but this idea came to nothing. For some time it was used as a costume store by Southwark Council's Entertainments Department, until in 1999 a serious proposal for its conversion to a community centre was pressed by the Caroline Gardens Residents' Association. This was supported by local MP Harriet Harman and Baroness Blackstone, Minister for the Arts, and pursued until at

least 2005. Eventually, in 2010, local artists Dido Hallett and Jo Dennis began to use the space as a not-for-profit venue for art and theatrical projects, exhibitions and photo shoots. A licence was secured for the chapel's use for weddings, and in 2013 a 12-year lease was taken in the name of Maverick Projects. The Council took positive steps in support of Maverick to ensure the chapel's future when, in the early months of 2018, it backed conservation work, guided by Historic England, with funding from The National Lottery Heritage Fund and the Architectural Heritage Fund, to partially restore the roof and portico. Further funding was awarded for ongoing restoration with the creation of a strong business infrastructure. The venue remains popular for couples seeking an unconventional romantic setting for their wedding day.

STAFFORD STREET CHAPEL

1834

This plain building began in 1834 as a Wesleyan chapel on the west side of Stafford Street (now Staffordshire Street) near the junction with Park Lane (now Goldsmith Road). This is a somewhat remote part of Peckham, steeped in history. Dr Milner's Academy, at which Oliver Goldsmith served as an usher, was on the opposite corner, William Penn is believed to have visited a nearby house in Meeting House Lane, and it seems likely that Peter Collinson's illusive garden was also in the vicinity. The chapel later became better known as the Peckham Settlement, and more recently functioned as an art gallery and studios.

During its initial phase as a chapel only a small number of worshippers were able to meet, and as the population of Peckham increased it became obvious that a larger building was needed. In 1864 an impressive, more traditional church was built on Queen's Road. The whole congregation of the Stafford Street chapel moved across.

Attempts to rent out the vacated building proved unsuccessful, and from January 1866 it was given over to a Wesleyan Day and Sunday school. Enlarged in 1875, the school continued, frequently in debt, until 1923, when the building was leased to London County Council, with a proviso for the Wesleyans to continue to use the school on Sundays. And so matters continued until May 1929, when the LCC unexpectedly decided to terminate the lease. The Wesleyan trustees had hardly come to terms with this grim news when, providentially, they received an offer from the Union of Girls' Schools Settlements (UGSS) to purchase the Stafford Street premises. This was gratefully accepted, subject to the survival of the Wesleyan Sunday School, which was able to continue for some years.

The UGSS, then based in Peckham, had its roots in a movement for social reform that had begun in London's East End in 1884. Reformers sought ways to address the deplorable conditions and grinding poverty which prevailed in some parts of Victorian England. One idea was to establish 'settlements', where benevolent mentors would live and work alongside their deprived

Present day view of Stafford Street Chapel, 2022

Peckham's Heritage – Past, Present & Future

View of Stafford Street Chapel, 1980

citizens, providing services such as day care, healthcare and education. The movement quickly spread to South London, described by one divine as having, "the biggest areas of unbroken poverty to be found anywhere in England". The scheme was taken up in Camberwell, where in March 1897, led by Jane Francis Dove, the campaigning founder of Wycombe Abbey School, a number of girls' schools united to open a mission in a building at 33 Kempshead Road.

This led to the formation of settlements in Calmington Road and Peckham Road, with an increasing range of supportive activities. Its diverse work continued until 1929 when the LCC announced that it required all remaining settlement sites for new housing. This prompted an approach to secure alternative accommodation in the Stafford Street school. In 1930 the settlement moved in, with a formal opening ceremony by Queen Mary on 18 March 1931.

In these unprepossessing buildings, augmented in 1933 by an added wing, the Settlement's mission to relieve distress and poverty expanded. It enjoyed the benefit of high level support, including, successively, the patronage of Princess Margaret and the Countess of Wessex. Some idea of the Settlement's social standing can be discerned from the evacuation of the school in September 1939 to Glyndebourne!

The history of the Settlement is largely one of outstanding achievement. An impressive range of social services for children, young and elderly people was provided by a dedicated team of staff and volunteers. Paddy Cribb, chair of the Settlement's Executive Committee until 2005, writing in the Southwark News in 2016, credited it as having initiated the provision of 'meals on wheels', and establishing the first children's nursery in London.

But towards the end of the 20th century the development of the welfare state and provision of local authority social services began to undermine the spiritual ethos of the Settlement and to diminish its funding. In the following years these ominous portends were to play out disastrously: a major redevelopment project collapsed, the Council withdrew its grant, and the trustees were beset with cash flow problems. Charitable social work continued, not least the establishment of a job club, thought to be the first of its kind, but in 2011/12 a series of complex financial and organisational problems led to insolvency. In August 2012, administrators were appointed, and the Settlement was closed and sold off.

The buyer, a Peckham resident, set about transforming the old building, refurbishing the interior, painting it white, and opening it to natural light. At its centre, what was the chapel is now a simple gallery space, with airy studios available for artists: a creative, not-for-profit venture in keeping with the cultural renaissance of Peckham, and the altruism of the building's heritage. Today, the site also hosts a popular family-run vegan restaurant.

THE NAZARETH COMPLEX

1857

This story begins with a convent called Nazareth House, situated on a triangular site bounded by Gordon Road and two railway lines running east from Peckham Rye Station: one of only two buildings on land otherwise given over to a formal plan of trees. Quite when it was built is uncertain but it can be said that for some years it was occupied by the Sisters of Christian Retreat, a Roman Catholic order committed to celibacy, poverty and obedience, which originated in France at the time of the Revolution. Blanch records that the Sisters came to Peckham in December 1848, moved two years later to Kennington Manor House, before finding peace at Nazareth House in 1857. That tranquillity was short-lived. When the railways arrived in the 1860s the convent was no longer a place for quiet retreat. The nuns departed, and the house and grounds were bought by the Camberwell Board of Guardians for use as a 'supplementary establishment' to house some 110 aged and infirm men who, if their health allowed, engaged in a variety of activities including the cultivation of the four-acre grounds, and caring for pigs and poultry.

Any notion of idyllic Christian altruism was dispelled in 1878 when a huge workhouse building with a very different purpose was erected alongside the former convent. The Poor Law, not replaced until 1948, was by then deeply entrenched. The overriding concern was to limit public expenditure, with a reluctance to provide financial relief to people who could possibly fend for themselves. Provision was meagre and confined to cases of extreme poverty. Those in receipt of relief were labelled 'paupers': the ultimate degradation.

In 1832, a Royal Commission was charged to conduct a root and branch review of the Poor Law. Its primary concern was to reduce expenditure. In its report of 1834, the Commissioners took the view that able-bodied paupers had everywhere demonstrated 'idleness and vice', and that in most cases pauperism could have been averted by ordinary care and industry. These were people regarded as being largely to blame for their own condition and it was concluded that the provision of relief merely

Gordon Road Resettlement Centre, 1986

Peckham's Heritage – Past, Present & Future

tended to encourage their feckless mode of living. The Commissioners felt that the moral, as well as the economic, argument must lie with the utmost restriction of relief.

On 14 August 1834, an Act for the Amendment and Better Administration of the Laws Relating to the Poor in England and Wales set a harsh paradigm which would survive for years. Under the centralised authority and guidance of three Poor Law Commissioners small parishes were grouped together as Poor Law Unions, each providing a workhouse, which as far as possible should be the only relief offered. Such institutions were not new, but this legislation marked the beginning of their systematic deployment. Here was a system of relief so irksome and disagreeable that no-one would seek to receive it who could possibly do without it. Workhouse inmates were expected to carry out menial tasks at set times in return for lodging. Favourites were breaking stones, chopping wood and picking oakum using a large nail or 'spike', and, also for women, work in the laundry. Workhouses were not prisons, though they

often had similar characteristics: minimal and unvaried food, rough uniform clothing, fixed waking hours, the separation of family members, and crowded conditions.

By 1868, Poor Law Unions had been established across Britain, each working through an elected Board of Guardians. To meet its obligations, the Camberwell Union set up a competition for the design of a workhouse. It was won by architects Berriman and Sons Ltd, whose plans led to the construction of an austere, forbidding building costing some £964. It comprised a central administrative block connected through covered walkways with two dormitory wards, one for men, one for women, with space for a total of 743 'residents'. Accommodation for vagrants was added in separate buildings.

Nicknamed 'The Spike', the Gordon Road institution opened in 1879 as the Camberwell Workhouse, unashamedly living up to its name until 1930, when the Poor Law Unions and their Boards of Guardians were abolished. Responsibility was transferred to local authorities, and the Gordon Road unit became one of many rebranded as public assistance institutions. It passed to London County Council and became known as the Camberwell Reception Centre, catering largely for homeless men.

In 1966, there was yet another change, when the Camberwell Reception Centre became a Department of Health and Social Security Resettlement Unit. This was an important development, because the government was now directly responsible for action to address the plight of 'unsettled' people, a problem that had become of great and increasing concern. Speaking in a House of Commons debate on 26 March 1969, Norman Pentland MP briefed members on the current dilemma - nationwide accommodation was being provided for upwards of 1,200 men in 18 reception centres, nearly half at the Camberwell institution, which was the largest in the country, indeed in Europe. On very cold nights up to 900 men would sleep there, in dormitories filled with 120 beds each. Those who stayed with a view to resettlement were only a little better housed. All shared one enormous dining room with bare wooden tables. Pentland noted: "It looks what it is: a Victorian workhouse of the 1870s in which people are trying to do a 1969 job of work."

On 2 August 1972, Christopher Mayhew MP, speaking in the House of Commons, drew attention to the plight of single homeless people, many mentally sick, "rootless, homeless and utterly miserable". Mayhew had visited the Camberwell Reception Centre and had been told that there were more mentally ill people going through it than went through the average mental hospital. He said: "It is an appalling building.

I do not know in Britain I have seen such an appalling structure. It would be tempting to say 'Knock it down', but we cannot afford to do that until other provision is made for the 8,000 single homeless people who go through the centre in a year." The ministerial response accepted his analysis, stating: "Of some 8,000 passing through the centre in 1970, 1,400 suffer from mental illness, 1,500 from personality disorder, and 2,000 from alcoholism. We all recognise that the Camberwell centre is out of date and that it should be replaced."

The history of the Gordon Road institution is a sorry chapter of Peckham's history. Through all the changes of name and administration the challenges faced through the years remained much the same. An internet search of each of its identities yields a tsunami of data across its 106-year history: case studies, sociological dissertations, parliamentary questions and media comment all speak of perennial problems: poverty, alcoholism, homelessness, mental illness and the failings of social care provision.

On 20 November 1981, following an internal review, a programme for the closure and replacement of the Camberwell centre was announced. Aside from its many deficiencies it was a considerable financial burden. The outlay for the financial year 1981/2, excluding building maintenance and repairs, was £2,065,286, a staggering sum far higher than the spend on any of the other resettlement centres. It finally closed in 1985, and after being squatted for several years it was redeveloped for housing in 1991.

Nearby Nazareth House had a separate history, ending in its total demise. Acquired by the Greater London Council in 1965, it was taken over by Lewisham Council in 1972, and used as a hostel for homeless families until 1979. Although eventually sold for development in 1987, the house remained empty for the next four years, left to be vandalised, until in 1991 it was severely damaged by a spectacular fire. There were vague hopes that the building could be restored, and it took some time to get round to its demolition. But in 1995, today's Cross Close (a reference back to the cross which surmounted the original convent) was developed on the site by Hyde Housing.

PECKHAM RYE STATION

1865

Here on Rye Lane is a majestic edifice, an architectural treasure, which is now undergoing a glorious revival, having been hemmed in and hidden by other buildings and neglected over the years.

As this book goes to publication, in 2023, work is underway on Southwark Council's project to create a new public square in front of Peckham Rye Station, with the demolition of the 1930s arcade revealing the Grade II station building in all its original splendour.

At the same time, in sensitive conservation works carried out by local architect Benedict O'Looney, a much-needed £3m project has been funded by Network Rail to restore the exterior of the station building. The Victorian cast iron cresting has been carefully fabricated and restored to the main roof and 1860s patent clay tiles have been re-made for the four lower wing roofs. Window and door joinery has been restored, the brick and stonework has been cleaned, and architectural lighting has been applied to the front of the station. The elevations have been returned back to the station's original Victorian design, so well documented in the 19th century contract drawings and period photographs.

Network Rail has obtained planning permission and listed building consent for alterations to Peckham Rye Station, including improved access, better connections to the surrounding public realm, new lifts to all platforms, accessible toilets, wider platforms and entrances. A funding request for these works will be made to government.

Peckham Rye Station opened on 1 December 1865 to serve passengers using the London, Chatham & Dover Railway. A few years later, they were joined by travellers on the new suburban line created by the London, Brighton and South Coast Railway, both lines scything through the back gardens of South Grove (now Holly Grove) and Blenheim Grove. Peckham Rye thus became a key south London interchange, not least for Crystal Palace with its Great Exhibition.

The station building, a favourite of John Betjeman, was listed Grade II in January

The Old Waiting Room, 2019

ABOVE
An early view
of Peckham Rye
Station shortly
after the building's
completion, circa
1866

OVERLEAF
South section
through Peckham
Rye Station,
Contract Drawing
number 6. This
drawing cuts
through the Old
Waiting Room and
shows the now lost
plaster ceiling in
that tall space, 1865

2008. The English Heritage citation identifies three areas of special interest: a vast, double-height booking office; a "dramatic" stone staircase of considerable artistic quality; and the large former first class waiting room. English Heritage saw Peckham Rye Station as "impressive" in a continental renaissance style. It is one of only four suburban stations of the London, Brighton and South Coast Railway in London that survive in the house style of the 1860s: an age of expansion in which railway companies typically sought to mark their identity architecturally.

The same report describes the group of shops built in the vicinity of the station frontage as: "hemming in the station and diminishing the impact of its architecture on the streetscape". A modest row of small shops had appeared in the station forecourt by 1914, with an access

space on each side. These were replaced in about 1936 by an arcade designed by the practice of famous architect JJ Joass. Though initially attractive it had, over the years, been much adapted and degraded. None of the original shopfronts survived, and what was left was a run-down, poorly lit walkway between the station and the arcade, through arches supporting twin tracks. As one of primary gateways into Peckham, the first impression of the town centre presented an underwhelming vista, with the entire facade of the station obscured and compromised.

It was back in the winter of 1997 that the Peckham Society News first reported a suggestion that the arcade in front of the station be demolished and replaced by a grand piazza. The idea gained widespread support and, in the autumn of 1998 secured

PECKHAM

RYE LANE №6

Rail

CROSS SECT[ION]

SCALE 4 FEET

OUTH COAST RAILWAY

ON LINE

Floor

Floor

Floor

Floor

Level

A

CHIEF CIVIL ENGINEER'S OFFICE
PLAN Nº 12 2613 E / 08.
WATER STATION

229232

View from Rye Lane with station visible in background, 1927

an encouraging response from Railtrack, the predecessors of Network Rail.

Gradually the proposal took shape. In spring 2009, it was reported that Southwark Council had agreed that, "over time, the buildings around the station will be removed and an open courtyard will be created". And in 2016, after a lengthy period of planning and consultation, planning permission for the demolition of the arcade and the creation of a piazza was granted.

The creation of the new public square has been carried out in phases, beginning with the refurbishment of the Art Deco building on the corner of Rye Lane and Blenheim Grove, designed by Landolt + Brown to create new community facilities, and spaces for business and tenants formerly in the arcade.

Over many years, the listed station building has been carefully restored. Since 2005, various collaborations between architect Benedict O'Looney and the Peckham Society, Peckham Vision and the Rye Lane & Station Action Group, Southwark Council, the Railway Heritage Trust, Southern Rail

and Network Rail, have led to projects to renovate areas of the building that were bricked up and abandoned in 1962. Benedict O'Looney Architects has led, and helped raise the funds for, six projects at Peckham Rye Station. These include unbricking and re-fenestrating the Old Waiting Room, restoring and re-making the windows to the forecourt, restoring the north wing with its lost 1930s 'Sanitary Courts' (the boarded up former station loos). The north wing of the station is now a popular restaurant.

In 2016 a new stair was built above the Victorian south stair to give independent public access to the Old Waiting Room at Platform Level. 20 new windows and doors have been re-made, 45 original windows have been restored, The spectacular restoration of the Old Waiting Room has revealed its barrel vaulted roof structure.

There is common consent that Peckham Rye Station is a building of great merit, a splendid Victorian junction station, It is also the focus of a remarkable regeneration as hordes of people continue to flood through its Victorian portals.

Peckham's Heritage – Past, Present & Future

ABOVE
Peckham Rye
Station forecourt,
1969

RIGHT
Bomb damage
to railway tracks
during World War
II, 1944

PECKHAM RYE STATION:
A STORY OF COMMUNITY ACTION

Peckham Rye Station has been the focus of community campaigns since 2004. These have shaped and informed the dramatic changes now emerging in the spaces around the station. This summary outlines the community action, giving a sense of the debates, discussions, campaigns, and partnership working over the years.

RAISING AWARENESS

In 2004, local resident Eileen Conn, in discussion with the head of Southwark Council's Peckham Programme, Russell Profitt, set up the Rye Lane & Station Action Group (RLSAG), with the aim to clean up the public spaces around Peckham Rye Station. The discovery of a digital version of an early photograph of the station helped raise awareness of the group, bringing wider attention to the significance of the building, which lay hidden behind the shopping arcade. The idea of listing the building, first proposed by the Peckham Society in the late 1990s, was publicised by the RLSAG and was eventually achieved in 2008.

Peckham Vision community meeting on 2nd August 2012, the first evening of the 3 day town centre exhibition in the Old Waiting Room

RESCUING THE OLD WAITING ROOM

From 2006 the RLSAG devised an action plan, supported by Peckham Vision, the Peckham Society and Network Rail, to restore in small stages the derelict space above the station's ticket hall. Led by architect Benedict O'Looney, the Old Waiting Room as it became known, was restored for meanwhile use by 2010. In 2012, Peckham Vision organised a three day exhibition about the town centre in the Old Waiting Room, attracting over 700 visitors.

After the extension of the staircase to the room in 2016 enabled public access, the Friends of the Old Waiting Room (FOWR), which emerged from the long effort to restore the room for community use, arranged some further events. Clarity over the long term future of the space was affected by Network Rail's sale in 2017 of the long lease to The Arch Company. The FOWR continue to seek a community managed lease for the space amidst further delays caused by the planned station works.

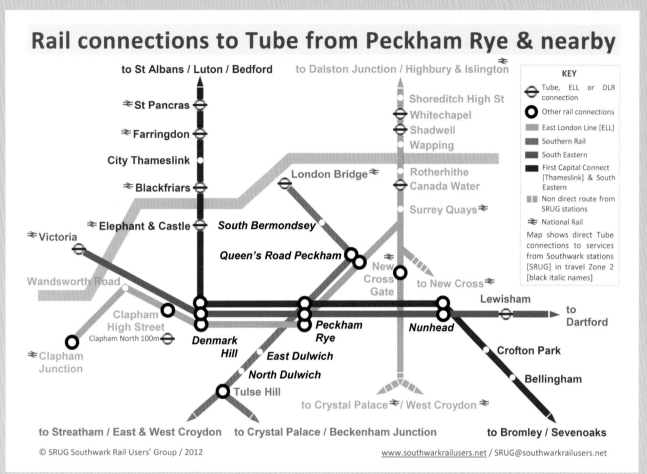

Rail connections to Tube from Peckham Rye & nearby

to St Albans / Luton / Bedford
to Dalston Junction / Highbury & Islington

St Pancras
Farringdon
City Thameslink
Blackfriars
Elephant & Castle
Victoria
Wandsworth Road
Clapham High Street
Clapham North 100m
Clapham Junction

Shoreditch High St
Whitechapel
Shadwell
Wapping
Rotherhithe
Canada Water
Surrey Quays

London Bridge

South Bermondsey
Queen's Road Peckham

New Cross Gate
to New Cross
Lewisham
to Dartford

Denmark Hill
Peckham Rye
East Dulwich
North Dulwich
Tulse Hill

Nunhead
Crofton Park
Bellingham

to Streatham / East & West Croydon
to Crystal Palace / Beckenham Junction
to Crystal Palace / West Croydon
to Bromley / Sevenoaks

KEY
Tube, ELL or DLR connection
Other rail connections
East London Line [ELL]
Southern Rail
South Eastern
First Capital Connect [Thameslink] & South Eastern
Non direct route from SRUG stations
National Rail
Map shows direct Tube connections to services from Southwark stations [SRUG] in travel Zone 2 [black italic names]

© SRUG Southwark Rail Users' Group / 2012

www.southwarkrailusers.net / SRUG@southwarkrailusers.net

Pocket-size map developed by Peckham Vision from 2011 in association with Southwark Rail Users Group (SRUG). This version was created and distributed from 2013, with the following explanatory note on the reverse. Concept and design by Eileen Conn and Corinne Turner.

Peckham Rye station – rail connections to the tube
Peckham Rye station is almost like a tube station - 9 to 15 minutes from six different Tube lines - Victoria, District, Circle, Bakerloo, Jubilee, Northern. Publicise this to your friends and visitors; support the campaign to improve the frequency; tell us your views on this map.

IMPROVING RAIL SERVICES

In 2007, Peckham Vision set up the Southwark Rail Users Group (SRUG) to campaign to save the South London Line (SLL) for services between London Bridge and Victoria through Peckham Rye station, and to improve other services from and to central London. As part of this campaign, Peckham Vision created a pocket-size map showing the direct connections from the station to the Tube. The campaign for the SLL was lost in 2012, the year which marked the arrival of the Overground. This new rail service significantly increased passenger numbers. This pressure proved the tipping point, after years of campaigning, to push through plans for the redesign of the station's access while preserving the original Grade II Listed station building. In a project to be delivered by Network Rail, subject to funding, all four platforms will be made step-free, improving access and safety, with completion envisaged by 2028.

SELF-REGENERATING ECONOMY

Peckham Vision's 2006-2009 campaign against the tram depot to be built on land opposite the station on the east of Rye Lane (see Bussey Building, page 102), led to the development of a community alternative plan to reflect the potential of central Rye Lane as a cultural quarter. This work highlighted how small businesses around the station, and in Copeland Park and the Bussey Building, formed part of a self-regenerating local economy.

PLANNING STATION SQUARE

By 2008, community publicity efforts had led to all-party agreement for the Council to remove the buildings in front of the station and develop a new public square. In August 2011, then Mayor of London Boris Johnson offered £5m funding to any projects ready for decision in London boroughs affected by the recent riots. This, plus £5m from Southwark Council, enabled the plan to create a new square.

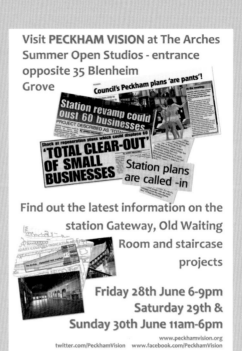

Visit **PECKHAM VISION** at The Arches Summer Open Studios - entrance opposite 35 Blenheim Grove

Find out the latest information on the station Gateway, Old Waiting Room and staircase projects

**Friday 28th June 6-9pm
Saturday 29th &
Sunday 30th June 11am-6pm**

www.peckhamvision.org
twitter.com/PeckhamVision   www.facebook.com/PeckhamVision

Poster for the Peckham Vision stall at the Open Arches weekend 28th to 30th June 2013, to publicise the issues arising from the Peckham Rye station redevelopment plans

Network Rail and Southwark Council consultation in January 2014, where the community rejected plans to demolish all commercial buildings on the station site and clear out all businesses

At this point Network Rail presented Southwark Council with a plan to clear the whole site, replacing all commercial buildings around the station with new blocks up to seven storeys high. This proposal was met by strong local opposition: while the creation of a Station Square was widely supported, the scale of the site clearance and proposals were not. This opposition led Network Rail and the Council to rethink. In 2015, a new proposal was accepted. Slated for completion in 2024, this confines the plan to the new square and a two-floor addition to the Art Deco building on the corner of Blenheim Grove and Rye Lane.

During the campaign, particular attention was drawn to the plight of the businesses in the buildings earmarked for demolition in front of the station. As a result some were to be relocated to the new premises and some to Peckham Palms in Atwell Road off Rye Lane - which Southwark Council created as a centre for Black hair, beauty and lifestyle. This provided space for the Black hair stylists moved from Blenheim Grove but did not meet the needs of all. Peckham Palms is run by an independent organisation leasing the premises from the Council. It is now fully let to 100% female black owned businesses.

SAVE PECKHAM'S
ART DECO QUARTER

Peckham Vision's graphic poster to publicise from 2014 the existence of the Art Deco buildings clustered around Peckham Rye station

INTRODUCING THE ART DECO QUARTER

As part of its work to develop alternative plans for central Rye Lane, Peckham Vision coined the phrase 'Art Deco Quarter' to draw attention to the important 1930s Art Deco heritage in the buildings clustered around the Victorian station building. These include the two storey buildings immediately in front and along the side of the station, as well as three large retail buildings: 72-76 Rye Lane, (now McDonald's), 117-125 Rye Lane (see pages 108-109), - the building between the railway lines opposite the station, and the former Holdron's store now occupied by Khan's at 135 Rye Lane (see pages 72-77). This helped to strengthen the case against the scale of the new buildings originally proposed around the station.

CAMPAIGN FOR PUBLIC TOILETS

In 2013, a petition organised by Peckham Vision and the Rye Lane Traders' Association for public toilets in central Rye Lane was presented to the Council with over 4,000 signatures. As a result of these efforts, the planning permission of 2016 for the new public square incorporated public toilets in the arches in the passage leading to Holly Grove.

Collecting signatures on the petition in 2013 for public toilets in central Rye Lane

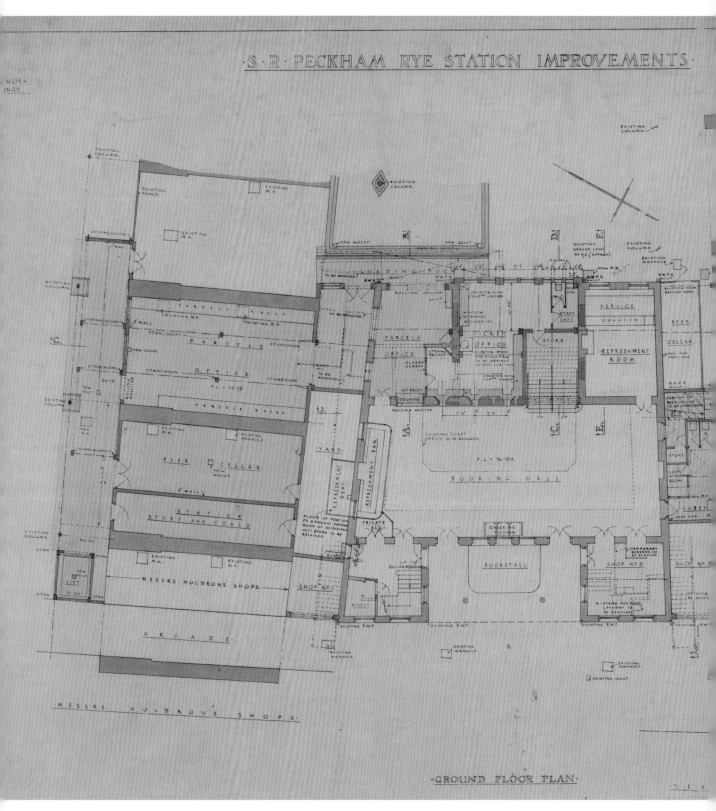

Peckham Rye Station - Contract Drawing number 1, ground level plan, 1935

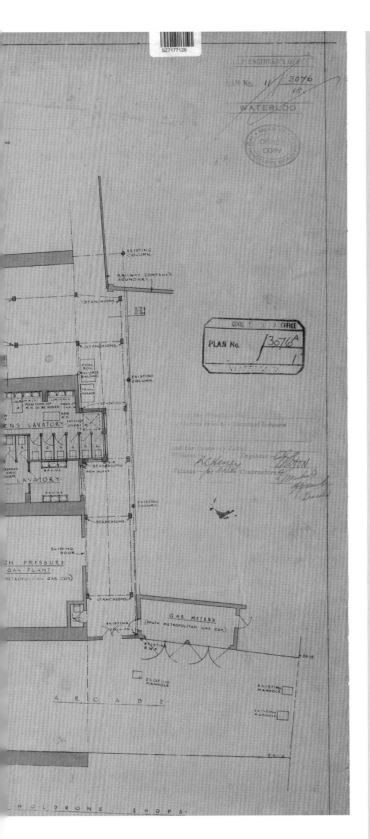

ARCHITECTURAL NOTES

The Grade II listed Peckham Rye Station is the most important Victorian building in Peckham's town centre.

The London, Brighton & South Coast Railway Company (LB&SCR), which built the station, was known for its architecturally exuberant station designs. The architect, Charles Henry Driver FRIBA (1832-1900) was well able to deliver a building with considerable architectural chutzpah. Peckham Rye is one of the grandest of more than a dozen stations Driver built for the railway company.

The Station is a railway junction where once, three platforms for the LB&SCR on the south side, met the two of the London Chatham and Dover Railway on the north. Just to the west of the station the railway passes through Denmark Hill so the lines are at a high level on a tall brick viaduct. Driver's design, with its generously proportioned central façade and two wings, fills the entire space between the railway lines and its tall façade rises to the platform level and beyond, where an immense General Waiting Room formed a spacious upper part to the station.

Like C.H. Driver's other stations, the architecture is a free mix of Renaissance and Gothic detailing favoured by exuberant civic architects in the High Victorian period.

The overall form of the station, with its mansard-style zinc roof, is in the French-inspired 'Second Empire' style. Its architectural antecedent must be the magnificent Grosvenor Hotel at the London Terminus of the LB&SCR in Victoria, designed by the architect James T. Knowles a few years before. Peckham Rye Station borrows the hotel's architectural approach and palate of materials: buff facing brickwork with florid Bath stone decoration.

Typical of Victorian architecture, the front façade of Peckham Rye Station is showy and decorative, and the rear and side facades are plainer. The front face is formed in handsome Suffolk 'white' bricks with its fine-grained clay in pink and cream tones. The Victorians loved this material, and you can find it around London, particularly on Peabody housing estates. Its bright hues stood out in the sooty 19th and 20th century city. Now cleaned and re-pointed, the field of these subtle two-tones of bricks to the Peckham station front looks spectacular.

Further architectural detail to the façade is in honey-coloured Bath stone. Deeply cut crocket capitals form string courses to the ground and first floors.

Typical of C H Driver's showy architecture, all of the front façade windows have oversized keystones with incised 'modern gothic' ornament. A Beaux Arts oeil-de-boeuf cartouche forms a centrepiece to the central roof pavilion.

Further enrichment to the station was given by the cast iron structure and decoration. In addition to his work as an architect, Charles Henry Driver was a prolific cast iron designer for one of the premier cast iron manufacturers in Britain – Walter McFarlane's Saracen Iron Works in Possilpark, Glasgow. His brilliance lay in making complex, beautiful plant forms cast in iron for prominent architectural elements like columns, balustrades, beams, fascia & cresting. In using modern iron foundries Driver's design brought advanced artistic ideas into the everyday lives of Peckham's station users. Alongside other progressive designers like Christopher Dresser and Thomas Jeckyll, Driver helped develop a new decorative language for this new Victorian building type 'the railway station'. The twisting foliate forms of the balustrades and canopy structures anticipate the Art Nouveau of the late 19th century, but are also splendidly functional. Behind these striking decorative forms Driver used modular dimensions allowing the cast iron and terracotta components to be used in diverse architectural settings across the LB&SCR network.

Sadly, much of the cast iron work at Peckham Rye Station was lost in the two re-orderings of the station, first in the 1930s and then with the total rebuild of Peckham Rye Station's platforms circa 1962. Victorian photographs show an elaborate iron and glass entrance canopy that met the station's former courtyard. Also lost are the tall cast iron columns supporting the platforms on either side of the brick railway viaducts. Decorative cast-iron cresting was set on the roof's ridges. On the platforms, canopies, handrails and columns had florid cast iron detailing. Internally the tall, ground-level Booking Hall had a mezzanine gallery that allowed passengers to interchange between the northern platforms and the southern platforms without descending to the ground level. Surviving original drawings show a cantilevered circulation gallery supported by large cast iron brackets.

One can get a strong sense of what was lost by visiting Denmark Hill Station where the roof cresting, iron work and handsome iron platform columns are wonderfully preserved. Platform 1 at Battersea Park Station survives with all its details intact including its timber boarded floor and platform columns.

The 'rediscovery' in 2005 of the lost cast-iron and stone stairs in the bricked up south wing of the Peckham Rye Station was welcomed as a significant remnant of Victorian cast-iron surviving these reorderings: a powerful testament to C. H. Driver's brilliance as a designer.

The 1960s was the nadir of appreciation of Victorian architecture. All across Britain 19th century railway stations, commercial buildings and houses were being denuded of their decorative detail or being demolished. At Peckham Rye Station the cavernous General Waiting Room and south stair wing were bricked up and eight out of ten of the station's chimney stacks were removed.

The most spectacular space at Peckham Rye Station is the former General Waiting Room at the top of the building. One suggestion for the impressive scale – 70 feet long, by 31 feet wide, by 25 feet tall – was that Peckham Rye was an important interchange for travellers to the Crystal Palace, re-erected on Sydenham Hill in the mid-1850s.

In the seventy years since the arrival of the railway and partly because of it, Rye Lane had grown into one of the most popular shopping destinations in South London. Department stores on the Lane such as Holdron's and Mark & Spencer's were rebuilding their premises in the fashionable Art Deco style. Following suit, the Southern Railway commissioned one of London's leading commercial architects John James Joass (1868-1952) to develop their sites on both sides of Rye Lane.

On the west side of the 'Lane' the present shopping arcade was built, and two storey commercial buildings were constructed along Holly Grove to the north and Blenheim Grove to the South. On the east side Joass' Art Deco 117-125 Rye Lane department store was built.

From the bricking up of the station in the sixties to the early 2000s Peckham Rye Station was at a low ebb architecturally. The 1962 reordering saw the northern third of the booking hall lopped off by a tall new wall, with a betting office established on the other side, from the front to the back of the station. A period photograph shows a wholly remodelled ground level façade in modernist green tiles and a glass block window. The Victorian glass and iron front canopy was removed around this time, and the station forecourt was dominated by a central news kiosk. Above these depredations to the building, the southern platforms were reordered, with the removal of the timber platforms and cast iron and timber canopies and the creation of the 'current island' platforms 1 & 2 on the south side. The former General Waiting Room, by then a billiard hall, was bricked up and abandoned.

By the mid-1980s Peckham Rye Station was keenly in need of a thorough maintenance programme.

A plaque in the booking hall records a general restoration of the station by British Rail. The modernist betting office elevation to the north wing was restored to the Victorian design and the Booking Hall was restored. The zinc roof with its fish-scaled central pavilion was renewed in the late 1990s.

With the arrival of the London Overground service in Peckham in 2012, four railway lines now serve Peckham Rye Station. The 1930s period circulation routes are overcrowded at peak times and the platforms have become unsafe. Network Rail has obtained planning and listed building

consent for a bold scheme to create a new western atrium to the station with wider stairs and lifts to all platforms. The existing west elevation will become an internal facade to a tall, partly glazed public space. The 1930s booking office will be removed to create a wide opening at ground level facing west. The restored Victorian booking hall will then connect with this new atrium with a gate line in this location. For the first time in Peckham Rye Station's history the station will be accessible from both Rye Lane and a new western entrance accessed from Blenheim Grove and Dovedale Court.

The arrival of the railway and Peckham Rye Station transformed Peckham from a genteel early Victorian suburb to a part of the urbanised capital within a generation. With the planned new extension the long and complex building history of this doughty Victorian railway gem continues!

Staircase at Peckham Rye Station, 2019

OUR LADY OF SORROWS

1866

This impressive, neo-gothic Roman Catholic church lies at the junction of Friary Road and Bird in Bush Road. Designed by Edward Welby Pugin (1834-1875), son of the more famous Augustus Pugin, it remains substantially unchanged.

As Blanch pointed out in his 1875 history, Capuchin Franciscans were principally poor and struggling people, therefore ill equipped to raise the funds needed to build the first Catholic place of worship in Peckham. Moreover, despite the Emancipation Act of 1829, Catholicism was not popular in England. A Papal Bull of 29 September 1850 to re-establish a Catholic diocesan hierarchy was widely seen as an aggressive intent to return Britain to Roman Catholicism. It is therefore not surprising that it took seven years to bring the Friary Church in Peckham to fruition. That so beautiful an edifice was eventually created is mysterious. Blanch has it that one of the earliest contributors was the King of Naples, but the fact that all difficulties were eventually overcome suggests a zeal and fervour inspired by

Peckham's Heritage – Past, Present & Future

Exterior view of Our Lady of Sorrows, adjacent to Friary Hall, 1972

the Reverend Father Emidius, Superior of the Peckham Order. Italian by birth, he became a naturalised British subject, seen by Blanch as "much beloved not only by members of his flock, but by Protestants of every denomination".

In 1854, while in Rome, Emidius chanced to meet the Rt. Reverend Dr Thomas Grant (1816-1876), the first Catholic Archbishop of Southwark. Emidius took the opportunity to seek Grant's consent to create a new Capuchin Order in London, to which Grant is said to have readily agreed.

Work began in 1857. First "a small and poor but decent chapel and a school were erected in the Park Road, Peckham." Several prelates preached there, including Cardinal Wiseman, who "pleaded the cause of the poor Catholics of Peckham", many of whom had arrived following the great famine in Ireland. After a few years, this provision proved insufficient for a greatly increased congregation, and it became imperative to erect a much larger building. The foundation stone of the present

church was laid by the Rt. Reverend Dr Grant on 7 July 1859; he opened the resultant church on 4 October 1866 in the presence of the Superiors of the Religious Orders in England and Ireland and most of the Catholic clergy of London. Wiseman preached in the morning, and Amhurst, Bishop of Northampton, in the evening.

The building's designer, E.W. Pugin, was baptised an Anglican, but brought up as a Catholic following his father's conversion in 1834. St. George's Church (now Cathedral) was designed by Augustus Pugin, and opened by Wiseman on 4 July 1848. E. W. Pugin was invested a Knight of the Order of St. Sylvester by Wiseman on the gift of Pope Pius IX in 1858.

Known as the 'Capuchin Franciscan Church of Our Lady of Seven Dolours' the church flourished. Yet, while there remain around 11,000 Capuchin friars practicing around the world, and four friaries in the UK, Peckham is no longer one of them, having passed to the Catholic Archdiocese in 2000.

ARCHITECTURAL NOTES

The Church and Friary of Our Lady of Sorrows on Friary Road was designed by the intriguing Victorian architect Edward Welby Pugin (1834-1875). E.W. Pugin is overshadowed by his famous father Augustus Welby Pugin, the co-designer, with Sir Charles Barry, of the Palace of Westminster, perhaps the most important early Gothic revival building in Europe.

Happily in Peckham we find that the younger E.W. Pugin was a talented architect in his own right and the Church and Friary show this to great effect.

North Peckham was developed in a later period than Peckham's town-centre nucleus and its character was more industrial with the Surrey Canal serving a range of factories and timber yards including the large South Metropolitan Gas Works. Its rapid development in the second half of the nineteenth century soon delivered a substantial population housed in terraces of modest character filling the spaces between the factories. Churches were built to enlighten and morally improve new generations of Peckham residents, many of whom were immigrants to Britain arriving from Catholic nations such as Ireland and Italy.

Our Lady of Sorrows is one of four remarkable 19th Century Gothic churches in this area. The other three are: St. Andrew's Glengall Road, built 1864, and 1868's Christ Church Old Kent Road – both designed by the architect Enoch Bassett Keeling (1837-1886), and St Mark's on Coburg Road, designed by Richard Norman Shaw RA (1832-1912), built in 1879, and now a mosque.

E.W. Pugin and E.B. Keeling were known as 'Rogue Goth' architects, their churches and public buildings used bold structural polychromy. This is when a building's facing materials are chosen both for their performance and robust qualities, and their intrinsic colour able to deliver strong patterns like the stripes of Blue Staffordshire bricks set against a field of buff London bricks, enlivened with the rich tones of gothic Bath Stone detailing, at Our Lady of Sorrows.

One of the innovations of these talented Gothic revival architects is their ability to handle diverse programmes on a single urban site. At Our Lady of Sorrows in Peckham, a substantial church is combined with a friary and a school, all interlocking on a corner site. The original impression was even more powerful before wartime bombing destroyed a Gothic revival range further north on Friary Road where the present post-war school now stands.

Our Lady of Sorrows is designed in the High Victorian Gothic Style. E.W. Pugin's church was opened first in 1866 with the Capuchin friary, designed by the skilful Liverpool architect James O'Byrne, following in the 1880s.

Both the Bird in Bush Road and the Friary Road elevations are very fine. The latter deftly combines symmetry and asymmetry with a series of gables meeting the road in slightly different ways. The street corner is particularly impactful with the tall east end of the church, magnificent central rose window, battened buttresses and aisles coming to an abrupt, stripy crescendo at the pavement edge.

The interior is equally impressive and consists of a broad nave with a tall sanctuary and a cheerfully painted arch braced and panelled timber roof.

THE OLD FIRE STATION

1867

This is an outstanding example of a superb restoration of one of Peckham's historic buildings. Historic in that Peckham's old fire station at 82 Peckham Road was the first purpose-built fire station in London, probably one of the earliest in the country, constructed shortly after the formation of the London Metropolitan Fire Brigade and opened in 1867.

Originally called Camberwell Fire Station, it boasted not only two appliances but was also home to the firemen and their families.

It served the people of Peckham until 1925, when it was replaced by a new station better equipped to meet the needs of the day, manned by crews working to a new

Streetscape showing the Old Fire Station to left of billboards, 1979

The Old Fire Station, converted and restored for South London Gallery by 6a architects, 2018

shift pattern. The redundant fire station was acquired by Kennedy's sausage company, and became its headquarters from 1934 to 2007. The building was then sold by auction in 2008 and listed Grade II in the same year. The Historic England citation indicates that this was on account of its: "special architectural and historic interest as the earliest surviving purpose-built fire station in London, if not nationally, designed in the Gothic style with a degree of civic character which distinguishes it from contemporary stations that were adapted older buildings." But it was in poor condition and remained unoccupied, deteriorating with water ingress and dry rot.

Rescue came in 2014, when the dilapidated building was anonymously donated to the South London Gallery. With the benefit of wide ranging consultation and research a restoration project was put in place. Thanks to financial support from The National Lottery Heritage Fund, the Mayor of London and the Arts Council England the old building has been transformed, giving the SLG almost twice as much space in which to support British and international artists and the local community. Its facilities now include gallery spaces, an archive room and artists' studios. The archive has both the proud history of the SLG and material relating to social and architectural past times.

While much of the original interior fabric of the building has been lost, this remarkable achievement, opened to the public on 22 September 2018, is an object lesson not only of conservation, but also in promoting beneficial use into the future; boosting Peckham's artistic reputation.

Peckham's Heritage – Past, Present & Future

ARCHITECTURAL NOTES

In June 1861, a few miles to the north of Peckham on Tooley Street, there was a spectacular fire, thought to be the worst since the Great Fire of London. It burned for two weeks and the superintendent of the London Fire establishment James Braidwood was killed fighting the fire. The subsequent Parliamentary enquiry initiated the 1865 Metropolitan Fire Brigade Act which led to the creation of this pioneering fire station on the threshold between Peckham and Camberwell.

The urban fire station was one of many new building types, including railway and underground stations, and Board Schools developed in the mid 19th century.

London's earliest fire stations had typically been simple sheds designed to house fire pumps. With the introduction of the Metropolitan Fire Brigade in 1866 new purpose-built fire stations were devised to house horse-drawn pumps, equipment and stabling. The celebrated Peckham horse-drawn bus operator Thomas Tilling, supplied horses to the Fire Brigade from one of his stables, next door, at Pelican House.

The Peckham Fire Station's architect, Edward Cresy Junior (1824-1870), was the son of an architect and civil engineer. Cresy Jr designed a number of early stations for the new fire brigade on behalf of the Metropolitan Board of Works. At Peckham, Cresy designed an imposing building faced in buff brick with red rubber brick detailing. A big street-facing gable and tall chimneys, now lost, evoke the Queen Anne architectural style beginning to be fashionable in the 1860s.

To the ground floor, three substantial timber doors announce the 'appliance bays' where the latest in Victorian mobile pumping equipment was housed ready for the next 'shout'. The upper stories of the building contained residential accommodation for the district's fire officers.

A generation later, a group of talented young architects working for the new London County Council designed fifty fire stations for the rapidly expanding capital, creating a family of modern, truly artistic, fire houses of international significance. Highlights of these include the New Cross Fire Station, down the road in Lewisham, the Euston Fire Station and the Fire Brigade headquarters in Southwark, many of which are much loved neighbourhood landmarks, still in active use by the Fire Brigade today.

With the advent of motorised fire engines in the early 20th century, Cresy's Victorian fire station's days were numbered. In the 1920s R. P. Whellock's handsome Camberwell Library, next door to the west, was demolished and a new fire station was built beside the old. This was in turn demolished in the 1980s to make way for the cheerful post-modernist Peckham Fire Station still in use today.

6a architects' thoughtful restoration of the old Fire Station to create an annexe to the South London Gallery is a joy to experience. New galleries are created in the east appliance bays and in the upper stories. The west appliance bay is opened up vertically into a tall entrance and circulation space featuring a beautifully detailed cast iron stair.

The original stable paving is retained to the floor, and the old fireplace to the lost first floor is left un-decorated high up on a wall, poetically communicating the previous life and uses of this space.

This re-use project won a RIBA national award in 2019. Further excellent work by 6a architects can be seen at the main buildings of the South London Gallery across the street.

Detail of lantern on building facade, 2022

OLD MILL BUILDING

1870s

Situated at 72 Copeland Road, this compact, robust and attractive industrial building dates from the 1870s. Its former owner, William Woodhams, features in the Post Office Directory for 1876 as a vinegar maker, an undertaking that soon extended to the manufacture of "British wine". Woodhams died in 1883, but the business continued to trade in his name until 1950, overlapping at the same address for about the last five years with a company making liquid soap, which operated there until 1960.

Ownership of the Old Mill Building - a moniker the Peckham Society's Christine Camplin explains as probably deriving from the milling of malted barley used in vinegar-making, then passed to the borough council. Over time the building was abandoned and neglected, until eventually in 2007, it was leased to Communities Outreach Ministries, a Pentecostal church.

The interior has since been restored, decorated and brought into use both as a place of worship and a centre for community activities. The Old Mill Building was included in Southwark Council's proposals for Blackpool Road Business Park, a large, mostly industrial site designated for redevelopment in the 2017 preferred option version of the New Southwark Plan.

The proposals indicated demolition of all buildings on the site including the Old

Mill Building, one of Peckham's undoubted heritage assets. Peckham Vision launched a vigorous campaign drawing attention to the presence of the important Victorian industrial building on the site, and conducting a series of open building visits and a survey of local people about the significance of the building.

The auguries were not good for the Old Mill Building but as a result of the campaign the Inspectors agreed the building was of merit and their report on the Examination in Public (EiP) in 2021, noted that the New Southwark Plan should reference the Old Mill Building as an important heritage asset of local interest.

Peckham Vision will continue to campaign to protect the Old Mill Building by encouraging local people to nominate it for inclusion on the Heritage Local List, which will afford it some protection in any redevelopment plans.

ABOVE
Present day view of the Old Mill Building, 2022

BELOW
Blackpool Road with Old Mill Building in distance, 1982

Peckham's Heritage – Past, Present & Future

Choumert Square,
1982

CHOUMERT SQUARE
1876

This is one of the gems of Peckham. It is not a square, simply two facing terraced rows of small cottages with tiny front gardens separated by a pathway leading to a communal garden delineated from the gardens of the Rye Lane shops by a brick wall, dating from the development of the Square. It is a gated community, but the gate never seems to be locked.

The development began around 1876 as a single row of cottages (1-24, 45 and 46), infilled on land behind a large double house (now 134-138) on Rye Lane. Subsequently a second row (25-44) was added a year or two later, on the garden of the next Rye Lane house to the south (now 140-144).

Little is known of George Choumert (1746-1831), the French entrepreneur for whom the square, and several Peckham roads are named. We know that he came from Lorraine, moving to England when he married into

the wealthy Fendall family of Bermondsey, becoming a British citizen in 1796. A Patent Office record of 7 August 1783 shows the grant of a patent to "George Choumert of Five-foot Lane, Bermondsey Street, a tanner" for his invention of a machine for cutting, splitting and dividing hides and skins. Rate books have him in South Street (later Rye Lane) in 1818 and 1831. He went on to finance the development of several local areas. His wife, Lydia, died aged 82 on 10 February 1825, whereupon George inherited her estates in Bermondsey, which by his death in 1831 were producing an estimated annual rental of £6,000.

Choumert died around 45 years before the construction of Choumert Square. Deeds and indentures held by Southwark's Local History Library indicate the principal players in the building of the Square were Parker Todd and William Nunn, a surveyor and architect, resident in Peckham Lodge. Locals are said to have called the alley 'Cut Throat Lane', and census records indicate only a gradual population of the cottages. By 1891, the Square had attracted 106 residents, engaged in a wide variety of occupations, including a Commissioner of City Police.

When Charles Booth visited the area in October 1899, compiling his famous 'poverty' map of London, he deemed Choumert Square as 'fairly comfortable; good ordinary earnings', representing this for his map by the colour pink, hatched to indicate this assessment was variable. He commented, "north side: 4 room cottages; rents 6/- and 6/6; going up for newcomers; queer entrances behind out of a covered passage way; little garden fronts on each side, and 'all fronts' as an occupant said, proud, however, of her square. The south side very much the same, save that the entrances are in the front, 'more after the way of the world' ". Evidence of these disused doors remains. Booth further noted "No tenants are taken with children, and the whole place appears to be very quiet, select, old-fashioned, and quaint".

The so-called gardens were scarcely that - more just front yards until the early 80s, when they came into their own, tended with care by their owners, thriving on the rich soil that had once been part of Peckham's market gardens. The cottages survived the ravages of the Second World War unscathed; perhaps the earliest extant record of the Square community coming together to mark an historic occasion of national importance is a photograph of the 1946 VE Day celebrations taken in the communal garden.

Following the closure of the adjacent Quantock Family Laundry in 1984, two residents, Robin (a civil engineer and part

Choumert Square, early June 2010

of the team that masterminded the demolition of the old London Bridge that went to the USA), and his wife Ann Anderson, galvanised the community to pay for the paving of the central pathway. Ann, a keen horticulturalist, also redesigned the communal garden plot, which subsequently featured on BBC's 'Gardeners' World' three times; on Channel 4; in books and in many national and international magazines and newspapers. It has won three prestigious awards: Blooming Fantastic (Conservation Foundation, 2007), which cited Choumert Square as one of the inner city's 25 greenest corners; Southwark in Bloom' (Southwark Council, 2009); and London Squares (London Garden Society, 2017) when Choumert Square was awarded third place alongside St James's Square, Piccadilly and Arlington Square, Islington.

The Square is renowned not only for its 'secret garden' reputation. It is also remarkable for ingeniously making the most of its tiny two-storey houses. In 1999, the communal garden was paved with York Stone by four male residents and a Jack Russell terrier, closing the venture with a final feast. An official opening ceremony acknowledged the approaching millennium, as residents purchased their own beacon and joined together to set it alight at midnight on 31 December, to end the 20th century. Since 1983 residents and friends have come together at Christmas time to sing carols by lamplight, stimulated by goodly drafts of mulled wine.

THE RED BULL
1882

The Red Bull, 1995

There was a Red Bull public house on Peckham High Street more than 400 years ago. The first written evidence appears to be an entry in the diary of Edward Alleyn, founder of Dulwich College: "October 1, 1617- I came to London in the coach and went to the Red Bull". Two days later he records: "Went to the Red Bull and received for the 'Younger Brother' [a play] but £3.6s.4p".

The Peckham Red Bull was the meeting place of the Peckham Lighting Trust, set up under two Acts of Parliament in 1776 and 1787 for 'lighting and watching the villages of Camberwell and Peckham, and certain roads thereto: and for establishing a foot patrol between Peckham and Blackman Street in the borough of Southwark'. Those responsible for arranging these things "met at the Red Ball [sic], High Street Peckham". Patrols would leave and return every 30 minutes from the Bull to the Green Man turnpike in the Kent Road. The rateable value of the Red Bull about this time was £18, compared to the £80 set for Marlborough House.

The present building dates from the 1880s and was likely a rebuild as a consequence of the road widening of 1880-82. As is generally true of public houses, very little of its history has been recorded; yet it is at the heart of historic Peckham. Close by in Bull Yard was Thomas Tilling's Peckham workshops; his fleet of 150 horse buses were built there, and many of them worked the route between Peckham and Oxford Street.

In the early-2000s, The Red Bull was closed down, switched first to retail sales and then became a nail bar. It was repaired and restored in the first phase of the Peckham Townscape Heritage Initiative project between 2017 and 2019 and is resplendent once again. Its large mural by W. B. Simpson and Sons, depicting the trial of Queen Katherine from Shakespeare's 'Henry VIII' has been conserved Through the THI works, a new shopfront was installed with stall risers clad in Balmoral granite to match the existing pilasters. The upper storey brickwork was carefully repaired and repointed with lime mortar. Untidy surface clutter was removed, and sections or items of decoration were restored: for example, a missing section of decorative cast ironwork above the ground floor cornice was replaced, and the deep parapet cornice was repaired. The restoration also unearthed an unexpected delight - a beautiful delicate tiled frieze below the shop fascia, possibly from the workshop of William De Morgan. A missing tile section from the side return elevation was remade by hand and replaced.

THE GREYHOUND
1889

109 Peckham High Street, The Greyhound, stands on a prominent location, at the corner of Peckham High Street and Peckham Hill Street. Happily, it is one property that, without prompting, had been freshened up by its owner, Charrington's, before further repairs were carried out through the Peckham Townscape Heritage Initiative (THI). The present building dates only from the 1880s, and apart from television screens, is a specimen of an authentic Victorian hostelry, with old racing scenes on its walls and sculptures of greyhounds everywhere.

The site of this pub dates back to at least the 17th century and was situated at what was then the very hub of the village. I was already aware of a playbill from 1807 which located Peckham Theatre as "Opposite the Greyhound, Peckham", but was delighted to also find among Bill Marshall's papers at Southwark's Local History Library, a reference to rubbings of Greyhound trade tokens dating from 1660. Further enquiry disclosed a copy of these rubbings, inscribed on the obverse "WILL ERBERYAT THE", with a greyhound running, and on the reverse "GRAYHOUND IN PECKHAM", with the initials W.M.E.

This is interesting in itself, as greyhound racing is said to have originated only in the 19th century. Coursing preceded this, first described by Arrian in c.160AD, and codified in Britain during the reign of Elizabeth I though primarily as an aristocratic activity,

until the first club meeting, at Swaffham, Norfolk, in 1776. Here, perhaps, is something intriguing for canine historians.

Through the THI project, an initial detailed condition survey established the outline principles of the façade repair to this landmark building. Investigation of the existing tile work at lower level revealed fractures in the pilaster face, due to failing patched render attempts over the years. Repair required stripping back the tiles, restructuring the backing and facing with matching tiles. At lower level, all the old paint was removed from the ventilation grilles, the window frames, and the base of the stall risers, exposing the tile work. These areas proved to be in worse condition than anticipated, especially the tiled skirting and pilaster beside to this area being heavily used, missing moulded features were rebuilt in cement and the skirting was redecorated, resulting in the new skirting closely matching but being more robust and easily maintained than the original tile work. Following the success of the stained-glass restoration work at The Old Crown (119 Peckham High Street) the same subcontractor undertook the repair of the striking stained glass fan lights above the ground floor windows.

ABOVE
The Greyhound, 1979

BELOW
Greyhound token from *Trade Tokens Issued in the Seventeenth Century. A new and revised edition of W. Boyne's work,* by G.C. Williamson

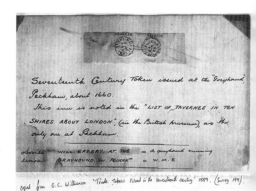

THE CROWN
1891

Located on the north side of Peckham High Street, next to the post office, this imposing building, now the Crown Hotel, was a prominent Peckham Townscape Heritage Initiative (THI) project. 119 Peckham High Street is a converted pub, formerly known as The Old Crown Hotel. There was a pub on the site of the current building by 1830, which was rebuilt in 1891. By the early 21st century the building was converted into two shop units, with flats above, and additions, clutter and disrepair crowded the facades.

Through the THI, the heavily modelled, richly ornamented upper facades were repaired. The upper cornice and elaborate parapet balustrade, ornamented with urns, was in poor condition. Missing urns and baluster bottles were restored or repaired. The distinctive window surrounds and rusticated quoins on the corners had been damaged, and before the facades were redecorated, all the defective fabric was repaired and made weathertight. New sash and casements windows were installed.

RIGHT
Site photo of restoration work underway at The Crown, 2019

BOTTOM LEFT
The Crown as the Tapas Room, 2022

BOTTOM RIGHT
The Crown on Peckham High Street, 1889

A new timber shop-front and entrance door to the corner was made to suit the original proportions of the existing timber windows to the main and side streets. Once on site, the far end shopfront window was uncovered, and a damaged but surviving stained glass detail was found, which was used to prepare a replica design and wording for new stained-glass panels along the Mission Place side of the building.

ARCHITECTURAL NOTES FOR
THE RED BULL, THE GREYHOUND AND THE CROWN PUBLIC HOUSES

The Victorian corner pub is one of the great building types in London's townscape and central Peckham has three splendid examples of them: The Red Bull, The Greyhound, and The Crown.

In the late 19th century, all across the capital, the former ale houses and taverns from the Georgian and the early Victorian period were pulled down to make way for the impressive new 'Public House' building type. These buildings made splendid use of corner sites with embellished corners and generous decoration, designed to catch people's eye from distance and lure them inside. The interiors did not disappoint either.

The Crown at 119 Peckham High Street, and The Red Bull at 116 Peckham High Street, are fine examples of the Victorian Italianate Style with their generous modillioned cornices and pedimented windows. The Crown was designed by the well-known pub architects Messrs Wilson, Son and Aldwinckle and opened in 1891. Thomas Aldwinckle (1845-1920) was a great innovator in Victorian architecture building important early public baths pools in Ladywell (1884), and Kentish Town (1900); the Brooks Hospital on Shooter's Hill in 1896 and a series of workhouses. These are ambitious well-engineered 'modern' buildings designed with considerable gusto in historically inspired architectural styles.

The Greyhound at 109 Peckham High Street is formed from Suffolk White bricks with lively terracotta decoration, the building is in the advanced Queen Anne or Aesthetic movement style still fashionable in 1889 when the present Greyhound was built.

Favourite Aesthetic movement floral motifs like the terracotta sunflower reliefs are combined with pretty wrought iron work, all topped with an alert-looking greyhound above the corner sign.

To the ground level the lovely later-Edwardian glazed tilework has recently been restored. Here you will find burgundy and cream tiles with a frieze in elegant Roman lettering announcing Charrington's ales and stout.

The interiors of these pubs are of considerable interest too. The current Red Bull was built in 1882 as a result of the widening of this part of the Peckham High Street. The treasure inside the Bull is a wonderful hand-painted tile mural showing the trial of Queen Katherine from Shakespeare's 'Henry VIII'. This is by the important tile studio W.B. Simpsons & Son's, St Martin's Lane, one of London's foremost tile decorators and contractors. As principal tiling contractors for the development of the London Underground from the 1890s onwards, most Londoners will have seen their work. There is a good chance that the ground level tilework at the Greyhound pub, across the street, is also by W. B. Simpsons.

In recent decades each of these three pubs have had their rear yards built over with modern flats. This has been done to a high architectural standard by the Dalston-based architects Kennedy Twaddle. Their carefully-detailed brickwork and zinc clad mansards show how modern extensions can respectfully co-exist with these characterful Victorian Buildings. While the upper floors are now flats, the recently re-opened ground level bars are doing a brisk trade.

What's next - perhaps the, now empty, tall corner signs can be re-created? Tom Phillips RA's beautiful corner mosaics nearby on Bellenden Road are an exciting precedent for this.

Glazed wall tiles uncovered during restoration of The Red Bull, 2018

THE TRIAL OF QUEEN KATHARINE. Henry VIII. Act II. Sc. IV.

Ceramic mural showing The Trial of Queen Katharine in The Red Bull, 2018

88 PECKHAM HIGH STREET
EARLY 19TH CENTURY
WITH LATER ALTERATIONS

88 Peckham High Street, like its neighbouring building, 86, was repaired and restored through the Peckham Townscape Heritage Initiative project (THI). Together, the two buildings create a vivid juxtaposition of Georgian and Victorian scale and styles. 88 originates in the late Georgian/Regency period, and its modest scale contrasts with its grander late Victorian neighbour.

The front elevation at 88 was rebuilt in the Edwardian period, with red brick bands and gauged arches, and a rear meeting hall was built at the same time. The Edwardian iron shop sign bracket survives on the front of the building, while the original brickwork can be found on the rear elevation.

By 2018, many of the original features, and the timber windows, were in a poor condition. Previous movement of the front wall had been repaired, by stitching the brickwork, and the insertion of a circular pattress plate at first floor level. Later structural repairs had disfigured the main elevation, and cement mortar, (which prevents the release of water-vapour and damages brickwork), had been used.

The THI works greatly improved the condition and appearance of the building. The brickwork was repaired, with cement mortar cut out and replaced with 'breathable' mortar made with a lime binder. A new shopfront was installed, with structural works required to create an upstand footing and create bracing at the top. The existing pilaster heads were conserved, and a timber fascia and cornice were reinstated with an electronically operating awning to suit. An internal grilled shutter was installed to maintain a lively street presence.

ABOVE LEFT & RIGHT
88 Peckham High Street, before and after refurbishment, 2021

86 PECKHAM HIGH STREET
1870s

ABOVE LEFT & RIGHT
86 Peckham High Street, before and after refurbishment, 2021

86 Peckham High Street is a handsome late Victorian red brick building which was repaired and restored through the Peckham Townscape Heritage Initiative (THI). By 2018, various inappropriate additions, clutter and disrepair had crowded the facade of this impressive building, reducing the splendour of many of its historical design features.

At ground level, the original granite pilasters had been damaged, and the Portland stone capitals were fractured. The brickwork was sooted, and the windowsills were unsuitably decorated. The sash windows had been replaced with PVC, and a separate residential access was in poor condition.

Through the THI works, the front elevation brickwork was gently cleaned – the panelled brickwork pilasters on either edge of the building have "cut and-rubbed" moulded borders where dirt and soot had built up. At the same time, the pair of carved Portland stone capital consoles at high level, and the attic storey pediment, were cleaned. At first floor, the plain stone band and the head of the first-floor window keystones were stripped of flaking paint, and delicate repairs to the stonework were carried out.

Structural repairs were also necessary: a weakened basement steel support was replaced, so the new timber shopfront sits on a new structural beam with new concrete pavement light at the threshold. A new residential door and dividing pilaster have been inserted, and new timber sash and casement windows have been installed.

LIVESEY LIBRARY

1890

The provision of privately endowed public libraries can be traced back to at least 1601 but it was not until 1835, that a Select Committee examining "the extent, causes, and consequences of the prevailing vice of intoxication among the labouring classes of the United Kingdom", were lobbied by radical social reformer Francis Place that "the establishment of parish libraries and district reading rooms might draw off a number who now frequent public houses". A bill to that end, presented by James Buckingham, followed but was met with strong opposition and failed.

In 1845, William Ewart contrived to secure the passing of a Museums Act, followed by one extending its provisions to include dedicated free public libraries, which, despite vigorous opposition, became the Public Libraries Act 1850. It excluded London, applied only to districts with a population of at least 10,000, and was made subject to acceptance by a two-thirds majority of local ratepayers in a referendum, and merely permitted English town councils to levy a dedicated half-penny in the pound rate to cover the cost of building, furnishing and employing staff (but not books!).

Five years later, the Public Libraries and News Rooms Act 1855 came into force. It extended the opportunity to provide free public libraries to London, and beyond municipal boroughs to parish vestries. It still required a two-thirds majority in favour but only of those at a public meeting. The population criterion was halved to 5,000, and adjoining vestries could join together to meet that requirement. The levy increased to one penny, and provision was made to acquire newspapers and specimens of art and science.

LEFT
Lending department at the Livesey Building, 1905

RIGHT
Livesey Library, likely to be 1905

Peckham's Heritage – Past, Present & Future

Exterior view of Livesey Museum, 1987

literature among the working classes had been met by James Fleming's 'penny-readings' at Peckham's Sumner Road. Action to adopt Ewart's Act was prompted by George Livesey, Chairman of the South Metropolitan Gas Company. On 27 March 1888 he wrote to the Camberwell Vestry, informing them that he had purchased 678-682 Old Kent Road and offered the site and a building for use as a free public library. A year later, five libraries were proposed: Old Kent Road, Knatchbull Road, Peckham Road, Rye Lane, and Lordship Lane. The first to open, experimentally, was 18 High Street. Peckham (later renumbered 20). It proved popular, its records tell us: "in September the Librarian was reporting daily average issues of 601 with 711 on a Saturday; the stock and staff were severely taxed."

The Livesey Library opened at 682 Old Kent Road on 18 October 1890. The building was badly damaged during World War II but was repaired. It served as a lending library until 1966, when Southwark Council decided to relocate its library services, and closed the building to the public. The library was eventually renovated and opened as a Children's Museum on 30 March 1974. John Betjeman did the honours. It was an apt choice. He was a founding member of the Victorian Society, remained a fervent defender of Victorian architecture, and had been created Poet Laureate two years earlier.

This was not a conventional museum of static historical objects, but one that sought to encourage children's creativity and imagination. By all accounts it was both popular and effective. This iconic building, at the heart of a proposed conservation area, was listed in its own right in 1998. Nevertheless, in February 2008, Southwark Council, hit by the Great Recession, voted

In 1858, a vote in Camberwell to take advantage of the 1855 legislation was soundly rejected. Ewart now brought forward an amendment bill to dispense with the population requirement, to allow it to be funded from the general rate, to need only a simple majority approval, and to extend the opportunity across the whole of the UK. This time it was warmly welcomed.

London authorities were still slow to react, vestries were fearful of the funding implications and middle-class ratepayers antagonistic to an additional burden. In Camberwell, from 1866, the thirst for

Mural at the Livesey
Building, 1980

to close the museum and save £140,000 in running costs. A storm of protest ensued. The Peckham Society deplored the decision, and a charity, the Friends of the Livesey Museum for Children was formed with a view to create a Trust and run it for the community. But it emerged that Livesey had included a protective covenant in making his gift, such that the building was not owned by the Council, and therefore could not be disposed of by it. A plan to use it as rehearsal space for Peckham Theatre failed, and in February 2010 it was occupied by squatters. Only in November 2012 was the charitable status of the building recognised.

It was agreed that the Livesey building should be held in trust for the people of Southwark and leased to Treasure House (London) CIC to run the building as an independent school for 14-19 year-olds unable to cope in mainstream settings.

George Livesey was knighted in 1902, and a statue of him in bronze by F.W. Pomeroy was created (1908-14). The family lived in Canal Grove, SE15 from 1840, before moving to a house in Consort Road. An estimated 7,000 people followed Sir George's coffin to be buried in Nunhead Cemetery in 1908.

ARCHITECTURAL NOTES

One of the Victorian architectural delights of the Peckham stretch of the Old Kent Road is the former Camberwell Public Library and Livesey Museum. It was built in 1896 by the talented architect Robert Phillip Whellock (1835-1905) and paid for by Sir George Livesey (1834-1908).

The Livesey Library is one of the best examples in Peckham of the Victorian Queen Anne style, popularised by the architect Norman Shaw RA, and adopted by advanced architects across the capital - immediately recognisable in Peckham's 'Board Schools'.

It is clad in rich red face brickwork with complex carved brick decoration in the free Renaissance manner. A great, projecting, bay window brings plenty of daylight into the former main reading room. A taller tower element to the north side is a tour-de-force of gauged brickwork detailing giving confident asymmetry to the composition.

Internally there is a magnificent arched timber roof structure over the reading room.

The interior, of this Grade II listed building, was reordered in the post-war period by the South London architects Myles and Deirdre Dove to create the children's museum.

This building can be seen in context of a series of exceptionally fine, philanthropic public educational buildings in the Peckham area, designed by some of the capital's top architects. The most spectacular must be Maurice Adams' Camberwell School of Art and The South London Art Gallery, on the Peckham Road built in 1891. Adams also designed the listed Passmore Edwards Library and Baths now in Burgess Park, constructed in 1903.

The Livesey Library's architect R. P. Whellock was a distinguished designer, based in Camberwell, for some years. He produced a number of noteworthy buildings locally. The showy, Renaissance-revival, Central Hall at 41 Peckham High Street (1894); the striking circular hospital tower on Havil Street; and Camberwell's splendid Central Public Library on the Peckham Road (1890), now demolished.

One of his most interesting surviving buildings is the Dairy Supply Company (1888) on Coptic Street in Bloomsbury. An extremely lively, stripy, red and yellow brick urban dairy with elaborate architectural sculpture, and even Art Nouveau lettering in stone and terracotta. Its generous spirit and big arched windows are similar to the Livesey Library.

Parked in the yard behind the former Library and Museum is an extremely fine bronze statue of Sir George Livesey (1909), on a tall stone base. The Livesey Statue was modelled by the prominent Edwardian sculptor Frederick William Pomeroy (1856-1922). Pomeroy was a leading light in the New Sculpture movement and his other public works in London include the colossal bronze figures on the piers of the upstream side of the Vauxhall Bridge, and the figure of Justice on the dome of the Old Bailey.

Statue of Sir George Livesey, 1980

This is probably Peckham's finest work of public sculpture. What a shame that it is hidden away, out of public view.

The bandstand on Peckham Rye, 1905

PECKHAM RYE PARK & COMMON
1894

Peckham Rye Common is known to have been used both as a deer park and for public recreation from at least the 14th century. Historically it was part of a much larger area popularly regarded as common land, but increasingly appropriated to private use and built upon. Local parishioners fiercely opposed building and other incursions on the Rye, not least the arrival in 1864 of 32 vans of Wombell's Wild Beast Show. In 1865 they took their objections to Parliament, where they were examined in committee. It was argued on behalf of Sir William Bowyer Smyth, the Lord of the Manor, that he had absolute ownership of the Rye, and was entitled to its full building value, there being "no copy-holder having rights over it". The contrary was put by the parishioners. The question was finally settled in 1882 when

Rye Common, along with those of Nunhead Green and Goose Green, were sold on to the Metropolitan Board of Works and secured for the public for ever.

The Common became hugely popular. In 1889 it inherited a bandstand from the Royal Horticultural Society's Kensington Garden (destroyed in the Second World War). Performances on the Rye attracted thousands of people. On public holidays as many as 70,000 people crowded the Common's open space. There was so much cricket, football and other games that it was bare of turf for many months of the year.

The idea of an extension on the adjacent Homestall Farm to help meet this demand is attributed to George Morley. In 1888

Peckham's Heritage – Past, Present & Future

Drawing of Peckham Rye Park looking south towards Forest Hill, 1863

his persistence over 20+ years led to the formation of the Peckham Rye Extension Committee. The committee made it known that the owners of Homestall Farm were agreeable to sell their land at £1,000 per acre. The chair of the Vestry, having by this time seen the crowds attracted to a Sunday band performance (established by Morley), threw its weight behind the committee's initiative and set in motion a successful appeal for funding with major contributions from the Vestry, London County Council, and the Charity Commissioner's City Parochial Charities Fund. The terms of sale in 1892 stipulated that 13 acres at the heart of the farm, along with the farmhouse (said to have been at least 200 years old) and a barn, which was home to owls and thought to have once been used by smugglers to store contraband goods, should be retained on lease by the vendors; this portion to be surrendered to the Council upon the death of its lessees, brothers C.W. and A. Stevens.

The acquired land formed an inverted horseshoe around three sides of the reserved land and was no longer seen as an extension to the Common, rather a park in its own right

enclosed by iron railings. On 28 February 1893, the LCC gave the go-ahead to the land's adaptation, and a year later resolved that it should be called Peckham Rye Park.

The opening on 14 May 1894 saw a huge procession march to the new park from Camberwell Vestry Hall (the former Southwark town hall) including traders, temperance organisations and friendly societies with their banners, accompanied by fire engines and bands. It was estimated that 100,000 adults and children assembled on the Rye to hear the opening speech from John Hutton, Chair of the LCC. The new park inspired the removal of old buildings, the fencing of boundaries, the preservation of existing trees and shrubs, and the excavation of an ornamental lake. The latter was fed by a small watercourse running through the grounds, formed by dams into a number of ponds. 24 and a half acres (of a total of 49) were given over to tennis, cricket and playgrounds.

Little changed in the following twelve years, save for the addition of a drinking fountain donated by Edwin Jones (of Jones & Higgins) in 1898. C.W. Stevens died before the end of

the century, but his brother lived on until 30 November 1906. His death finally enabled the LCC to secure the reserved farmland. It possessed great natural beauty, and was well wooded but the old farmhouse, too dilapidated for future adaptation, was demolished. Arthur John Ashmore, who had helped John Sexby, the LCC's Chief Officer of Parks to lay out Dulwich Park, went on to create several new features including: an American Garden, modelled on that at Dulwich Park, an Old English Garden (in 1910 renamed the Sexby Garden in memory of the renowned champion of public parks), and an arboretum to the south of that garden.

In 1910, work was begun on a Japanese Garden designed to mark the Anglo-Japanese Festival of that year, completed in 1914 with the placement of an ornate shelter, donated by the Municipality of Tokyo to celebrate the warmth of Anglo-Japanese relations. A bowling green was added in 1911 and under Ashmore's superintendence Peckham Rye Park took on the basic character that we know

today: a succession of contrasting gardens set among trees, composed as a series of ornamental spaces, joined by pleasant walks, and sheltered among a wide variety of trees. In 1937 the travel writer H.V. Morton wrote: "London does not possess a more beautiful park than Peckham Rye".

There were allotments on the Common during the Second World War, after which the iron boundary railings of the Park, sacrificed for the war effort, were replaced. But there were

Peckham's Heritage – Past, Present & Future

THE SEXBY GARDEN PECKHAM RYE PARK M 1952

no major changes until 1950 when the present main entrance and the nearby oval bed were created, and the properties on the north west corner removed. This was followed in 1953 by the fashioning of a sensory garden between the Sexby Garden and bowling green.

The centenary of the Park in May 1994, was followed in 1995 by the formation of the Friends of Peckham Rye Park (FOPRP), a group of volunteers dedicated to preserving and maintaining the historic beauty of both the Park and the Common. The Friends have since been instrumental in shaping the future of this historic community space and respecting its past.

The FOPRP supported a £2.37 million Heritage Lottery Fund bid which Southwark Council applied for and delivered along with £557,000 Southwark Council match funding. The funding facilitated the draining and refurbishment of the lake, replacement of the associated water system, the return of the Sexby Garden to its former glory, clearance of decades of unwanted vegetation in the overgrown shrubberies, making-good of paths, rockeries and structures, renewal of the Japanese Garden's shelter and bridge, erection of a new pavilion, replacement of the water fountain with a replica, and extensive new planting of shrubs and trees, bringing the park back, if not quite to its former Victorian elegance, at least to a state that earned it a Green Flag Award in 2007.

In 2005, the FOPRP came up with the idea of a Community Wildlife Garden on a site once occupied by 1897 greenhouses that had become derelict. Work began in 2010. This lovingly-created haven opened in April 2012 as a precious addition to the Park's attractions. It remains as a tribute to communal endeavour, funded by the FOPRP, maintained by its members, and encouraged by the local authority. Subsequently the Friends also secured funding from Queen Elizabeth Fields in Trust, Southwark Council and FOPRP to revive another derelict site at the northern edge of the Park which they transformed into a fernery of shade loving plants. And in 2017, a Southwark Council regeneration team embarked on a further major project to design and build a play area, inspired by the Tumbling Bay Playground in the Olympic Park. It opened in July 2018,

close to The Round café, with a children's playroom, new changing rooms at the eastern edge of the Park, and a re-sited car park.

Most recently, another group of volunteers led by Californian researcher Nancy Coleman-Frank has formed a charity, supported by the Friends and expert advisors, to revamp the American Garden to an ambitious new plan. This rejuvenated space was launched in December 2020, when Harriet Harman MP and then US Ambassador, Woody Johnson` helped out with the planting of ten trees. It reopened in July 2022, replete with many varieties of plants and trees in honour of Peter Collinson, the botanist who lived in Peckham from 1696 to 1749.

ABOVE LEFT
Water fountain at the entrance to Peckham Rye Park donated by Edwin Higgins, 1914

ABOVE RIGHT
Postcard of the Old English Garden in Peckham Rye Park, 1904

BELOW LEFT
Religious gathering on Peckham Rye Common, 1953

BELOW RIGHT
The opening of Peckham Rye Park. Banners belong to trade union whose members took part in the procession from Camberwell Vestry Hall, 14 May 1894

BEST WESTERN PECKHAM HOTEL

1900s

Various websites, including those of the hotel, refer to it dating "from 1849" or it being "170 years old". Not so. The Amalgamated Society of Engineers (ASE) was founded in 1851 but it was only in 1899 that it acquired the land in Peckham Road on which to build its headquarters, raising £3,500 from its branches to do so. Back in 1851 the census shows four occupied houses between Grummant Road and Lyndhurst Way, which later became known as 1-4 Lyndhurst Place. There was a toll house, a school for girls run by the Misses Gales (2), and the rest were family homes. The 1894 OS map shows these same houses, with a chapel adjacent to Grummant Road, named on the 1901 census as the Mizpah Baptist Chapel, and all so remained until at least the census of 1911.

By 1900 the ASE had moved into a house on the Lyndhurst Road side (1), holding its first executive council meeting there on 1 October. There was a renumbering in 1901. 1 became 110, and the census of that year shows the ASE office there, with the Society's secretary living with his family at 108. Quite when the present flamboyant premises were built is not entirely clear, certainly after 1911 and during or before 1914, when plans show three buildings on the site, which were brought together in 1916. It may be significant that over a door on the west side of the building is carved "Be United and Industrious 1815 and 1916".

The building, described in the Peckham Society News as a "Jacobean or Renaissance revival", had its roof blown off in the air raids of the Second World War, but continued to serve as a trade union headquarters until the Amalgamated Engineering and Electrical Union, as it had been renamed, moved out of Peckham in 1996. The first change to be carried through, following planning consent in November 1997, was the conversion of part of the building fronting Lyndhurst Way to form 14 self-contained flats, given the name Berkeley Court. On 14 August 2000, permission was sought to convert the existing building to a 93-bed hostel, establishing a budget hotel known as Peckham Lodge Hotel. It survived a threat of demolition in 2004, and so remained until late 2015, when the premises were taken over by the Best Western franchise.

The recent planning history of the site is long and complex. Particularly interesting is the fact that there was a Second World War bunker some five metres below the garden forecourt accessed from the hotel basement. Initially the bunker was used for storage, later converted into a breakfast room. Permission to extend it to provide for a fire escape and a lightwell was granted on 19 August 2010. A planning statement submitted with the application gives details of the location and construction of the bunker.

133 RYE LANE
1908

This distinctive red-brick building is best viewed from Blenheim Grove, on the other side of Rye Lane. It stands in front of, but separate from, the gigantic Bussey Building, and has its own identity though a recent extension means large black rectangular blocks obscure the original roofline.

The original purpose of the building, which dates from 1908, is unclear. However, soon after it was constructed it was partly taken up by the Electric Theatre, an early cinema, the shell of which survived at least until 2016. There was also a billiards hall with 14 tables on the floor above.

Although not built as a cinema, the space suited the needs of the Electric Theatre and marked the third London cinema opened by former Wall Street stockbroker George Washington Grant. Not long after its launch in August 1908, Grant opened another cinema nearby called the Gem at 121 Peckham High Street.

The Kinematograph & Lantern Weekly of 24 June 1909 observed that the Electric Theatre had been specially designed for kinematograph shows, with seating for 450, "nicely upholstered tip-up seats" and "the glow of roseate electric lights around the theatre", which "heightens the effect of the beautifully lighted pictures projected onto the screen".

Leslie Wood described the exterior in his book The Miracle of the Movies:

"The frontage was the size of a large shop; its pay-box was set between twin pairs of swing doors. The handles and footplates of the doors were of gleaming brass. The entire frontage was painted white, with the words Electric Theatre picked out in naked electric-light bulbs which burned even during daylight hours…The notices with which the doors were painted, in gold leaf, stick in the memory as symptomatic of the frantic efforts of the period to establish the cinema as a respectable form of entertainment."

The enterprise, begun only 12 years after the first public film show in Britain on 21 February 1896 (when the Lumière brothers brought the wonders of their cinématographe machine to the Regent Street Polytechnic), came to an end in May 1915, superseded by the Tower Cinema on the other side of Rye Lane.

Subsequently number 133 served as a sports arcade, then a penny bazaar and a clothing retailer, before enjoying a resurgence as a Lyons tea shop, which opened in 1921 and was part of the Holdron's parade. Criminal defence lawyer Ralph Haeems, whose clients included the Kray twins, later had an office on the upper floors. By 2006 the building, still imposing at the front, housed a meat and fish shop at street level, and a Redeemed Christian Church of God above.

Some years later, the building was purchased by a private owner who submitted plans for residential development. In response, in 2015, a major campaign, led by Peckham

133 Rye Lane, 1981

ARCHITECTURAL NOTES

133 Rye Lane is the most prominent of a number of Christopher Wren revival or 'Wrenaissance' buildings erected in Peckham in the early 20th century.

This English Baroque style was used from the 1880s through to the inter-war period. Also known as the 'Free Renaissance' style, this architecture was adaptable to different building types. Its decorative brick and tile work could be quite jolly, so was well suited to pubs, theatres and early cinemas, as at 133 Rye Lane. Add a bit of Portland Stone and this (often exuberant) baroque revival was also ideal for expanding London's new town halls, schools and fire stations. Sir Alfred Brumwell Thomas' 1905 Woolwich town hall, is probably the most spectacular example in South East London.

133 Rye Lane's blocked rustication and blind circular windows with tiled keystones, channels Christopher Wren's work at Hampton Court. Interestingly, behind its fine red facing bricks is one of Peckham's early steel-framed buildings. The complex stepped gable concealed a steel and glass vaulted hall to the top two floors. This was sadly removed in the building's recent redevelopment.

Vision, Copeland Park, CLF Art Cafe and other entertainment and leisure businesses nearby, was mounted to prevent the site from being converted into flats, with Southwark Council's website temporarily stalling under the weight of the 13,000 objections submitted. The subsequent conversion into a space for businesses came about after this campaign, in parallel with Southwark Council's work in negotiating a scheme with the owners for a suitable redevelopment of the building.

In 2017 there was great excitement when Maverick Projects and The Peckham Society took over the former Electric Theatre space for one night, to present an evening of archive films, photos and live music celebrating the streets of Peckham and Southwark over the decades.

Today, following a major remodelling, 133 Rye Lane provides modern professional co-working space; an elegant ground floor frontage with shops and food bars; Tonkotsu restaurant (where something of the old decor has been retained); and rooftop bar Forza Wine, with its stunning views.

Other Wren-revival buildings in Peckham include the characterful former Bun House at 96 Peckham High Street, Central Buildings at the north end of Rye Lane, 41 Peckham High Street, 114 Rye Lane with its impressive baroque gable, the former Sainsbury's at 61-63 Rye Lane, even the Neo Georgian architecture of the former post office at 199-201 Rye Lane is a part of this family of late-classical buildings in Peckham's town centre.

These attractive buildings are united by spirited classical detailing in Kent and Surrey red brick and tile, and timber windows with divided lights.

Happily two of the original shopfronts of this group survive at 61-63 Rye Lane, and partially at the Bun House on the High Street.

PIONEER HEALTH CENTRE

1935

This is a well-known story and an initiative, which made Peckham famous. It was conceived by two doctors, George Scott Williamson (1884-1953) and Innes Hope Pearse (1889-1978), who both worked at the Royal Free Hospital in north London, the former as Director of Pathological Studies. In the 1920s they came up with a revolutionary idea: a model of health, which would rely on people coming together to take responsibility for their own health. They chose Peckham as an area conducive to experiment with a variety of income levels and a spread of occupations. Their objective was to answer the question – What is Health?

To explore this, they set up a health centre at 142 Queen's Road in 1926. It served as what Pearse noted was, "a family health club which was also a biologists' research laboratory". Participating families tested the practicalities of following a healthy life rather than relying on medical interventions to cure the consequences of poor health. Families paid five pence a week to make common cause in keeping well, a charge which covered periodic examinations and counselling, if needed.

The centre was used by 112 families, some 400 men, women and children, and proved popular. Though opposed by some GPs it flourished for three years, when

it was recognised that something more ambitious was needed. Funding was raised for a purpose-built centre, designed by the illustrious engineer, Sir Owen Williams. The Pioneer Health Centre opened in Frobisher Place, off St Mary's Road in May 1935, an art-deco creation of concrete and glass, which came to be known as the 'Peckham Experiment'. Available for leisure use by up to 1,000 people, it remained true to its original principles, but was now equipped with a full range of facilities including a swimming pool, gymnasium, theatre, nursery, provision for various games rooms, consulting rooms, a medical laboratory and a cafeteria selling organic food. Staffing included four doctors, two nurses and three laboratory technicians. There were periodic medical checks, and

Pioneer Health Centre, St Mary's Road, Peckham: the swimming pool, 1990

information was given on the state of the health of each family, but the operating principle was one of encouraging members to choose their own activities, and take control of their lives.

Two impediments stood in the way of this vision. First, although the cost of £38,000 for the building and its equipment had been raised, funding remained a constant problem. Second, tension with the medical establishment continued to simmer. Though widely recognised as a dynamic seminal enterprise, it is inescapable that the 'experiment' was fully operational for only a little over four years. Vacated on the request of the police during the Second World War, its glass facade was seen as a potential beacon for enemy aircraft. They had a point. A 1945 survey found that half of Peckham's houses had suffered bomb damage, with at least quarter made uninhabitable. The Centre remained empty until 1942, when it was rented out as a factory making radar

Queen Mary visiting Pioneer Health Centre, 1948

equipment until April 1946, before returning to its original purpose. The building was by then quite dilapidated, but a grant of £10,000 enabled its reopening. Research resumed, but only in a restricted way. By this time government plans for health reform were being laid.

The NHS arrived on 5 July 1948. This national illness service was at odds with the philosophy of Williamson and Pearse. The Centre was unwelcome to much of the medical establishment and funding for the Peckham Experiment dried up. In 1950 the Centre was taken over by King's College Hospital as a medical clinic. It was bought by the London County Council in 1951, its leisure facilities run by Southwark Council, and in 1970 was used by Southwark College for adult educational purposes. It was in this function, on 27 September 1972 that Historic England gave the building Grade II* listing, noting its "revolutionary idea and design".

But ideas do not die. The Pioneer Health Foundation continues to promote its legacy. The Centre attracted wide interest. A film, 'The Centre', was produced by Paul Rotha, first shown in July 1948, and was followed by a visit from Queen Mary and the Prime Minister, Clement Attlee. Wise commentators continued to believe that 'prevention is better than cure' and that concepts explored during the Peckham Experiment have their place in health provision and prevention. It has inspired a massive output of literature and lectures.

The building itself was converted into flats in 1998/2000 in what was widely seen as a sympathetic development by architect Alan Camp, It was also at this time that the landscaping of the site was completed with a

new cycle store, tennis court, trees and other planting. As part of the refurbishment works the pool was adapted to provide a shallow children's section and an adult swimming area, achieved by creating a new stepped structure within the shell of the original pool.

There are 34 apartments in total. 22 two-bed duplex apartments spread across the ground and first floors, and 12 second floor single level one- and two-bed apartments with access to private roof terraces. A total of 14 new houses were also built in the grounds as part of the redevelopment in 2000 (each with their own garden space) along with a communal garden area shared by all residents.

The former Centre was awarded a Southwark blue plaque in May 2006. 142 Queen's Road still stands. An English Heritage blue plaque honouring Dr Williamson and Dr Pearse was unveiled there on 26 March 2009.

THE PECKHAM MULTI STOREY

1982

OPPOSITE ABOVE
Glass screens dividing the cafeteria from the kitchen, 1935

OPPOSITE BELOW
Swimming pool at Pioneer Health Centre, 2018

ABOVE
View looking west along Moncrieff Street towards Peckham Multi-Storey Car Park east elevation, 2012

Back in 1977, the Peckham Society proposed the creation of seven conservation areas. Particular consideration was given to two areas threatened with demolition. One of these was a large part of Moncrieff Street, where a residents' association was opposing a plan to knock down houses to create a multi-storey car park in the town centre, primarily for the customers of a new Sainsbury's store that would front the building.

Inevitably business interests prevailed. A planning application to replace Sainsbury's 1931 store at 61-63 Rye Lane with a new supermarket on the Moncrieff Street site

was approved by Southwark Council and the Greater London Council in 1978. The scheme was to accommodate a new store and 720 cars at a projected cost of around £2 million.

The Peckham Action Group, an offshoot of the Peckham Society, called a public meeting in January 1980, and took its objection to the scheme all the way to a public hearing in 1981. To no avail. Much of Moncrieff Street was demolished in 1982, to be replaced by the enormous car park.

Following the opening of a new superstore at Dog Kennel Hill, Sainsbury's decided

Looking north-west towards corner of the Peckham Multi-Storey Car Park south and east elevations and south passage, 2015

to close their Peckham store in 1993. The vacated store was quickly converted into the successful Peckhamplex cinema, and the multi-storey car park was operating as a public car park run by Southwark Council for the town centre for a number of years but was poorly used.

Things began to change in 2008 when not-for-profit arts organisation Bold Tendencies, founded the previous year by local gallerist Hannah Barry, held an exhibition of large-scale sculpture on the upper floors of the car park, with the benefit of a short lease from Southwark Council. Frank's Café, with its now famous rooftop views, followed a year later. New visual art and architecture have been commissioned and the space has become the venue for an award winning live events 'summer season' programme, including performances by the Multi-Story Orchestra, working with local young musicians.

Meanwhile in September 2010, Southwark Council commissioned a town centre parking review. It reported that the multi-storey car park appeared to be underused: occupancy was no greater than 10%, while the general environment was deemed "not very welcoming": the lifts were dark and dirty, and a general lack of activity added to a feeling of this being an unsafe space. In 2012, the Council's Peckham and Nunhead Area Action Plan proposed that the building should be demolished and the site redeveloped.

But following objections at the statutory Examination in Public in order to adopt new planning policy in 2013, the Planning Inspector decided that the building's long-term future should be reconsidered. The car park was therefore removed from the Area Action Plan, and there was broad community support to implement the Inspector's recommendations to consider the building's

Peckham's Heritage – Past, Present & Future

long-term potential, while in the meantime repurposing the empty levels.

Southwark Council invited tenders for possible ways of using the space only in the short-term and in July 2016 Make Shift (working with Turner Works Architects), was awarded a contract to utilise the empty levels for just the following five years. Having previously managed the successful Pop Brixton, a project that turned a disused site in SW9 into creative space for local independent businesses, its plan was to transform the multi-storey car park into a vibrant collective under the banner 'Peckham Levels'. The enterprise opened in December 2017.

Peckham Vision meanwhile continued to campaign against the threat of demolition, urging wide public discussion about the sustainable, long-term potential of the existing building. In October 2017, Southwark Council agreed to remove the car park from the impending New Southwark Plan and announced that Bold Tendencies, Peckhamplex and Peckham Levels would have their leases extended. The following month the Council accepted Peckham Vision's nomination of the building as an Asset of Community Value, to remain on its list for five years, with a restriction on its title at the Land Registry. However, they ignored the Inspector's recommendation for examination of the long-term potential of the car park.

View looking south-east from Cerise Road roundabout towards the Peckham Multi-Storey Car Park north elevation, 2013

At the end of 2021, Peckham Levels was bought by the Really Useful Group. The building as a whole is a thriving hub for events, art, food, music, cinema, and culture, with 200 small independent businesses supporting 400 jobs. Its vast capacity, particularly in Peckham Levels, includes a children's area, viewing spots, and places for meetings, conferences and community activities, as well as many studios and other working spaces. Peckham Vision has successfully renominated the building as an Asset of Community Value, and it has been relisted for five years from August 2023.

ABOVE
The Food Hall: the main public space at Peckham Levels for the community, 2023

BELOW LEFT
The Auditorium: a smaller event space at Peckham Levels, 2023

BELOW RIGHT
J Walshe and T Conrad perform at the London Contemporary Festival of Music at the Peckham Multi Storey, 2013

ARCHITECTURAL NOTES

Sainsbury's has taken a particular interest in architecture and interior design since its first grocery shop founded on Drury Lane in the 1860s. This can be seen on two sites in Peckham where noteworthy Sainsbury's buildings have been built.

In 1931, Sainsbury's built the attractive Wren-revival shop at 63 Rye Lane. This building has one of the last original hardwood shopfronts in Peckham. Above this is a handsome Queen Anne period façade in red facing brick with tiled details in the Classical style. The interior walls of this shop were clad in pretty decorative tilework. This tilework survived its transformation to a Clark's shoe shop in the 1990s. However much was unnecessarily lost in the spring of 2022.

In 1982, a very new type of Sainsbury's came to Peckham, on a much larger scale, when they opened a new 'supermarket' with a ten-level car park above. The new Sainsburys was designed when developers and planners believed that car ownership would be universal and town centre car parking would be essential for the success of any supermarket development.

In connection with this, it is worth noting that Peckham narrowly escaped a stretch of the GLC (Greater London Council) promoted 'Inner Ringway 1' motorway, which proposed an eight-lane elevated motorway connecting Peckham with Brixton and Lewisham, roughly where Choumert Road is today. Thankfully, after the construction of a section of the elevated inner ring, the 'flyovers' in Notting Hill and Hammersmith, the public and local authorities rebelled against the GLC plan and Peckham's Holly Grove conservation area was saved.

The new Sainsbury's on Rye Lane was designed in what you might describe as an 'expressive late-modern style' by the brand's own architects and engineers department. The building's concrete frame is expressed in a bold geometric way with different tones of brick infill panels. Above, a profiled metal clad roof. The Sainsbury's archive shows views of a lofty, brightly lit, tiled interior.

In the late 20th century the Sainsbury family commissioned many notable buildings showing the architectural possibilities of this new building type: the supermarket. Nicholas Grimshaw and Partners designed the canal side housing and supermarket in Camden Town in 1989 (now Grade II listed); Ahrends Burton and Koralek designed a masted High-Tech supermarket in Canterbury, 1982; Norman Foster completed the Sainsbury Centre museum at the University of East Anglia in 1978 (Grade II*).

Sainsbury's new supermarket in Peckham was short-lived. Since 2008, the upper parts of the car park have been reused as a popular outdoor sculpture park with new commissions added each year. This aerial civic garden for Peckham benefits from a spectacular panorama of London from Wembley in the west, Westminster and the City, to the Docklands in the east. Refreshments are housed in a striking covered café made from scaffold planks and tensioned truck tarpaulins playfully designed by Practice Architecture.

The comprehensive re-use of a former Sainsbury's supermarket and multi-storey car park into diverse and productive community activities is one of Peckham's most unique success stories. It is a triumph of the community, entrepreneurs and Southwark Council working together for Peckham's benefit.

Part 4
Oral Histories

'Grow Our Histories' is an oral history project produced by the South London Gallery in partnership with the Peckham THI, exploring the history of Peckham through the first-hand experiences of local people. Written extracts from the recorded interviews are included here.

The full interviews and summaries can be accessed on the South London Gallery website www.southlondongallery.org/archive-room/archive-and-local-history/oral-history-peckham

The interviews and summaries will be held permanently at Southwark Archives. www.southwark.gov.uk/libraries/southwark-archives

SLG

OPPOSITE 25 inch Ordnance Survey map CIII, 1897 edition

AREA 10
DIMITRI LAUNDER
AND ANILA LADWA

DIMITRI LAUNDER was born in Surrey in 1974 to a Greek mother and a British father. He spent his childhood living in different locations around the UK and Europe, as both parents were artists and travelled for work.

ANILA LADWA was born in London in 1971. Her great grandparents came from Gujarat and settled in Zimbabwe where she spent her childhood, returning to the UK when she was 19.

Dimitri and Anila met when they were both studying at Camberwell School of Art. In 2002 they set up Area 10 in an abandoned timber yard in Peckham. Area 10 was a cultural space for artists, live music and mixed media arts events until 2009. Dimitri is now co-director of Arbonauts and Anila is a creative producer working in interdisciplinary social arts practice.

PART 1:

D: People walked into the space and immediately said 'Wow!' And because of security, we kept the front door to be a domestic front door off Peckham Square, so going through this domestic door into this huge cavity, it was constantly this breath-taking effect. It was vast, it was 8 meters high, 25 thousand square foot, it had car-parking, it had loads of interesting access and hundreds of tonnes of material, mostly in the form of timber in storage bays that the timber yard were leaving behind.

A: People thought they were in Alice in Wonderland because there were these difference spaces and as artists we worked on the unexpected. There were mazes, there were spaces where we could just unfold our imagination. We understood that we could make wonderful artworks with people and in that way we engaged in conversations about our practice and people were really interested, and we had started developing a language, which was very much processed-based.

D: The way that ethos translated into Area 10, was that we shared practice, we shared techniques, we shared tools, materials and audiences. The structure evolved organically in those early days.

A: And we functioned on these pepper-corn licences and occupied the building with no funding and no money in the bank. The site was really exciting, it was the size of an air craft hanger and there wasn't much else around and we became really popular immediately.

At the time, Peckham had a very negative stigmatisation from Damilola Taylor's death and the then Regeneration Department in the Council, Peckham Programme had

Area 10, 2002

a tonne of funding to spend in Peckham. They took an interest in us, because part of their remit, was to use arts and culture to turn the tide, on what was seen negatively about Peckham and to use local arts and culture to bring up the profile.

D: Area 10 created a structure that was quite permeable and open and we remained open to how artists came in, not only by being in a critical structure with other artists, but engaging with the community as well. We were a brown box, not a white cube, we were process-led, we loved the idea of create, collaborate and communicate, these statements created a position around what we were doing and it lent itself to the passion of the people who participated.

A: We tried to be very democratic and in the way we did things. We took proposals and the one criteria, was that people had to make work that was site specific. We had visual artists and performers form companies and the work that was shown there, was the most exciting I ever experienced, aerial work, light shows and digital work, all came together around a narrative for those shows. The things that came out of Area 10 were really important works.

We also built things around arts education. The children around the building used to throw things at us when we were first in there. But a couple of years later, they could actually have a conversation about what live art was. We invited them in, we hosted them before the actual shows. Those kids grew up knowing what art was and I hope went on to appreciate or become artists themselves. But we had this impact and we engaged with local businesses and communities.

It was the catalyst, alongside 'I Love Peckham', which was a platform for all sorts of other things to happen in the area. I think our period that time, was a catalyst for Peckham and loads of organisations exist today because of the work of Area 10.

D: Also, because we were open till late at night, we had a seismic effect on the public space of Peckham Square. It was dangerous and there were drug exchanges and prostitution and you would be concerned about travelling across it, but those things changed in the time that we were there.

And we always put extra time in. If someone knocked on the door, we wouldn't say we were closed, we would give them the time to have a conversation, if not to invite them in to see what was happening. It was part of our generosity of approach throughout the whole thing.

A: Our shows were mixed media and we hosted a lot of music and there was nowhere to go in Peckham to see live music or theatre, or have a dance and we were young! There was also a lot of live art and you might have your mother visiting, the show opening and then some naked woman would be walking around or climbing out of clay as performance! Those were unexpected happenings which we hosted.

D: We had one event where there were 2000 people in the middle of winter. It was a lot to deal with, because it was our names on the papers, in terms of our personal responsibilities and liabilities.

PART 2

D: One of our favourite shows was called Destination Area 10. The idea was looking at Peckham as a kind of landing site for people from different countries, it was a refugee gateway, there were asylum seekers and we really wanted to express that in a multimedia show.

A: Back then things were different, Camberwell College students would never want to venture to Peckham, they always hung out in Camberwell and didn't come here. I think people may have done some local projects, but it was always about extracting cultural references; the existing shops and the multi-cultural nature of it, I mean they extracted bits from the community for work, but that never went back into that community.

D: And at certain times of night Peckham was a place that didn't feel safe. I certainly got mugged immediately on moving into Peckham, literally with a duvet under one arm, although they didn't take the duvet! And again towards the end of us being in Peckham, on a bicycle I was attacked with a broken bottle. So there certainly were issues at certain times of night, but in general I don't think it was a no-go area.

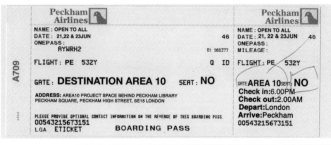

Airline ticket flyer for the Area 10 show 'Destination Peckham', 2007

And in relation to Destination Area 10 as a project, it was a changing cycle of different cultural influences and the time we were there we saw that, we saw different asylum seeker communities come in and out of Peckham as a gateway, changing the profile of the shops and the cultures there.

A: There was no economy for us to consume in Peckham either at the time. There were no coffee shops or catering, there weren't any cultural spaces beyond South London Gallery, there wasn't that step into the area necessarily and it was therefore new territory for us too.

The beauty of the Destination Area 10 as a project, was having all these different people, especially through the music, we invited performers from different ethnicities to perform different types of music in the building. We had a tabla player and an opera singer, just this crazy diversity of multi-culturalism which was happening over three nights.

D: And it was a particularly big group of artists, it was over 60 artists. The audience was also very mixed, local people, literally our neighbours coming, and we would go out and specifically flyer our neighbourhood, so they become regulars and they would come back again and again asking what have you got next. We didn't have issues with our neighbours.

A: Although the building did seep noise. So we had to let them know and that was a difficult thing to manage.

D: But we had conversations and we chatted with people about this

A: So for Destination Area 10, there were lot of installation works and multimedia work and our own projects were in there too, but we also put a lot of effort into show-casing diversity. With the art world you get so stuck in your own little thing, that you forget about the importance of engaging different kinds of cultures.

A: It was just really good energy, a really good celebration. And you got a plane ticket, which was our flyer, saying 'Destination Area 10 in Peckham'.

D: It said Peckham Airlines and you could tear it off.

A: With a pigeon as an icon, because we did have a lot of pigeons in the building.

D: So I think that the legacy is invisible. I think that what we did in Area 10 was to create a sort of rhizomatic or

mycorrhizal network of cultural actors and practitioners, which have developed in all sorts of different directions and have established a cultural quarter in Peckham, that we couldn't even have visualised, no way! Initially, we just worked inside our bricks, because there was just so much to deal with and then slowly, we started for example with the I Love Peckham Festival, we started working outside. But then I think people saw what we did, saw the confidence that we did it with and that confidence led to a shared confidence and other people then taking it on and taking it forward, so we were the flag-bearers for that. I think our legacy is there, but quite invisible.

A: The legacy I agree, is very invisible, but it was a catalyst, alongside I Love Peckham, which was a platform for all sorts of other things to happen in the area that exist today. Peckham Platform as well, where I spent five years working with the Regeneration Team on having that space built, is really successful today. Hannah Berry Gallery or Bold Tendencies in the car park rooftop, I think our period, our time was a catalyst for Peckham and I am quite pleased we can make claim to that. There are loads of organisations from that time that exist today.

D: Our energies at the time were recognised, in other groups who were doing what we were doing as recent graduates. There were undergraduates like Lucky PDF, who graduated in 2007, who showed with us and then took their work off to the Venice Biennale. Over the years, we had over one thousand five hundred artists work with us and regularly had events with over a thousand people in the audiences. The numbers were massive and the responsibility was too.

BARRY JENKINS

BARRY JENKINS was born in Dulwich in 1944 and has lived and worked in Peckham all of his life. He recalls a time when people flocked to the shops in Rye Lane and Peckham was a busy, affluent shopping centre. Barry worked for several local vehicle repair companies including Brenda Car and Coachworks, J. H. Sparshat and Freeman Motors and he owned Barry's Accident Repairs. Barry reflects on the many changes he has witnessed and shares his memories of local characters and the people he worked with around the Bussey Building and in Peckham in the 1960s.

RYE LANE AND ITS CHARACTERS

Rye Lane Peckham, up until the middle 1970s was a very, very good shopping centre and there were a lot of people working there. When I was a young man of 19, there was a lady's dress maker there and five tailors and we used to have our suits made in Rye Lane, but those places have all gone now., There were very good department stores but they've all gone. The Peckham area rivalled Oxford Street - in the money it took… it was the place to shop. It's hard to imagine now, there was even a shop called Home and Colonial in Peckham!

I can remember going in to Jones and Higgins, the department store with my mother and a man would come up to her and say, 'Can we help you madam?' It was all, 'Yes sir' and the staff looked after you - well that doesn't happen anymore. It was a very good shop, it was very big and went all the road. Inside it had lots of different departments and it sold all sort of things, furniture, clothes and everything else, you could even buy pianos there! But it changed and became the Houndsditch and things went downhill.

In those days, the difference between then and now was that everyone didn't have to buy their own house, but the people who lived here in Peckham, they were dockers and printers and these people were the people who were earning the money, so Rye Lane Peckham catered to them. It was a very good shopping centre, this was in the late 1950s-60s but when they left, a lot of the good shops left too. This happened when they closed the Docks down, people moved on and the people who moved in were different people as such.

Barry wearing a suit bought on Rye Lane

There was even an Omega dealership in Rye Lane, selling Omega watches in a shop. When the man went to the moon, they strapped an Omega Speed Master watch onto one of the rockets and I bought one of them from that shop in 1971, it cost a lot of money then. There were very good jewellers on Rye Lane. But in the early 1970s, London Borough of Southwark was rumouring that they wanted to build a town hall at the bottom of Rye Lane, where there was a mixture of people running different shops, but they all left. They never built the town hall, but that put the wind up a lot of people. People say it will come back, but I don't think it will.

I also remember the local characters, like Johnny Cambridge who was known as the Tomato Man, because he sold so many tomatoes. He had a stall opposite Marks and Spencer's, just selling tomatoes and he earnt a good living there and he attracted long queues. He sold a lot of tomatoes, although he also had fruit and veg stall up at the top end of Rye Lane, where Asda supermarket was until recently.

Another popular character was Dubonnet, said to have been a member of the French Resistance in WWII. He worked as a night security guard under the arches of Peckham Rye station, then drove his three beautiful daughters to the French Lycée in Chelsea and then went on to his day job. We couldn't pronounce his name, so he called him Dubonnet, the name of the aperitif and the only French word we knew. Now we've passed the nickname to one of his daughters.

Revd Bob Hurley was a vicar who knew how to get things done! He came to All Saints Church on Blenheim Grove in1996, on a promise to double the congregation and install heating. He achieved both in a matter of months, so saving the church from demolition and he went to achieve a lot more. I helped him find a belt for the organ and he did me the favour of taking some bread I'd baked down to Plymouth to give to my son who was studying there.

Hugh Leach was another local, who was the last man to be seen wearing a bowler hat in Peckham. He was a man of many parts with an interesting past and he would have a cheery good morning for everyone, either in English or Arabic, as he strode out on his daily walk from Choumert Square to the Foreign Office.

In Bellenden Road, there was a wooden building behind one of the shops which belonged to Sid the Safe. Sid used to repair safes and when they tried to get a safe open and they couldn't do it, Sid was the man who you got in to do it, to the extent that Sid couldn't go anywhere. If Sid decided he was going to go to Southend for the day, the police had to authorise it, because he was a master safe opener. He was the man who repaired them for the insurers, but he was so deadly, that they wanted to know where he was, coz he could open any safe. And if he sold you a safe, he would have two keys, one for him and one for you. He was a professional in that place. He was one of those wonderful characters, who rolled their own cigarettes and he used to say, that the one he had in his mouth, he'd had it there since 1936!

Barry being presented with a certificate by the Princess Royal after completing the Venice Marathon in 2000 and raising money for Save the Children (of which she's the President)

THE BUSSEY BUILDING

If you go into the Bussey building from Rye Lane, you walk up an alley way and at the end of the alley way, that's the Bussey Building. The building that you are walking past, used to be a cinema and that was only the entrance and that big chimney on the right that goes up the top of the front, that was a lift for the cinema.

On the ground floor there was a Joe Lyons and there were two Joe Lyons in Rye Lane, that shows you how busy it was. If you had one, it was a good shopping centre, Joe Lyons had two. One there, and one down the bottom of the road.

In the Bussey Building itself there was a junk jewellery manufacturer, a tent manufacturer, I remember them. When you come out there it comes into the open and that was Freeman Motors on the right and there were petrol pumps too. At the end of it, was a car show room and I helped build the front piece of it, but they have blocked it off now. There was also a big unit there where we used to do the body work, as you went in from Copeland Road along the left hand side.

The one on the right hand side was the Commercial Plywood Factory, what made Plywood. There was a lot of churches in there for a while and all, African churches in the big building. There was also a Roots Motor Dealership, which was a subsidiary of Freeman Motors, and that's where we had the car showroom, with the Roots cars in. My first car was a Humber Super Snipe from there.

Memories, I have so many memories of that area, the characters and all the people that I worked with, who taught me everything. They were men who had been in the war and

they taught me everything and some of them had been wounded. It was the places where they were living and all, there was a lot of prefabs in Peckham and they were living in them and some of them couldn't go to work, they weren't getting much of a pension, I remember things like that and their families.

I worked for the old man Fred Crocker, owner of F S Crocker's Coachworks in Alpha Street and eventually he ended up working for me till he was 100 and he lived to be 103. I also worked for Brenda Khan Car and Coachworks at 9 Blenheim Grove and Freeman Motors and they all ended up working with me, and in the end and they left me all their tools - so I guess I couldn't have been a bad bloke.

Just up around the corner from there, was this place between the houses called Meridian Bronze, and they just sold bronze and copper and things like that in there. I remember going there and you had to be introduced. My son, he went to Camberwell School of Art and he and he was making things out of copper, he was very good with metal. The woman there liked him, so she

was letting him have all the stuff cheap and I couldn't work this out. So if we wanted anything, we used to send him round there. I remember going round there one day and there was no staff about, but someone in there said that they were all in court, because someone had bought some metal from them and was knocking out pound coins and they had tracked the metal back to there! They've shut now and moved away for more room.

At the bottom of Bellenden Road, there is a group of arches which go over to Lyndhsurt Way and that was J.H. Sparshat. That was one of the largest wood body builders in Western Europe, Leyland dealers. And Brenda Khan Coachworks used to send me down there, to do the stuff that had a wallop that was coming in and I was only young and mucking about. The Guvnor, used to come up from Portsmouth every day and there was one time that I was ill or not at work and he rung up the firm where I worked for and asked 'Where is he? Where's Barry?' And they said, 'Why? What's he done this time?' And he said, 'He's not here, he's bleeding hopeless, but he's great for moral!'

DR CHARMAINE BROWN

Dr Charmaine Brown is an education expert and senior lecturer at the University of Greenwich. Charmaine was born in Kingston, Jamaica in 1962 and came to the UK in 1964. She has lived in Peckham since 1987. Between 1989 -1994, she was education manager at the Peckham Literacy Centre, known as The Book Place, which was on Peckham High Street. Charmaine recalls the presence of a lively Caribbean community in Peckham and has witnessed both their struggles and successes.

CHANGE AND TRANSFORAMTION

I came to Peckham in the 1980s and I have lived in the same house all the while I have lived in here. But where I live is now in a conservation area, it's quiet and tree-lined and everyone has big gardens and it's far removed from the high street.

When I come out of my house, I enter the high street and I am in another world and I only tolerate that for a short time span, so it doesn't matter too much to me. Rye Lane is very much a local high street, but you go onto Bellenden Road and that's fully gentrified. It's another world and another mind-set and the two worlds don't really meet. Some people go to Rye Lane to buy what they call 'exotic' fruit and vegetables, but it is two different worlds, existing in parallel streets.

Then there is the Bussey Building on Rye Lane, it's very vibrant and has social events, it's on Rye Lane, yet people from the local community who shop on Rye Lane all the time, they don't know it's there. It's just through an archway, but if they went down that archway to the Bussey Building, they would still feel it is not a place for them. These days, Peckham seems very segregated.

The thing about the Caribbean community when they first came here, was that they integrated a lot and it didn't matter which Caribbean island you came from. There was a lot more integration in those days and the Caribbean community felt more settled, there was more provision for the community and there was a buzzing social life, both in the day and in night life.

By then, a lot more people from the Caribbean had purchased their own houses and there were certain houses where there were weekly parties called Shebeens, basement parties, sometimes in the very big houses. There were daytime social clubs like the Dominoes Club run by Dominicans, which became a club in the night time. There was also a famous club on Peckham High Street called The Bouncing Ball, which was called Mr B's at one time. It was a prominent Peckham night club which attracted international artists from all over, but especially from Jamaica. And that was the place where you went to in South London on a Saturday night. The local pubs with Caribbean landlords would also do a social, so they would have sound systems on particular days and that would be a venue for socialising and dancing.

The Caribbean community have left a legacy in Peckham because they have invested in the social capital. They went from being tenants in one room, to end up owning their own houses. In certain areas, especially the gentrified area around the Bellenden Renewal area, there were quite a few Caribbean people who owned their own houses and on the back of this, they created their own jobs and businesses through things like hairdressing in the home, setting up nurseries, shops and clubs. They also had their own financial system, like a credit union, called a Pardner, because they weren't able to go mainstream to borrow money and this was going on in the properties. Lots of things were built up from this system. The barber shops also had a big role in terms of legacy. There were many barber shops which the younger generation inherited, or were paid-for outright and these were leased or sold to up and coming young people.

The first set of families came to Bellenden Road because it was affordable, but also because a person was prepared to sell their house to

Charmaine when she was Education Manager at the Peckham Literary Centre (The Book Place), 1991

them. You see, because of the prejudice of the time, some people would refuse to sell their house to Black people who wanted to buy it. But it happened in Bellenden Road, so from there, other families came to realise that we can buy, they will allow us to buy, so it built from there and quite a few Caribbean families had houses on the Bellenden Road.

But Peckham had gone into some decline in the 1980s and I think that was a natural thing, but during that decline, a good percentage of the Caribbean community moved out of Peckham, because they felt it was a bit run down now. The Bellenden Road, which at first had lots of independent shops, became run down and a lot of them closed and looked derelict. And as the Caribbean people moved out, the Nigerians came in, but not in the same parts of Peckham, because the parts of Peckham that the Caribbean moved out of, those are the areas that became gentrified. Where they called it Little Lagos, was predominately Choumert Road, where there were Nigerian businesses at one stage and then Nigerians began to rent out spaces for churches and it went from there.

I've lived in Peckham for 35 years. When I became Education Manager at the Peckham Literacy Centre (The Book Place) on Peckham High Street, that part was a very creative community hub. The Book Place attracted communities who wouldn't usually have gone into a book shop, like Caribbean communities and others. There were also community businesses, a Jamaican green grocers and restaurant next door. The Women's Centre which was for women of all cultures, was across the road. Quite a few Caribbean enterprises sprung up on that stretch of road and initiatives sprung up with different communities. At the time it was a nice community feeling and people supported each other and each other's initiatives.

HOW A MURDER SHOCKED PECKHAM

The North Peckham Estate which bordered the High Street, was notorious for crime and gangland violence in the 80s and 90s. You literally didn't go on the estate, unless you lived there.

But the rest of Peckham was still predominantly houses, as opposed to flats. Rye Lane was bustling, Bellenden Road which is now the gentrified area, had become run down, because when I moved there first, it is was a nice little community. But then it became rundown, the houses became run down, lots of shops were closed and Rye Lane was the main road to be on to shop and socialise.

Peckham was going through a transition then and there were riots, there was an uprising at one time, in the 80s, after the Brixton riots, there was the Peckham uprising. It was for similar reasons, it was all about injustices and policing, is still a heavy topic in Peckham, although because of gentrification, you hear less sirens and there are more undercover cars. But back then at the time, the one thing you heard was the police sirens, very piercing and there was a lot of that and the sirens were disturbing and it would be multiple sirens and two, three, four police cars racing along. And I used to think, what it is now? It made me feel sorry for the young people, because the stop and search was rampant then. You would see these school boys all lined up, the police would pull down their trousers and they be searching them these little boys were in hand-cuffs. I had to intervene a couple of times and ask, have you called their parents?

Peckham High Street used to be called the 'Front Line' for the Caribbean community and you'd have people who'd hang out there, like Brixton had their Front Line on Railton Road.

And that stretch where The Book Place was, where I worked, was on the Front Line. This was a place where people just gathered to talk, to socialise, but often there was an undercurrent to do illicit things, like drug exchanges, but the socialising aspect was people playing music and people just hanging out all day and in the evening.

The police were always policing the Front Line and they were always doing drug raids. It was nonstop, non-stop! And you'd hear

Damilola Taylor, Evening Standard, 28th November 2000

WEST END FINAL

Evening Standard

LONDON, TUESDAY, 28 NOVEMBER 2000   www.thisislondon.com   Incorporating THE EVENING NEWS   35p

MURDERED

10-year-old boy stabbed by London bullies and left to bleed to death

by JUSTIN DAVENPORT
Crime Correspondent

A 10-YEAR-OLD boy bled to death in his school uniform alone on a London estate after being stabbed by a gang of bullies as young as 11.

Damilola Taylor — who had arrived in England only a few months ago — died on a stairwell on the North Peckham estate. He had been knifed in the leg and desperately tried to crawl or hobble 100 yards before collapsing in a pool of blood.

The boy had left an after-school computer studies unit at Oliver Goldsmith primary school in Peckham minutes before he was apparently attacked last night by three youths aged between 11 and 14.

Police and paramedics were called by a member of the public who found Damilola barely conscious on a first-floor stairwell at 4.50pm. Paramedics carried out emergency treatment but the boy was dead on arrival at King's College Hospital in Camberwell.

Two hours later his mother — unaware of

the tragedy — was scouring the estate for her son who had failed to arrive home. He had told her he was being bullied and yesterday she took him to school. Scotland Yard said the attack is being treated as murder. A post mortem is taking place today.

Police said they had been called to an incident in nearby Blakes Road at 4.45pm when a fight between a group of youths was reported. Officers arrived but could find no sign of a fight.

Detectives now believe Damilola was attacked at that point and managed to stagger away in a bid to escape his attackers before collapsing.

Police are hunting three black youths dressed in dark, hooded jackets who were seen at the foot of the stairwell where the boy was found and later spotted running from the scene. Anyone with information

Continued on Page 2 Col 3

Damilola Taylor: he managed to stagger 100 yards from the scene in an attempt to escape his attackers before he collapsed dying from his leg wound

CAN YOU HELP POLICE? PHONE 020 8247 4567 OR CRIMESTOPPERS ANONYMOUSLY ON 0800 555 111

about it. So you didn't really go out there in the evening, unless you had a purpose there. Even if you were going out there to buy food, because there were quite a few fast food shops on the Front Line and I used to go there to get food if I wanted to, but then you had to weave between groups of men and some of the same men, would stay in the shops to get their customers. You had to have tunnel vision, literally focus, get what you want and come straight out. They wouldn't trouble you, but they would encourage you to purchase something, it was more that kind of thing, but not aggressively.

Then there was the North Peckham Estate, which stretched from Peckham High Street to around Burgess Park I think, and because of the nature of the estate, it was like a maze and it was interconnected to other estates by walkways. There would have been a lot of murders before Damilola Taylor, but his murder was the most prominent one. And the reason it was prominent, was there was camera footage of him skipping to his death and that is the image that was left in people's minds and the fact that he didn't know what was going to happen. Those people, they picked on him because they knew he stood out as a newcomer, because they said his exterior clothing was very strange and you don't wear that if you lived in London. And the fact that they could stab someone and leave him there to die.

I mean things happen and years later you start to rationalise and since then, you come to realise that for some gangs that was a rite of passage, so to be initiated in a gang, you had to stab someone in the leg. But they left Damilola there to die; either they knew he would die, or they were ignorant, because they could have done it as a rite of passage and moved on. But it just so happened, that where he fell, he wasn't discovered. But that was the image in people's minds that marked Peckham, but to tell the truth, there would have been a lot of murders before then, that did not make the news.

And I didn't know how prolific Peckham was for gang violence, especially on the North Peckham Estate. I didn't realise and all the time, I'm teaching on the estate, or I am at The Book Place, I wasn't aware that all this was going on, because it wasn't my reality, it wasn't my world.

I think about all the time I was at The Book Place and I wonder if some of my students were involved. But it is just a different world, a different world and it's so sad when you can be at the heart of it and not know what is going on. And I think, all this was happening, but where was I? How come I didn't see that?

CLEMENT OGBONNAYA

Clement Ogbonnaya was born in Lagos, Nigeria in 1981 and came to the UK as a child with his family in 1986. After university, Clement worked in events and hospitality, organising upscale late night entertainment. When he purchased a rundown pub in Peckham, he went about transforming it into The Prince of Peckham, which opened in May 2017. He talks about his vision for a local community pub and the vibrant mix of local people in Peckham, as well as making a change and adding value to the local community.

THE PUB

I'm a great believer in 'if you make magic, you will make money', because when I was buying this pub, I wasn't looking to mess up. I was one hundred percent in my head saying, this is going to work. I said to my wife, 'I'm one hundred percent going to buy a pub'. My family thought I was nuts! But my business plan was incredible, I still big it up now.

I knew that I wanted a pub and I wanted a community pub, but it had to represent the community and it had to represent me. I wanted it to really change this community. I wanted a ripple. I wanted people to understand that the business is here and it is theirs, whether they be white, Black, old or young, students, workers, it's for everyone. A space for old and new Peckham. I wouldn't have been in the position that I am in now if I hadn't created a business plan that was centred on community.

The Prince of Peckham name came from the show 'Desmond's'. It was the first TV show that I watched with my family that I could relate to. They were Black people on television, who had come from Guyana. They were here, in London, just like me & my family's situation. The character of Lee, the Peckham Prince Stanley, was a Black wide-boy. Cockney one second, patois the next, it was fantastic. Everyone wanted to be the 'Prince of Peckham' or the 'Peckham Prince'.

When I coined 'Prince of Peckham' for the pub, I was saying that we are all royal. We are regal and we should realise our value and our worth. When we painted, 'Welcome to Peckham' on the front wall, as soon as you walk into our space, you are all Peckham. It doesn't matter if you are from out of town, no one should make anyone feel less than. We treat everyone the same and that was the whole message behind it.

Mural by Artfuldodger at the entrance to the Prince of Peckham circa 2019

Putting the Black boy and the Black girl mural on the front was important because there are so few images of normal, everyday Black people around. Normally the only Black people represented are athletes or musicians. I wanted young Black kids passing the pub to go to school to see themselves and think, 'Yo! This could be us'.

I closed the pub for three months, refurbished it, as much as my small amount of money could do, and I reopened it on the 16th May 2017 for a soft launch. I opened Prince of Peckham to the public on Thursday 18th May and it was incredible. There was such a range of people there and it was packed. I was like 'Yo! This is madness!'

I've got this picture of me on the first day of the opening of the Prince of Peckham, I'm in my traditional Nigerian wear, I'm behind the bar and I'm like, 'Welcome everyone!' I'm chuffed and I'm thinking, this is mad, I'm a Black guy who owns a pub in Peckham!

MELTING POT

I always say to people that Prince of Peckham isn't a Black pub, I never ever wanted it to be. I'm the owner and I happen to be Black. I also have the long standing strategy of excellence and we strive for that. But I hear it all the time, I can't believe a Black guy owns it! And I'm like, 'Why? Why can't we believe that we are incredible?' There are other Black pub owners, I'm not the first and I'm sure I won't be the last, but I want what we offer to be better than any other pub and I want us to create a truly inclusive space. This pub isn't for just one type of person, this pub is for all of us and it's important that this is the message. If people don't like it, they can go to Wetherspoon's.

We are located near an estate area so I wanted to make sure that I am present with the residents, to talk to people and engage

Prince of Peckham with Clifton Estate's Witcombe Point in background circa 2019

with them so they know what we're about. There are local boys and girls who grew up nearby who have bad reputations, but they come to the pub and they never give me any trouble. It's our approach that makes a difference.

One of my favourite things is when I see some of the local Black boys playing 'Ghetto-opoly' next to a table with people who have clearly just bought a three bedroom flat on Bellenden Road. You can see the integration because the common goal is for everyone to enjoy themselves and they all feel part of this community. We also make sure our events cater to everyone, like our queer nights, because we want to create safe spaces for the underrepresented. This pub is for everyone.

I feel that as a pub owner, we are just custodians to something that has been here for generations. The pub needs to remain the public house. Back in olde England, you could pop into any town and you would see

two things – a church and a pub. Somewhere where you sin and somewhere where you can repent. Pubs should be a home from home and if you can get people to spend more time in your pub than in their front room, then you have done good. We are achieving that.

I look at other places in Peckham and it seems they are just doing what they know and are appealing to who they can appeal to. Whether I agree with it or not – and more often I don't, I will still come down and support them but I know that I will always choose to do things differently. I'm going to make a positive change and add value to this community.

Growing up, I couldn't have imagined how Peckham would eventually evolve. I didn't know about Peckham's creative side. I did not know there was affluence here. I'm happy that this ecosystem has changed and that there are more creatives. For Black children, the fact that they can be creatives today in such a locality, is great. Don't get me wrong, it's still definitely a minority of Black people. In Black families there's still pressure to earn money doing sensible jobs like being a doctor or an engineer. But to know that Peckham is creative, more so now than it ever has been, opens up things for everyone to enjoy.

It's great to see that there are more Black social enterprises appearing and that working class kids from the local area, of all ethnicities, are doing positive work in the community. It's really exciting to see and I get a lot of them coming into Prince. That's what I like about Prince – allowing all these like-minded individuals into one space, to exchange ideas and to feel happy, to feel valued, to feel that they can make a change.

I'm really proud that there is a space that they can all congregate in.

I think the transformation of Peckham isn't a problem. I guarantee that if you asked people who grew up in Peckham in the 1990s, nine out of ten would say they want Peckham to improve. When regeneration is done responsibly, information is afforded to all and there are opportunities for those that live there.

The best thing for me about Peckham is that it's such a melting pot. Everyone is their own character and there is a lot of individuality. There is no more vibrant a place in London than Peckham. This is a fact.

Prince of Peckham seen from corner of Clayton Road and Queen's Road circa 2019

EILEEN CONN

Eileen Conn was born on Tyneside in 1941 and has lived in Peckham since 1973, when she set up her first home. Eileen is a community activist and founder of Peckham Vision. She has campaigned to get people involved in working together on their mutual interests in their shared local physical and social environment. Eileen recalls the changes she has observed in Peckham town centre, and the campaign to protect the historic rooftop view from the Peckham Multi Storey.

NOTICING CHANGE AND DIVERSITY

I've lived in Peckham for 50 years and I've watched Peckham get to the point at which Islington was, when I lived there. I've watched it happen for 40 odd years and when you get to my age, you've got an experience of the waves of social change, which are not in a straight line.

The place's social memory is very different, because of the different ages of people here. So, there are some people who've been born in the last 25 years and their understanding of what Peckham is, is totally different from mine. This is because they were born into a place that had become what it is, only in the previous 10 to 15 years and they imagine that it was like that forever, and they're surprised when there are more changes, but actually the thing that they think was permanent has only just arrived.

Peckham is very diverse, it's at least one of the most diverse places in London, on just about every single social characteristic, or economic characteristic you can think of. And that's happened, while I've lived here, it was not like that when I came. Back then, there were two main ethnic communities living in Peckham when I arrived in the 1970s; there was a big Afro Caribbean population and there was a big, very longstanding south London white population. It was lower levels of income, but not poor. A lot of people owned their own houses and a lot of people were in council housing. It's totally, dramatically changed since the 1970s and now we are a microcosm of the world.

And there are big issues arising from that, not surprisingly, because people have completely different understandings of who a human being is, what kinds of behaviour is appropriate, different kinds of belief systems about why we're on earth in the first place and all kinds of things.

The kinds of shops have totally changed. There were two big department stores, one at the north end of Rye Lane and one at the south, Jones and Higgins in the north and the Co-Op in the south. I used both of them, for household things, because I was just establishing my own house, so I'm very familiar with those. You could get everything in the Co-Op and Jones and Higgins but they've both gone. The buildings have both gone, except there's a remnant of both left. With Jones and Higgins, we've still got the tower which is the only bit left, and with the Co-Op, all we've got left is a symbol of green and pink on the side of a building, which is twice as high as the Co-Op building.

We had a shop of every kind, we also had an electricity showroom, The London Electricity Board and South Eastern Gas Board, they were all state-owned companies

Little did I know that I was going to be there for 50 years. At that age, you don't think about the length of time that you're going to be doing anything for really, but there I am, I'm still in the same place. When I did my house up, in those days, all the stuff that you needed for repairing and renovating a house, was actually available in shops in Rye Lane. So, I remember those shops, which are long since gone, that I used to go and queue in to get all the colours and the papers and the doorknobs, and all the rest of it, that I needed for my house, which needed to be renovated from top to bottom, inside and out.

I don't recall Peckham being dirty then, but the overriding feeling now is that it's dirty, there's a lot of rubbish, but then, of course, society's changed, there wasn't so much rubbish 50 years ago. Everything's packaged now and so there's so much rubbish and waste packaging, which everybody has to dispose of.

PROTECTING THE ROOFTOP VIEW

The Council's original plan was to demolish the multi-storey car park and the cinema. In Peckham Vision, we started a campaign in 2013 about protecting the rooftop view, because we knew that if we worked hard to draw attention to the demolition plan, we'd probably get a long-term life for that building, so that the view would remain a significant local asset that deserved protection.

There were ten levels, in what was the car park, and the top three levels had been occupied in the summer since 2008, by a project called Bold Tendencies and Frank's Café, which became very well known, because of the amazing view from the roof. Looking out from the rooftop over the Thames flood plain, with no tall buildings in front, the multi-storey building gives a dramatic experience and perspective of the meeting of sky and earth, as well as a spectacular view east and west across London.

In terms of the view, one of the things that is a contribution of ours, is that this is a historic and heritage view. And we know that, because in the 17th to 18th century, a well-known English writer called Daniel Defoe, was writing that one of the best views in the British Isles, was from Peckham looking towards the city, toward the river.

The reason for that is, that it is the Thames floodplain, so the land is almost completely flat from Peckham to the river, which means that you have an uninterrupted view of Central London. It's a very extensive flood plain of about three miles and it may be the longest and the widest in the whole of south

London. Certainly Daniel Defoe was talking about this amazing view, which at that time, he could get at street level, because of course, there were very few buildings.

Now, that view is available from the top of the Bussey Building and the multi-storey car park building. It is the same view, although what you are seeing is different, because of all the urban developments, but it's actually the same view, the same perspective. We think that also archaeologically, historically, it's actually an important view to protect and we still have a campaign to protect that view.

We worked to get the council to rethink and eventually they agreed to take the demolition of the multi-storey car park out of the New Southwark Plan and to rethink the future of the building. This led to a new business

The Council plans to redevelop the Peckham Multi Storey building and site after 2023.

Peckham Vision is campaigning to have the plan reviewed as the Planning Inspector recommended.

Peckham

Multi Storey

©Peckham Vision 2015 First edition www.peckhamvision.org

Peckham Vision works to inform people of local changes and how to take action. www.peckhamvision.org email: info@peckhamvision.org

Find out more, follow Peckham Vision on Facebook and Twitter. Peckham Vision shop: Holdrons Arcade 135A Rye Lane, Saturdays 2-5pm.

Community campaign merchandise item co-created by Corinne Turner, Clyde Watson and Eileen Conn. Black on pink t-towel with information text about the campaign, 2017

The wide, expansive rooftop view showing the meeting of the sky and earth and sweeping from east to west across the Thames floodplain towards central London

in the empty levels called Peckham Levels, run by a company called Makeshift, who created workspaces for local businesses and public facilities for the community. The dramatic view is also available from those levels. However the view is still under threat because of the continued proposals for tall buildings for the Aylesham Centre redevelopment.

JOY GREGORY

Joy Gregory was born in Bicester, Oxfordshire in 1959 to Jamaican parents. Like many creative people, she was drawn to Peckham and has lived in the area since 2013. Joy is an international artist working with photography and related media. Her practice is concerned with social and political issues which reference history and cultural differences in contemporary society. She reflects on how the area has influenced some of her work and the benefits and drawbacks of gentrification in Peckham.

I LIKE LIVING ROUND HERE

I like living round here. I used to live in another part of south London which used to be called Stockwell, but is now called Nine Elms, because it has its own tube station. But that area feels more transient, especially now with all those big buildings which have gone up, I don't even think the buyers live in this country.

Peckham feels more solid, but also because I work here and I feel very connected to the South London Gallery and I feel very connected to the Camberwell School of Art next door, because it's my neighbourhood and my closest friends live in Peckham.

I think gentrification is something that has happened across south London. When I first came to London when I was living in Brixton when I was at the Royal College of Art and people used to ask me, 'Why are you living there, it's so far out?' But it's only four stops on the tube. Back then, south London was like a no-go area and Burgess Park, nobody would ever walk through Burgess Park, you'd be lucky to get to the other side unscathed!

It's changed, for me it's safer, but for me the bad side, the sad side, is that a lot of people that have just ordinary jobs, they might work in the local shop or they might work at the hospital, or they might run a cab, they can't afford to live here anymore. And so they've had to move out. So the demographics, the diversity has sort of changed and you end up with two worlds. You end up with people who live in local authority housing, who are more and more in need to get that help, then you've got all the new builds. I've no idea who can afford to buy these half-work-half-live places this 'affordable' housing, you'd have to be on £50-£60K a year and most people I think are on £24-£25K.

Invisible lifeforce of plants – Chamomile. Print on silver gelatine paper by Joy Gregory, 2020

Yes things have improved and people want to live here, because it's hip and trendy and there is a lot going on. People are interested that there is a lot going on and that is right across the board, but it's whether or not you can afford to access the things that are going on. I mean how much does it cost to have a drink in the carpark bar?

Peckham has attracted a very artistic and creative community, I think it always did, but maybe they weren't as visible as they are today. I also think we have more 'tourists' coming in, because there are more clubs and bars and things happening, and those new-builds will be young people moving into the area, so they can be close to the heart of what is happening, it's pretty much what happened in Hoxton. I remember going to Hoxton to the Blue Note Club, I used to live around there in Wentworth Street which is near Liverpool Street, and people being horrified that I could live in such a terrible area. It was awful, almost derelict with broken windows with dirty net curtains hanging out of them. But I now feel the same thing has happened in Peckham, those places that no one would even look at, have now been improved.

I don't think I'm part of gentrification because I've never had any money. I think gentrification is about access really, things that were there before but also about nostalgia, so people don't like change whatever the form the change comes in, whether or not the newsagent closes down or the pie and eel shop isn't there anymore, those things shift gradually and change for different reasons. So whether or not its young people coming into the area, which is a natural thing, because young people become older people, then old people, it's part of the cycle of life, and they tend to stay if they like it a lot, or they move out depending on what it is they want to do.

My friend, who has lived in Peckham for 20 odd years, came here as a young stripling of 18 or 19 and lived in Peckham when it was a bit edgy, she now has her own children and still lives in Peckham. She has moved to six or seven different places and could never imagine moving outside of the area, but she has been very clever and every time she has bought, it's something investment wise. She's part of the gentrification in a way, but it is her home and she's part of Peckham and she's very involved in different community groups. But I think it's about whether or not you make it your home, or whether it's an investment, that's for me what matters.

What happened to that Windrush generation is they had to buy, because nobody would rent to them and they brought through informal banks. They never had to move out, they died off, or they sold up for a vast sums of money and went home. But their children who lived in the area, could never afford to buy here, because they didn't get the jobs or have those opportunities, so their children had to move out of the area, they moved out to Croydon or beyond!

I think, here it feels normal. I go to where I used to live, where my flat is, which I rent out so that I can afford to live round here, and its beyond gentrification, my place is next to a tube station which is in Zone 1! But I think I'm going to stay around here, I'd love to stay here, but I don't think I could afford to buy anywhere around here now.

THE BREATH IS INVISIBLE

At the beginning it was frightening and first of all, I didn't believe it. And when we did lockdown, suddenly it was so silent and even the sky was silent, there was no planes in the sky, and in London you are so used to the noise, and for there to be no noise in London, especially central London, was quite a scary thing.

I started taking walks in Burgess Park which is near where I live, as you were allowed out for an hour, and I went out for an hour and a half of course, I think everyone did the same, and I actually started to enjoy it. I started watching the weather change, I enjoyed watching the plants change, I enjoyed the silence. I enjoyed nodding to people or noticing people at first, you know people who

I'd never seen before and eventually starting up conversations with people.

Burgess Park is a corridor, a big expanse of land between Peckham and Camberwell which brings both of them together. And it's quite interesting the park and how it's changed a bit now, but prior to Covid, you could really tell the differences between the populations. So towards the Camberwell Road end of the park with the tennis courts, there would be people having picnics with glasses of wine and hanging out, and then you go to the other side of the bridge and there would be families with millions of children, going wild on the playground and they would be much more diverse, whereas it is was less diverse the other side. But it's much more mixed now, I think the pandemic has actually shifted things in that respect.

It was great to walk there in lockdown and I saw people that I knew and I used to bump into people all the time who knew friends of mine. I used to walk around the whole expanse of the park and I remember towards the end, it would take me two and a half hours to walk round the park, because I'd be stopping to chat with people. I feel that Camberwell and Peckham almost merged into one because of the park being a shared space and it was where people were hanging out and taking their exercise.

But one of the things I did, was that I had some boxes of photographic paper which I was never going to use and I started picking up plants off the ground on my walks. I have all sorts of rules that I never pick anything, so I'd pick up plants which had been discarded and bring them back home and put them on this silver gelatine paper and just watch the colours change, because there was nothing else to do. It was very meditative. I started

to make these prints and one of the things I noticed was that if they were fresh, they created an aura around them that was like the breath of the plant, this invisible breath. And it made me think more about nature and how dependent we are on nature and how we are part of nature.

Prior to that, when you are running around the city, you don't think you are part of nature at all, because you are clamped onto your phone and the next task that you have to do. And I think being immersed in nature, even in the city and suddenly hearing birds and having time, because of lockdown, to notice that plants breathe and they are breathing out oxygen and taking in carbon dioxide, whilst we breath out carbon dioxide and breathe in oxygen – that interdependency inspired that work and it became work, but it didn't start off like that. And having time to observe things, I would never have had that time before.

During Covid, we were afraid of breath, if someone breathed on you, you could 'pop your clogs', or so you believed at the time, because we didn't know anything about this new disease. And at the same time, George Floyd's death happened and it brought home how important breath is to you and I was really struck by that.

I was so struck by this that I actually went on marches! I can't believe I went on marches in lockdown. It was an awakening! What was important was obviously there were lots of young people about, but it wasn't just Black people out, everybody was out and everybody was angry. That was quite empowering and it also made me feel quite emotional that things might be better for the next generation.

KARIN GREENE

Karin Greene was born near Bridgetown, Barbados in 1948. Like many Caribbean people of The Windrush Generation she answered the call to come to the Motherland in search of work and opportunities. In 1967 she left her family home and travelled to England, where she braved the cold and met with racism and discriminatory attitudes. In spite of the difficulties Karin faced, she also found freedom, independence, and a place to raise her own family. Karin reflects on her experiences of migration and settlement.

ENGLAND NEEDS YOU

I came to England when I was 21 and I thought it was freedom! I wasn't frightened at all, I was excited! You know, getting away from restrictions, not having to come in by 8.00 or 9.00 at night. At home, I didn't go anywhere, apart from church functions and things like that and I was studying, doing a bit of shorthand and stuff.

I came by plane in 1970. We had two stop-over flights, one in Grenada and one in Bermuda and then we flew into Heathrow Airport. At that time, the Barbados High Commission had people who would put you up in their homes, so before you came, you had arranged a place to live and you had rented accommodation, so that bit wasn't difficult.

But I didn't have the right clothes and it was freezing! And nobody said to get a coat. I was so lucky, because the landlady's daughter had all these lovely coats, fur, warm coats and she leant them to me and there were three of us, and when we got our first pay, we all went out and bought a coat of our own. But the cold hit you! But it didn't deter me, it made me more determined to see it out.

On the way coming from Heathrow, I was looking around me and there was so much smoke coming from chimneys, that we thought they was factories. But the guy with us said, 'Oh no they're not factories they are houses. They burn coal and they burn paraffin.' So that was an eye opener for me.

We were lucky, because we came to live with a Barbadian household in Grove Park Camberwell. The family had the ground floor and the lodgers were upstairs. It wasn't too hard to adjust, because we lived in a Black household in a three storey house. Juanita, one of the daughters of the household, took us out one Saturday and we walked from

Karin, London, 1971

Grove Park to Peckham and she showed us the different shops and the area.

In Choumert Road they had all this West Indian food and there was a market, and then we were free and by that time there were stalls catering for Asians and West Indians and all. We did our own cooking and there were two gas cookers upstairs in the house and we had our own paraffin heaters in the bedroom, so you could put the kettle on in the morning to make tea and wash in the bathroom.

I used to walk to Peckham from Grove Park to Choumert Road to do my shopping. When I first came there was a shop that sell everything from hairs pins to any practical thing, it was a real old fashioned shop you can have Vicks vapour rub, you can have Benji's Balsam, you can have a tonic, whatever you want… you can have a bucket. It was interesting and it spread out. There was a butchers on the opposite corner which sold everything, offal, anything you wanted. There was a fish shop on Rye Lane and after a while if he know you, you say what you

wanted and he'd have it ready for you when you came back.

We didn't have to go into town at all. I didn't go up the West End until the 80s, I didn't have to, because we had all the shops along Rye Lane and we had Sainsbury's and further down and at the other end we had Tescos, we had all the West Indian shops along Choumert Road and we had a Kennedys. We also had Jones and Higgins the big department store, they had all the floors, everything you want, furniture, haberdashery everything you didn't have to go up the West End to get anything, we had the choice

There was the indoor market, opposite the Clarks and you could get in from Rye Lane or one of the side streets and they had furniture shop in there, they meat shops and West Indian food shop Jack, they had hairdresser in there at the end, we had everything we need in Peckham.

I wasn't homesick, but I missed my dad and my son, I missed my mum a bit too. I missed my dad, because we were like two peas in a pod and I would write letters fairly often. My dad had put up his land as collateral, so that I could come to England and we had to pay it back, the money for travelling by a certain amount of time, if not, they would forfeit the land.

Fortunately, the Barbados High Commission had organised an interview for me at a Lyon's Corner Shop and they had the job waiting for us. I ended up working in the City at London Wall where all the City gents would come in with their bowler hats and an umbrella on their arms, briefcases and pinstripe suits. One of my favourite customers at Lyons Corner House was Willy and I knew what time he came in and he used to always have the same, two poached eggs on toast. And as soon as he cracked open the door, I would put his eggs on to poach the way he liked

them and by the time he sat down and that, I'd got it ready and was bringing it over to him and one day he said to me, 'Don't you do that my dear, you're not a slave' and I appreciated that. They were mostly friendly, only one was beastly and I put him in his place and I nearly walloped him.

I worked Monday to Friday, came home and do the washing or shopping, get up early on Sunday do the cleaning. I used to go out Friday night, Saturday night and Sunday night and then back at work again on Monday morning. I also went to events run by Barbadian Overseas Friends Community Association or BOFCA and they had gatherings and get-togethers. There was quite a large Barbadian community in Camberwell, Peckham and Brixton, although Brixton was more Jamaican.

PECKHAM LIFE AND POLICE

No need to fear for your life or anything in Peckham. I felt safe in Peckham there was no problem whatsoever, I felt safe and just because you are Black every person would say Hello! They didn't care which country you come from you know, it was just a good community and we didn't have all this fighting and thing.

Yes, I had a few negatives, when I first came, when white people come along, a white woman especially, she will put her handbag in at the front or clasp it tightly, because they think you are different and you are going to rob them, so there was that aspect in the mid 70s, especially if you go to a place where they didn't have many Black people you will see them grabbing their handbags, so that was the negative bits. When I feel really

frustrated I say, 'You don't have anything that I want!' because sometimes I'm human and you reach the stage when you think, this is annoying.

But actually it got worse in the 80s than when we first came here, because they think you are a Black person and you are going to rob them.

I faced prejudice, but nothing I couldn't handle, because I grew up with all men in the house and they taught me how to look after myself. But I learned to walk away, because someone told me that if I did anything, I would end up in prison because of my colour and that, you know. And my landlady said, don't retaliate against anybody, but I used words instead, I like using words.

Because if you didn't get used to it, it would annoy you and if it annoy you, then you are going to over react and if you react, then you are going to be put in a cell. And being a Black person in a prison cell wasn't going to be a very nice thing. There was a lot of prejudice from the police and they didn't know any better. Sometimes we spoke up and they said we had a big mouth and they didn't like it because we weren't humble. We knew humility, but we knew when to speak up, but that was the way it was.

I stayed away from the police, but saying that, if I got lost, I'd say, 'Excuse me officer,' or I say, 'Good morning,' because coming from the West Indies, you do not pass a person without saying good morning or good afternoon and the few times I had to speak to a police officer, they were helpful, but I stayed away from them as much as possible.

Peckham has gone through a lot of changes over the years, it's become more gentrified, certain parts are nice and certain parts are not very nice. It's in perpetual change, with different people and cultures coming here. Some of it I enjoy because it's a different avenue and one should not have a closed mind. It's not impinging on my life and some of it is enhancing my life and you get to see different things and different aspects of life and in the end, the changes might be for the greater good. But whilst it is happening, like when Black people first came to Peckham and people perceived it as going a certain way, it can be tough, but over the years, it's become acceptable to think, that we can contribute to society and everyone is contributing somehow.

We have to live together and we can all learn from each other and we don't have to adapt to each other's life-style. We can accommodate each other. When we first came here, some people accommodated us and some didn't. So its perpetual change and if we learn to live with it and learn to live as the human race, not of people of different colour, creed of religion, that we are one race, the human race. If we accept that, whatever come in our way we can adapt to it. We are all human beings first of all.

BUILDINGS REPAIRED AND RESTORED THROUGH THE PECKHAM TOWNSCAPE HERITAGE INITIATIVE

The Townscape Heritage Initiative (THI) has contributed to the special character of the Rye Lane Peckham Conservation Area by supporting works to the external fabric of key buildings and shopfronts. Nine properties clustered around the junction of Peckham Hill Street and Peckham High Street have been repaired and restored through the THI. Building owners have contributed to the costs, and the works have been carried out according to the specific standards required for conservation projects, using appropriate materials.

Thank you to the building owners who have contributed to this project.

THI project delivery team
Architects: Jan Kattein Architects
Project Architect: Felicity Barbur
Project Managers: Faithful & Gould
Cost Control: William G Dick Partnership LLP
Contractors: Triton (Phases 1 and 2)
Standage (Phase 3)

For more information on the THI building projects, see Peckham Heritage website peckhamheritage.org.uk

This map opposite shows the completed THI projects within the 'heritage cluster' around the junction of Peckham Hill Street and Peckham High Street

The THI buildings are:

Peckham High Street north side
1. 105 Peckham High Street
   Manze's
2. 130 Peckham Hill Street
   Filishack
3. 109 Peckham High Street
   The Greyhound
4. 119 Peckham High Street
   The Old Crown Hotel

Peckham High Street south side
5. 86 Peckham High Street
   Acuherbal
6. 88 Peckham High Street
   Mama
7. 100 Peckham High Street
8. 102 Peckham High Street
   The Peckham Cobbler
9. 116 Peckham High Street
   The Red Bull

PECKHAM HERITAGE
REGENERATION PARTNERSHIP

PECKHAM HIGH STREET HERITAGE CLUSTER

Library

Library

CANAL HEAD
PUBLIC
SQUARE

El Sub Sta

El Sub Sta

Posts

TCBs

TCBs

165

Orchard
Mission
Hall

MISSION PLACE

121a

PO

121 to 125

PH

109

13 to
115

119

126

131

107

99

91

CR

Ward Bdy

6.5m

71

77

67

PECKHAM HIGH STREET

PH

116

BULL YARD

118

120

122

PH

PE

Central
Buildings

99

The Aylesham Centre

Morrison's

Posts

Posts

RYE LANE

El Sub S

Posts

Posts

Car Park

217

BUILDINGS REPAIRED AND RESTORED THROUGH THE PECKHAM TOWNSCAPE HERITAGE INITIATIVE

PECKHAM HIGH STREET NORTH SIDE

105 Peckham High Street
Manze's

130 Peckham Hill Street
Filishack

109 Peckham High Street
The Greyhound

119 Peckham High Street
The Old Crown Hotel

PECKHAM HIGH STREET SOUTH SIDE

86 Peckham High Street
Acuherbal

88 Peckham High Street
Mama

100 Peckham High Street

102 Peckham High Street
The Peckham Cobbler

116 Peckham High Street
The Red Bull

ACKNOWLEDGEMENTS

History – Derek Kinrade
Architectural notes – Benedict O'Looney
Oral History extracts – Sarah Gudgin
History of community action – Eileen Conn
Graphic design and layout – Laura Mingozzi-Marsh
Image research – Angharad Davies
Community action image research – Corinne Turner
Additional historical research – Deborah Elliott
Editor – Claire Davies
Contributing Editor – Kate White
Project coordination – Claire Hegarty

Inception comment
Julie Mallett
Kate White
Mark McGinlay
Nancy Coleman-Frank
Rebecca Wilmshurst

Oral history subjects
Anila Ladwa
Barry Jenkins
Dr Charmaine Brown
Clement Ogbonnaya
Dimitri Launder
Eileen Conn
Joy Gregory
Karin Green

Comment on text
Clyde Watson
Deborah Elliott
Eileen Conn
Julie Mallett
Jonathan Wilson
Lorelie Wilson
Michelle Shaw
Nancy Coleman Frank
The Pioneer Health Foundation Trustees

Southwark Council
Thanks to Magda Bartosch, Michael Tsoukaris and their colleagues in Environment, Neighbourhood and Growth for comments and insights

Southwark Archive
Thanks to Dr Patricia Dark, Helen Savage and Chris Scales for assistance in image research

South London Gallery
Thanks to Ben Messih, Carey Robinson and Eleanor Costello for development and delivery of the 'Grow Our Histories' oral history project

SELECT BIBLIOGRAPHY

Allport, Douglas, (1841). *Collections, Illustrative of the Geology, History, Antiquities, and Associations, of Camberwell, and the Neighbourhood.*

August, Mabel, *Life in Old South London.*

Beasley, John D, (1973). *Peckham in the 19th Century.*

Beasley, John D, (1974). *Labouring for Posterity - the Story of Peckham Methodist Church.*

Beasley, John D, (1985). *Building Together - the Story of Peckham Methodist Church.*

Beasley, John D, (2009). *Origin of Place Names in Peckham & Nunhead: Amberley.*

Beasley, John D, (2009). *Peckham & Nunhead Through Time:* Amberley.

Beasley, John D, (2012). *Peckham & Nunhead Residents and Visitors:* Amberley.

Beck, William & Ball, Frederick T, (1869 reprinted 2009): *The London Friends' Meetings:* Pronoun Press.

Beecher Hogan, Charles, (April 1947). *The Manuscript of Winston's 'Theatric Tourist' (1805).* Theatre Notebook, vol.1, no.7.

Blanch, William Harnett, (1875). *Ye Parish of Camerwell. A Brief Account of the Parish of Camberwell, its History and Antiquities.*

Butler, David M, (1999). *The Quaker Meeting Houses of Britain:* Friends Historical Society

Butt, Stephen, (2011). *Paranormal Leicester:* Amberley.

Charlesworth, Tim, (1988). *The Architecture of Peckham*: Chener Books.

Cleal, Edward, (1908). *The Story of Congregationalism in Surrey:* Kessinger.

Conford, Philip, (2020). *Realising Health: The Peckham Experiment, its Descendants, and the Spirit of Hygiea:* Cambridge Scholars Publishing.

Constanduros Mabel, (1946). *Shreds and Patches:* Lawson & Dunn.

de Crespigny, Richard Rafe, (2017). *Champions from Normandy, an Essay on the Early History of the Champion de Crespigny Family 1350-1800:* Anne Young.

Defoe, Daniel, (1978). *A Tour Through the Whole Island of Great Britain (1724-1727):* Penguin Classics.

Dyos, Harold James, (1961). *Victorian Suburb: A Study of the Growth of Camberwell:* University Press.

Edwards, Edward, (2010): *Free Town Libraries, Their Formation, Management, and History:* Cambridge University Press.

Glucksberg, Luna, (2013): *Wasting the Inner-city: Waste, Value and Anthropology on the Estates.*

Guillery, Peter, (1998). *Royal Commission on the Historic Monuments of England survey report.*

Guillery, Peter, (2004). *The Small House in Eighteenth-Century London:* Yale University Press.

Hahn, W J A, (1950). *Camberwell Golden Jubilee booklet.*

Harry, Florence. Gentrification: *Peckham and The Future of The Metropolis.*

Hartnoll, Phyllis (Ed), (1951). *The Oxford Companion to the Theatre:* Oxford University Press.

Hewison, Robert (2022) *Passport to Peckham: Culture and Creativity in a London Village:* Goldsmiths Press

Highfill Jr, Philip H, Burnim, Kalman A & Langhans, Edward A, (1973). *A Biographical Dictionary of Actors, Actresses, Musicians, Dancers, Managers and Other Stage Personnel in London 1660-1800:* Southern Illinois University Press.

Hodgson, Norma & Baker, Sarah, (1952) *Studies in English Theatre History:* Society for Theatrical Research.

Holmes, Isabella M, (1896): *The London Burial Grounds: Notes on Their History from the Earliest Times to the Present Day:* T. F. Unwin.

Inwood, Stephen, (1999). *A History of London:* Macmillan.

Jones, Derek. *The History of Rate-Supported Public Libraries in London 1850-1900.*

Johnson, B H, (1952). *Berkeley Square to Bond Street: the Early History of the Neighbourhood:* John Murray.

King, Sam, (2004). *Climbing Up the Rough Side of the Mountain:* FastPrint.

Lennox-Boyd, Arabella, (1990). *Private Gardens of London:* Weidenfeld & Nicolson.

Macqueen-Pope, Walter, (1948). *Haymarket, Theatre of Perfection:* W. H. Allen.

McMenemy, David. *Public Libraries in the UK - History and Values:* University of Strathclyde.

O'Neill, Jean & McLean, Elizabeth P, (2008). *Peter Collinson and the 18th Century Natural History Exchange:* American Philosophical Society.

Pearse, Innes H, & Crocker, Lucy H, (1943). *The Peckham Experiment: A Study in the Living Structure of Society:* Allen & Unwin.

Pigot, J & Co, (1824), *Pigot & Co.'s Metropolitan Guide & Book of Reference to Every Street, Court, Lane, Passage, Alley and Public Building, in the cities of London & Westminster, the Borough of Southwark, and Their Respective Suburbs:* London & Manchester Directory Office.

Roethe, J & Smith, J, (2009). *Central Peckham, London Borough of Southwark: Historic Area Assessment:* Fort Cumberland: Historic England.

Rosenfeld, Sybil, (1970). *Strolling Players and Drama in the Provinces, 1660-1765:* Octagon.

Scales, Chris, (2017). *Peckham Streets a photographic history:* The Peckham Society.

Scott-Samuel, Alex, (1990). *Total Participation, Total Health: Reinventing the Peckham Health Centre for the 1990s:* Scottish Academic Press.

Sexby, J J, (2014). *The Municipal Parks, Gardens, and Open Spaces of London: Their History and Associations:* Oxford University Press.

Stallibrass, Alison, (1989). *Being Me and Also Us: Lessons from the Peckham Experiment:* Scottish Academic Press.

Stephens, Jennifer, (2022). *The Peckham Settlement, 1896-2000: A Story of Poverty, Privilege, Pioneering and Partnership:* Stephens Press.

Toksvig, Sandy, (2019). *Between the Stops: The View of My Life from the Top of the Number 12 bus:* Virago Press.

Williamson, George C, (1889). *Trade Tokens Issued in the Seventeenth Century:* Elliot Stock.

Wood, Leslie, (1947). *The Miracle of the Movies:* Burke.

Wulf, Andrea, (2008). *The Brother Gardeners: Botany, Empire and the Birth of an Obsession:* Windmill.

ADDITIONAL ONLINE SOURCES & PUBLICATIONS

- John Boughton: Municipal Dreams in Housing - municipaldreams.wordpress.com

- Charles Booth's poverty maps - booth.lse.ac.uk

- Damilola Taylor anniversary: Are Peckham Improvements Skin Deep?, The Guardian, 26 November 2010

- The Demographic Characteristics of Immigrant Populations; Council of Europe

- highwaymeninpeckham.co.uk/letters/

- The Friend archives

- Hansard

- Housing Today archive

- londongardenstrust.org

- Morning Advertiser archive

- Oremus, the magazine of Westminster Cathedral

- Peckham Heritage website (formerly Peckham Heritage Regeneration Partnership) www. peckhamheritage.org.uk

- Peckham Peculiar archive https://peckhampeculiar. tumblr.com/

- Peckham Society News archive www. peckhamsociety.org.uk/

- peckhamresidents.wordpress.com

- Peckham Rye Park website www.peckhamryepark.org

- Peckham Vision website www.peckhamvision.org

- Pioneer Health Foundation archive www.thephf.org

- Historic England Register of Parks and Gardens of Special Historic Interest historicengland.org.uk/ listing/what-is-designation/registered-parks-and-gardens/

- South London Gallery Archive for 'Grow our Histories: Peckham Heritage' oral histories www. southlondongallery.org/archive-room/archive-andlocal-history/oral-history-peckham/Southwark Council planning register www.southwark.gov.uk/ planning-and-building-control/planning-applications/ planning-register-search-view-and-comment-on-planning-applications

- Southwark Heritage website www.heritage. southwark.gov.uk

- Southwark News archive https://southwarknews. co.uk/

- William Marshall Papers, Southwark Archive

IMAGE CREDITS

46 (bottom)	Workshops built in the 1930s by the London Association for the Blind	© Southwark Archives
47 (top)	Corner of Rye Lane looking south before the demolition of the buildings on west side for the extension of Jones and Higgins premises, 1894	© Southwark Archives
47 (bottom)	Advertisement for a performance at Hanover Chapel, 1824	© Southwark Archives
48	Hanover Chapel in use as Peckham Picture Playhouse, c.1910 - 1914	© Southwark Archives
49	Plaque still visible on Rye Lane today denoting the site of Hanover Chapel, 1981	© Southwark Archives
50	Portrait of Peter Collinson, F.R.S, 1780	© The New York Public Library Digital Collection
51	Great Martigon …from Pennsylvania painted by Georg Dionysius Ehret. Originates from the library of Peter Collinson, who noted on the back that the Martigon was sent to him by John Bartram and flowered in his 'Garden at Peckham' in September 1736	© Nancy Coleman-Frank from folio belonging to the Earl of Derby.
52	Interior view of hallway in Peckham House, 1953	© Southwark Archives
53	Exterior view of Peckham House, 1953	© Southwark Archives
54	Peckham Secondary School for Girls, Camberwell, London: view of the gymnasium from the east, 1958	© RIBA Collections
55	Edward Hassell's 1831 image of the front of Marlborough House	© Surrey History Centre
57	Detail of Dewhirst map, 1842	© Southwark Archives
59 (top)	Aquatint of Heaton's Folly by John Hassell, 1804	© London Metropolitan Archives
59 (bottom)	Detail of Peckham town centre shown on OS Map, 1871	© Southwark Archives
60	Interior view of St Chrysostom, date unknown	© Southwark Archives
61	Exterior view of St Chrysostom, date unknown	© Southwark Archives
62 (left)	The Burning of Peckham Methodist Church, Queen's Road, 1972	© Southwark Archives
62 (right)	Present day Peckham Methodist Church rebuilt behind Cherry Tree Court, 1985	© Southwark Archives
63	Peckham Methodist Church before the fire, 1972	© Southwark Archives
64	Founders George Randell Higgins (left) and Edwin Jones (right) on Rye Lane, date unknown	© Southwark Archives
65	Jones and Higgins Rye Lane, date unknown	© Southwark Archives
66 (top left)	Jones and Higgins on corner of Peckham High Street and Rye Lane with its Victorian clocktower, 1910	© Southwark Archives
66 (top right)	Entrance to Jones and Higgins workshops and stables on Hanover Park, date unknown	© Southwark Archives
66 (bottom right)	Text reads 'Messrs. Jones and Higgins' original shop 3 Rye Lane, formally 1 Coburn Terrace, March 16 1867'	© Southwark Archives
67 (top left)	Jones and Higgins lighting department, 1884	© Southwark Archives
67 (top right)	Jones and Higgins delicatessen, date unknown	© Southwark Archives
67 (bottom right)	Poster advertising the Jones Girls fashion show, date unknown	© Southwark Archives
68	Jones and Higgins cafe, date unknown	© Southwark Archives
69 (top)	Jones and Higgins entrance below clocktower on corner of Peckham High Street and Rye Lane, date unknown	© Southwark Archives
69 (bottom)	The Clocktower on St Mark's Square, Venice, as drawn by Francisco de Holanda in his Álbum dos Desenhos das Antigualhas, 1538-1540	© WikiMedia Commons
70	Brewery worker with a glass of beer, 1860	© Southwark Archives
71 (top)	Gordon's Brewery, in The Building News, January 12th 1877	© Southwark Archives
71 (bottom)	Soldiers and horses from the Camberwell Division of the Royal Field Artillery on Lyndhurst Way (formally road), 1915	© Southwark Archives
72	Interior of Holdron's Arcade at 147 Rye Lane, circa 1927	© Southwark Archives
73 (top)	Holdron's Arcade, 117-125 Rye Lane, circa 1930	© Southwark Archives
73 (bottom)	Exterior of Holdron's main building, 135-147 Rye Lane, circa 1927	© Southwark Archives
74	Khan's Bargain shop, 135 Rye Lane, 2013	© Corinne Turner
75	Holdron's department store and arcade glass concrete roof, 1936	© RIBA Collections
77	Sketch by Benedict O'Looney, 2022	© Corinne Turner 2013
78	Crown Theatre (left) on Peckham High Street, 1905	© Southwark Archives
79 (top)	Crown Theatre, date unknown	© Southwark Archives
79 (bottom)	Gaumont Picture House on site of the Crown Theatre, 1979	© Southwark Archives
80	Crown Theatre Peckham published by the Libraries Department, London Borough of Southwark in 1977	© Southwark Archives
81	Poster advertising Carl Rosa Opera Company performances at The Crown Theatre by Smith and Bayley, 1903	© V&A Archives

PART 2: IN NEED OF RESTORATION

82-83	Peckham Rye Station forecourt, 1969	© Southwark Archives
86	Peckham High Street, 1979	© Southwark Archives
87 (top)	56-66 Peckham High Street by Charles Kirshaw, 1830	© John Doddemeade / John Beasley
87 (bottom)	Interior view of restoration and renovation work at 62 Peckham High Street in 2021	© Benedict O'Looney

89	A late nineteenth century painting (exact location unknown) showing the timber framed houses that characterised the village of Peckham, 1890	© Southwark Archives
90	Quaker Meeting House, 1982	© Southwark Archives
91	Frederick Farrand, (1786 - 1858) - Quaker and builder, who lived at Elm Grove, Peckham	© Farrand family
92	Shard's Terrace located at the junction of Peckham High Street and Peckham Hill Street, 1979	© Southwark Archives
93	Manze's after repair and restoration, with newly painted signage, 2021	© Elliot Potts
94 (left)	130 Peckham Hill Street before refurbishment, 2021	© Peckham THI
94 (right)	130 Peckham Hill Street after refurbishment, 2021	© Angharad Davies
95	Rye Lane Baptist Chapel, 1972	© Southwark Archives
96	Harvest Festival at Rye Lane Baptist Chapel, 1905	© Southwark Archives
97	Rye Lane Baptist Chapel, date unknown	© Southwark Archives
98	Exterior of Peckham Public Hall, 2022	© Angharad Davies
99	Central Hall, Peckham High Street, 1935	© Southwark Archives
100	The Central Hall, a grand space to the rear of 41-43 Peckham High Street, 2018	© Peckham Vision
101	Blackjack table at Maverick Club at Central Hall, 1966	© PA Images / Alamy Stock Photo
102	The Bussey Building, 2011	© Benedict O'Looney
103	Interior in the Bussey Building, with tall cast iron columns and pairs of steel windows.	© Sunset Studios/Alex Rimmer
105	Geo. G. Bussey manufacturers featured in Tatler Magazine, 1906	© Lorelie Wilson
107 (left)	Table Croquet set produced by Bussey's, date unknown	© Benedict O'Looney
107 (right)	Table Croquet set produced by Bussey's, date unknown	© Benedict O'Looney
108	C&A Modes at 117- 125 Rye Lane, 1981	© Southwark Archives
110	Peckham Library, 2008	Gerhard Bissell © RIBA Collections
111	View looking north from Rye Lane towards Peckham Library Square, canopy for Jones and Higgins department store in foreground with Whitten Timber Yard beyond, 1979	© Southwark Archives
112	Interior view of Peckham Library under construction, 1999	© Southwark Archives
113	Peckham Square shortly after construction of Peckham Arch, 1994	© Southwark Archives

PART 3: IN BETTER HEALTH

116-117	View from the top of Witcombe Point with Peckham Levels in foreground, 2022	© Angharad Davies
120	Wood's Road following renovations, 2022	© Angharad Davies
121	6-10 Queen's Road with neighbouring premises of Carter & Son vat makers (now 2 Wood's Road), 1980	© Southwark Archives
122	98-104 Peckham High Street, 2023. At the centre of this historic group, numbers 100 and 102 were repaired through the Peckham Townscape Heritage Initiative.	© Elliot Potts
123 (top)	100-108 Peckham High Street, 1928	© Southwark Archives
123 (bottom)	Peckham High Street, 1979	© Southwark Archives
124	Back of 98-100 Peckham High Street, said to be the remains of the Peckham Theatre, 2000	© Southwark Archives
125	Plaque from school that occupied 100 Peckham High Street from 1822 until 1880s uncovered during restoration, 2019	© Angharad Davies
126	Archival photograph of Licensed Victuallers' Benevolent Institution, date unknown	© Southwark Archives
127	Licensed Victuallers' Asylum, 1830	© Southwark Archives
128	Illustration of Prince Albert laying the foundation stone for the new wing of the Licensed Victuallers' Asylum, published in The London Illustrated News, 10 July 1858	© Southwark Archives
129	The wedding of Nancy Coleman-Frank and author Derek Kinrade at the Asylum Chapel, 2018	© Derek Kinrade and Nancy Coleman-Frank
130	Present day view of Stafford Street Chapel, 2022	© Angharad Davies
131	View of Stafford Street Chapel, 1980	© Southwark Archives
132	Gordon Road Resettlement Centre, 1986	© Southwark Archives
133	Exterior view of the Department of Health and Social Security, 1981	© Southwark Archives
134 (top)	Gordon Road Resettlement Centre Dormitory, 1986	© Southwark Archives
134 (middle)	The workhouse in Gordon Road, Camberwell nicknamed 'The Bastille', date unknown	© Southwark Archives
134 (bottom)	Gordon Road Resettlement Centre Chapel, 1986	© Southwark Archives
135 (left)	Nazareth House, 1984	© Southwark Archives
135 (right)	Gordon Road Workhouse Interior, date unknown	© Southwark Archives
136	The Old Waiting Room, 2019	© Quintin Lake
137	An early view of Peckham Rye Station shortly after the building's completion, circa 1866	© Southwark Archives
138-139	South section through Peckham Rye Station, contract drawing number 6. This drawing cuts through the Old Waiting Room and shows the now lost plaster ceiling in that tall space, 1865	© Network Rail Corporate Archive
140	View from Rye Lane with station visible in background, 1927	© Southwark Archives
141 (top)	Peckham Rye Station forecourt, 1969	© Southwark Archives
141 (bottom)	Bomb damage to railway tracks during World War II, 1944	© Southwark Archives

142	Peckham Vision community meeting on 2nd August 2012, the first evening of the 3 day town centre exhibition in the Old Waiting Room	© Adrian Perkins 2012
143	Pocket-sized map developed by Peckham Vision from 2011 in association with Southwark Rail Users Group (SRUG). This version was created and distributed from 2013, with an explanatory note on the reverse	© Peckham Vision 2013
144 (top)	Poster for the Peckham Vision stall at the Open Arches weekend 28th to 30th June 2013, to publicise the issues arising from the Peckham Rye station redevelopment plans	© Peckham Vision 2013
144 (bottom)	Network Rail and Southwark Council consultation in January 2014, where the community rejected plans to demolish all commercial buildings on the station site and clear out all businesses	© Corinne Turner 2014
145 (top)	Peckham Vision's graphic poster to publicise from 2014 the existence of the Art Deco buildings clustered around Peckham Rye station	© Peckham Vision 2014
145 (bottom)	Collecting signatures on the petition in 2013 for public toilets in central Rye Lane	© Corinne Turner 2013
146	Peckham Rye Station - Contract Drawing number 1, ground level plan, 1935	© Network Rail Corporate Archive
149	Staircase at Peckham Rye Station, 2019	© Edmund Sumner
150	Interior view of service taking place at Our Lady of Sorrows, 2022	© Angharad Davies
151	Exterior view of Our Lady of Sorrows, adjacent to Friary Hall, 1972	© Southwark Archives
153	Streetscape showing the Old Fire Station to left of billboards, 1979	© Southwark Archives
154	The Old Fire Station, converted and restored for South London Gallery by 6a architects, 2018	© Dan Weill
155	Detail of lantern on building facade, 2022	© Angharad Davies
156 (top)	Present day view of the Old Mill Building, 2022	© Angharad Davies
156 (bottom)	Blackpool Road with Old Mill Building in distance, 1982	© Southwark Archives
157	Choumert Square, 1982	© Southwark Archives
158	Choumert Square, early June 2010	© Rebecca Wilmshurst
159	The Red Bull, 1995	© Southwark Archives
160 (top)	The Greyhound, 1979	© Southwark Archives
160 (bottom)	Greyhound token from *Trade Tokens Issued in the Seventeenth Century. A new and revised edition of W. Boyne's work*, by G.C. Williamson	© Southwark Archives
161 (top right)	Site photo of restoration work underway at The Crown, 2019	© Jan Kattein Architects
161 (bottom left)	The Crown as the Tapas Room, 2022	© Angharad Davies
161 (bottom right)	The Crown on Peckham High Street, 1889	© Southwark Archives
162	Glazed wall tiles uncovered during restoration of The Red Bull, 2018	© Angharad Davies
163	Ceramic mural showing The Trial of Queen Katharine in The Red Bull, 2018	© Angharad Davies
164 (left)	88 Peckham High Street before refurbishment, 2021	© Peckham THI
164 (right)	88 Peckham High Street after refurbishment, 2021	© Elliot Potts
165 (left)	86 Peckham High Street before refurbishment, 2021	© Peckham THI
165 (right)	86 Peckham High Street after refurbishment, 2021	© Elliot Potts
166 (left)	Lending department at the Livesey Building, 1905	© Southwark Archives
166 (right)	Livesey Library, likely to be 1905	© Southwark Archives
167	Exterior view of Livesey Museum, 1987	© Southwark Archives
168	Mural at the Livesey Building, 1980	© Southwark Archives
169	Statue of Sir George Livesey, 1980	© Southwark Archives
170	The bandstand on Peckham Rye, 1905	© Southwark Archives
171	Drawing of Peckham Rye Park looking south towards Forest Hill, 1863	© Southwark Archives
172 (top)	Pond on Peckham Rye, date unknown	© Southwark Archives
172 (bottom)	Peckham Rye Lido, date unknown	© Southwark Archives
173 (top)	The Sexby Garden, 1938	© Southwark Archives
173 (bottom)	Whalebone arch, the remains of the whalebone shack, on Peckham Rye, date unknown	© Southwark Archives
174 (top left)	Water fountain at the entrance to Peckham Rye Park donated by Edwin Higgins, 1914	© Southwark Archives
174 (top right)	Postcard of the Old English Garden in Peckham Rye Park, 1904	© Southwark Archives
174 (bottom left)	Religious gathering on Peckham Rye Common, 1953	© Southwark Archives
174 (bottom right)	The opening of Peckham Rye Park. Banners belong to trade union whose members took part in the procession from Camberwell Vestry Hall, 14 May 1894	© Southwark Archives
175	Present day view of Best Western Hotel, 2022	© Angharad Davies
177	133 Rye Lane, 1981	© Southwark Archives
178	Pioneer Health Centre, St Mary's Road, Peckham: the swimming pool, 1990	Tim Benton © RIBA Collections
179	Queen Mary visiting Pioneer Health Centre, 1948	© Southwark Archives

180 (top)	Glass screens dividing the cafeteria from the kitchen, 1935	© RIBA Collections
180 (bottom)	Swimming pool at Pioneer Health Centre, 2018	© Angharad Davies
181	View looking west along Moncrieff Street towards Peckham Multi-Storey Car Park east elevation, 2012	© Corinne Turner 2012
182	Looking north-west towards corner of the Peckham Multi-Storey Car Park south and east elevations and south passage, 2015	© Corinne Turner 2015
183	View looking southeast from Cerise Road roundabout towards the Peckham Multi-Storey Car Park north elevation, 2013	© Corinne Turner 2013
184 (top)	The Food Hall: the main public space at Peckham Levels for the community, 2023	© Peckham Levels
184 (bottom left)	The Auditorium: a smaller event space at Peckham Levels, 2023	© Peckham Levels
184 (bottom right)	J Walshe and T Conrad perform at the London Contemporary Festival of Music at the Peckham Multi Storey, 2013	© Corinne Turner 2013

PART 4: ORAL HISTORIES

186	25 inch Ordnance Survey map CIII, 1897 edition	© Southwark Archives
188 (top)	Portrait of Dimitri Launder	© Dimitri Launder
188 (bottom)	Portrait of Anila Ladwa	© Anila Ladwa
189	Area 10, 2002	© Dimitri Launder
190	Airline ticket flyer for the Area 10 show 'Destination Peckham', 2007	© Anila Ladwa and Teresa Paiva
192	Portrait of Barry Jenkins	© Barry Jenkins
193	Barry wearing a suit bought on Rye Lane	© Barry Jenkins
194	Barry being presented with a certificate by the Princess Royal after completing the Venice Marathon in 2000 and raising money for Save the Children (of which she's the President).	© Barry Jenkins
195 (left)	Barry with a coach he worked on.	© Barry Jenkins
195 (right)	Exterior shot of Barry's garage.	© Barry Jenkins
196	Portrait of Dr Charmaine Brown	© Dr Charmaine Brown
197	Charmaine, when she was Education Manager at the Peckham Literary Centre (The Book Place), 1991	© Dr Charmaine Brown
198	Damilola Taylor, Evening Standard, 28th November 2000	© Evening Standard
200	Portrait of Clement Ogbonnaya	© Clement Ogbonnaya
201	Mural by Artfuldodger at the entrance to the Prince of Peckham circa 2019	© Clement Ogbonnaya
202	Prince of Peckham with Clifton Estate's Witcombe Point in background circa 2019	© Clement Ogbonnaya
203	Prince of Peckham seen from corner of Clayton Road and Queen's Road circa 2019	© Clement Ogbonnaya
204	Portrait of Eileen Conn	© Corinne Turner 2013
206	Community campaign merchandise item co-created by Corinne Turner, Clyde Watson and Eileen Conn. Black on pink t-towel with information text about the campaign, 2017	© Corinne Turner
207	The wide, expansive rooftop view sweeping from east to west across the Thames flood plain towards Central London.	© Elliot Potts
208	Portrait of Joy Gregory	© Joy Gregory
209	*Invisible lifeforce of plants – Chamomile.* Print on silver gelatine paper by Joy Gregory, 2020	© Joy Gregory
212	Portrait of Karin Greene	© Karin Greene
213	Karin, London, 1971	© Karin Greene
217	Map shows the completed THI projects within the 'heritage cluster' around the junction of Peckham Hill Street and Peckham High Street	© Peckham THI
218 (top left)	105 Peckham High Street Manze's	© Elliot Potts
218 (top right)	130 Peckham Hill Street Filishack	© Elliot Potts
218 (bottom left)	109 Peckham High Street The Greyhound	© Elliot Potts
218 (bottom right)	119 Peckham High Street The Old Crown Hotel	© Elliot Potts
219 (top left)	86 Peckham High Street Acuherbal	© Elliot Potts
219 (top centre)	88 Peckham High Street Mama	© Elliot Potts
219 (top right)	100 Peckham High Street	© Elliot Potts
219 (bottom left)	102 Peckham High Street The Peckham Cobbler	© Elliot Potts
219 (bottom right)	116 Peckham High Street The Red Bull	© Elliot Potts

INDEX

References to images are in *italics*.